I0752176

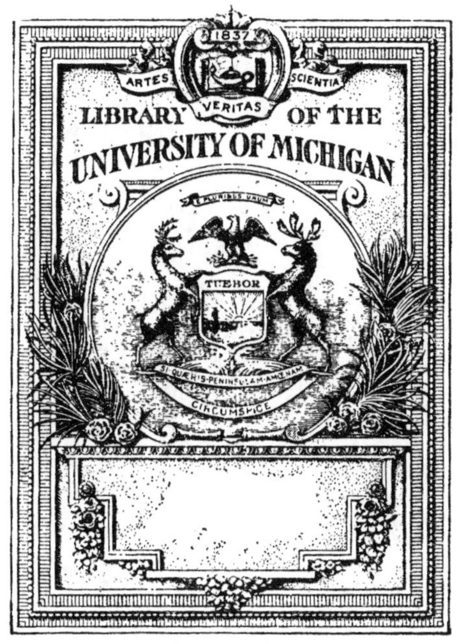
1837
ARTES
SCIENTIA
VERITAS
LIBRARY OF THE
UNIVERSITY OF MICHIGAN
E PLURIBUS UNUM
TUEBOR
SI QUÆRIS PENINSULAM AMŒNAM
CIRCUMSPICE

HOME SERVICE IN ACTION

A STUDY *of* CASE WORK IN THE HOME SERVICE SECTION OF THE NEW YORK *and* BRONX COUNTY CHAPTERS OF THE AMERICAN RED CROSS

By
MARY BUELL SAYLES

NEW YORK
NEW YORK COUNTY CHAPTER, AMERICAN RED CROSS
1921

WM. F. FELL CO. PRINTERS
PHILADELPHIA

CONTENTS

PREFACE

Home Service as a phase of America's war record has had a life extending over more than three years. It was born in an emergency; it found itself almost immediately with a full sized task for which almost no equipment had been assembled. The performance of this task was steady, high minded, and adequate. Its achievement is a monument to human resourcefulness and devotion and will form an enduring part of the heritage of Americans in whom the spirit of service moves.

The record of Home Service will prove a fertile field for students of every phase of American national life. It embraces experiments in organization, in finance, in the use of professional service, in civic relationships, in the development of an informed public opinion, which are highly suggestive for a nation working constantly to perfect its institutions and its social practices. No group of persons has a keener interest in the lessons of Home Service than that large body of social workers who have for a generation and more been steadily developing the equipment necessary for those who attempt to readjust disorganized human lives. Miss Sayles' study is an attempt to bring out the suggestive aspects of the Home Service experience for this group of workers as they were revealed in the work of the New York County Chapter of the Red Cross.

It is too soon to estimate with accuracy the effect of the war upon social case work. Toward such an estimate, however, many bits of evidence have contributed. Among them one of the most significant fostered by the experience of Home Service reveals the wide applicability of the combination of ideals, philosophy, methods, and purpose which is social case work.

Social case work developed directly out of the experience of the race in dealing with persons in need. The practice of charity was at first solely an act of mercy and consideration. A long line of leaders in work of this sort struggled to make charitable practice orderly. Their successors discovered the possibility of adding to consideration and order more or less scientific study of human needs and those race resources which could be used in alleviating them. For a period of years before the outbreak of the war social case work had been conscious of a scientific foundation. It had become an indispensable method of procedure in many fields where the readjustment of individuals is undertaken. It had been associated with the practice of medicine in medical agencies; it had found its way into procedure of courts and institutions dealing with delinquents; it had been incorporated into public school systems through the attendance officer and the visiting teacher; and it continued to be the fabric of all successful work in dealing with dependent children and family groups.

The service of social case work as thus organized was limited to those groups which are admittedly in need of service and leadership from community agencies. For the rank and file of self-maintaining men and women who control their own life routine it had not been made available, nor was there any evidence that such persons were conscious of its value to them. Many social case workers, however, had felt a growing conviction that the service of skilled case work was not inherently thus limited. Human beings are human beings in whatever status found. Human need is human need wherever revealed. The service to mankind which is the fruit of social case work is rendered through the medium of skill—skill in understanding human personality and the conditions which affect it; skill in adjusting human personality to the conditions of life. The service which such skill makes possible is applicable wherever such adjustments are needed. The experience of Home Service has demonstrated what leaders in the social case work movement had already perceived: that such adjustments are needed through the whole range of human life.

For the first time in the history of organized social service the war brought within the scope of such service men and women by the thousand who were not dependent, defective, or delinquent. They were men and women whose powers of self-maintenance were unimpaired, whose need was not economic, whose resourcefulness was ample, but who sought only the kind of leadership in a complicated situation which has been the finest development of social case work.

The significance of this can hardly be overestimated. It is not that the war forced grudgingly on social case work the assignment of a responsibility for which it was wholly unprepared. The discovery had been made by social case workers long before that organized helpfulness when voluntarily undertaken by one individual in behalf of another calls for the same qualities of tact, of understanding, sympathy, resourcefulness, and leadership which form the basis of all effective relationships in private life. The successful social case worker is one who brings these qualities to bear deliberately and quickly in professional relationships where he has not the advantage of a slowly maturing acquaintance and the confidence which it develops.

The application of these qualities is vital in any form of social case work. It is particularly difficult, however, with persons whose sensitiveness is born of pride in their own independence and their own powers of self-adjustment. The presence of so large a group of such persons among those who came to Home Service gave to social case work its greatest test. I believe that the greatest contribution of Home Service to American national life is its successfully meeting this test.

Professional case workers are indebted to Home Service for another demonstration. Whether social case work has become a profession need not here be discussed. If those already in the fellowship of professional status prefer not to admit social case work as yet, case workers can cheerfully content themselves with the consciousness that whether or not they wear the badge they have taken for their own the acceptance of responsibility, the reliance upon scientific method, the devotion to truth, and the ideals of service which distinguish the professional status at its best. Concern has sometimes been expressed lest, in maintaining for itself certain professional standards, social case work should become professionalized in an invidious sense. It has not been free from the danger of smugness, of static dependence upon methods already developed, of conventionalized thinking, of an uninspired reliance upon machinery to accomplish its needs. It has never succumbed to these dangers—if it had it never could have met the test which the war gave it.

As this study concedes repeatedly, abundant evidence of these facts can be found in the work of the permanently organized case work agencies in America today. The war emergency has passed, and the development of social case work as an honest, living, efficient force will continue in their hands, where it has been in the past. The struggle to maintain standards, to keep vision clear, to secure recognition for its real achievements has not been easy and will be no easier in the years ahead.

To cite the experience of Home Service as evidence that invidious professionalism can be avoided in social case work is not to reflect upon the older case work agencies, but is rather a heartening privilege. The record of Home Service contains its full share of instances of inadequate work, of opportunities missed, of superficiality where thoroughness was called for, but in the main the record is one of human service at its best. For over three years social case workers, in an environment in which overwork was incessant, never lost sight of standards, even when they had to be temporarily abandoned. They maintained flexibility of technique, they were alive to the spiritual factors in the situations which their clients brought them, and they rarely stood pat on any achievement as marking the high point to be striven for.

It is probable that in both phases of the Home Service experiment to which I have alluded—the range of its application and the living quality of the service—the general use of volunteers has been a factor. Volunteers are no new element in organized case work. It is doubtful, however, if in so small a space of time so large a number of them have ever carried so heavy a responsibility. Moreover, the policy of Home Service of maintaining one standard of efficiency for salaried and volunteer workers alike is significant for the future of case work. It furnishes one more bit of evidence that the social worker who qualifies as a professional worker does so because of a service which he is equipped to render and not by virtue of the status which he holds within an organization.

The spirit of service which the war engendered throughout the American people is responsible in a large measure for the willingness of volunteers to work and to work hard. That a corps of volunteers under such a compelling motive when adequately trained could do effective work should lead to earnest search for an equally compelling motive in peace times.

To social case workers the experience of Home Service would seem first to be a justification of their own faith in themselves, and second, a revelation of an opportunity for a much wider application of their distinctive contribution to human welfare than they had before the World War. It is both of these, but it is also the revelation of a high responsibility. There is in America today a more widespread interest in social case work, a more intelligent understanding of its possibilities, a greater readiness to accept it than ever before. It should be possible in the not remote future to make social case work available to the whole populace wherever there is need of leadership in matters of adjustment to life. Such leadership social case workers at the present time are equipped to render, but their equipment, compared with the implications of the task, is limited. It must be constantly enriched by broadness of conception, by advance in scientific method, and mellowed by a consciousness that its subject matter is very largely the spiritual needs of those it serves. Progress along these lines must be made by social case workers themselves. It will be the result of unceasing study of their experience and reflection upon its meanings —the result, in other words, of the same processes by which they brought their profession to the point where it would meet its greatest test.

Home Service was not the achievement of social case workers alone. It will be forever one of the glories of the whole American people. This nation, which perceived for the first time throughout its membership the possibilities of happiness and well-being which lie in organized human helpfulness will some day make professional social work, as a medium of such helpfulness, available for itself as are the resources of the other great professions. Home Service has gone far toward opening the way for this development. It has also revealed to the profession of social case work the spirit in which this development must be met.

PORTER R. LEE.

THE NEW YORK SCHOOL OF SOCIAL WORK.

INTRODUCTION

During the three years following the entrance of the United States into the World War in the spring of 1917 no fewer than twenty-five thousand families[1] of men serving in the Army and Navy, or men recently discharged, were brought to the attention of the Home Service Section of the American Red Cross for Manhattan and the Bronx.

Among these families were representatives of every race whose sons had been drawn into our armed forces and of nearly every race fighting with the Allies; also representatives, not only of the poorer among our fellow-residents, but of what, for want of a better term, we commonly refer to as the middle class. They came on their own initiative, or were sent to the Home Service office, for help in difficulties which varied all the way from failure to receive letters from a son or husband overseas to serious illness or complete lack of any means of support; oftentimes the problem they first presented proved to be less serious than others later brought to light. Many of these families can hardly be said to have been really known at all; others came to be known with profound intimacy during a period of months or years.

For each family or ex-service man with whom Home Service thus established relations, or who was referred to it, a case record was made, ranging in length from a mere report of an interview or a still briefer notation of an unavailing attempt to find someone at an address which was evidently incorrect, to a collection of sixty or seventy closely typewritten sheets, which, taken with the file of correspondence that accompanied them, tell the story of attempts to aid the family in the solution of a dozen different problems. These records, made up of entries originally dictated or written out in long hand from day to day by hundreds of different visitors with widely varying abilities and insight, working under terrific pressure, are many of

[1] Exclusive of homeless men cared for by the After Care Department of the Section of War Brides from overseas, and of Legal Committee information cases.

them fragmentary and ill organized. Yet they present a series of pictures of family life under the strain of deep emergencies which for variety and interest has never, we believe, been equalled by that presented in the records of any other single agency; and they reveal, in flashes here and there, not only the singleness of purpose and devotion which inspired the workers who made them but other qualities of mind and spirit which are well worth noting and meditating upon.

In the early summer of 1919, when the greater part of this vast mass of human documents had already accumulated in the files of the Section, Home Service was brought face to face with the question of its own tenure of life. The issue was raised by the chairman of the Section in what was known as the Supervisors' Meeting—a group made up of supervisors and assistants in charge of the various divisions and departments of Home Service, which met weekly to discuss and decide questions of policy and practice.[1] Was it desirable that the Section should continue indefinitely as a case work agency, or should it be discontinued as soon as its special war service had been completed? The power to decide this question of course lay with the executive committee of the New York County Chapter of the Red Cross; but the Home Service group, so far as it was concerned, concluded that its particular service would in another year or two be finished, and that its work should then be discontinued—a decision which the executive committee later confirmed.

Consideration of what this decision meant in detail may be left until the opening chapter of the study.[2] Here we are chiefly concerned with a second point which came to the fore while the question as to the discontinuance of Home Service was under discussion. It was then that a strong feeling began to manifest itself among the supervisors that if the work to which they had given themselves unsparingly for over two years were to end within a year or two, and the organization which they had built up with their chairman were to go out of existence, some permanent record should remain. They wanted not so much a formal report of the varied activities of the Section as an interpretation of what they felt had been in the nature of a distinctive contribution to case work on their part and on the part

[1] For further information regarding the Supervisors' Meetings see p. 32.

[2] See page 19.

of the large number of visitors and aides, volunteer and paid, who had worked with them. Such an interpretation could be made only by one who could give time to the reading of a representative number of records and who could enter into and become part of the Section sufficiently to grasp its spirit and understand the full significance of the forms of organization evolved. Only those who had worked with Home Service during its two years of greatest stress and strain could fully appreciate the heroism of its effort or the multiplicity and overwhelming burden of the difficulties met. On the other hand, those who had so worked were too much a part of the Section to be able to take the detached and impartial view essential to the appraisal contemplated, even if they had not been too much needed in the active work of the Section to be spared for such a task. An effort was made, therefore, to find a person able to undertake the study, and the present writer was selected.

The specifications for the study, as outlined by the chairman in the first interview, were as follows: It was to be a study of case work for case workers—not in any sense a piece of publicity or propaganda; it was to be absolutely impartial, aiming, of course, to bring out whatever was good and, above all, whatever was distinctive or in the nature of a fresh contribution to case work, but omitting none of the unfavorable aspects that might be revealed during the course of investigation. It was with this understanding that the work was undertaken. To insure the impartiality and scholarly standing of the study, Porter R. Lee, Director of the New York School of Social Work, was asked to oversee it.

The plan decided upon, after a brief general survey of the work of the Section, involved, first of all, the reading of representative case records from each of its nine divisions. Five of these divisions served the Borough of Manhattan—the upper and lower west side, the upper, lower, and middle east side; three served the Bronx; while the ninth took care of British and Canadian soldiers and their families, wherever in the two boroughs they might happen to live. All nine divisions occupied rooms set apart in the large central office of the Section. In each of these division offices were filed the case records of families under active care—"open" records as they are called; while case records on which work had been discontinued—"closed" cases—were filed in a central record room. It was felt that in an impartial survey both open and closed records should be examined, and that the work both of the period when we were actually at war and of the post-armistice period should be represented. In order to fulfil these conditions the device of taking a cross-section of the work of Home Service at two different dates was adopted. From books kept in the record room, in which were registered from day to day the new cases assigned to the various divisions for care, lists of cases were made out, beginning with May 1, 1918, and again with May 1, 1919, and these cases were withdrawn from the files for study. Of the total number of 454 cases chosen by this cross-section method, 217 were from May, 1918, 237 from May, 1919, in each instance at least one-fourth of the records of new families taken under care in the months indicated.

While the fact that these cases had been taken in the order in which they stood on the books, and comprised the intake of a week or more in each period, made them more nearly representative of the total of Home Service cases than so small a group chosen in any other way would have been, nevertheless there was an obvious probability that less than five hundred cases out of so huge a total would not afford a very large number of examples of the best work done by the visitors of the Section. To offset the danger of missing such examples—since the main interest of the study lay precisely in this best work—the supervisors of the Section were asked to select cases by which they would be willing to have their divisions judged. The total number of these selected cases read—out of a considerably larger number presented—was 77; limitations of time alone prevented further delving in this peculiarly fruitful field. It should be especially noted that wherever in this study citations from cases are presented, care has invariably been taken to distinguish between those "selected" by the supervisors and those chosen by the "cross-section" method, so that the reader might not be misled into accepting as customary or usual treatment that was perhaps more or less exceptional.

At this point it may be worth while to explain at some length the method of study adopted. First of all, the writer conceived that the study, as regards case work, was to be concerned chiefly, if not exclusively, with treatment. Naturally, if the investigation of a case or the diagnosis based upon it impressed her with its comprehensiveness and soundness, she would note the fact; or if a conspicuous lack of investigation or error in diagnosis had clearly undermined the treatment, these would not pass unnoticed. But no effort to evaluate the diagnostic process, case by case, would be made. The fact that diagnosis in social case work has been so much more fully and scientifically studied than has treatment had something to do with this decision;[1] the additional fact that Home Service seemed more likely to give an interesting yield on the side of treatment had more. A staff largely composed of devoted but only partly trained volunteers, facing a volume of emergency work such as might well overwhelm a highly trained professional staff, would be more likely to express itself in varied and resourceful forms of immediate and often intimate helpfulness than in a developed technique of investigation. Chiefly, however, the writer was influenced by the fact that she had been asked to make a study leading to an evaluation of case work, and "By their fruits ye shall know them."

Next, it seemed advisable to isolate for separate study the leading problems presented in the records read—problems of health, problems of relief, and so on. This analytical method involved, as is now realized more clearly than at the outset, grave disadvantages, since problems are not so isolated in everyday life; but we are still inclined to believe that the advantages outweigh the disadvantages, and indeed are unable to conceive of an orderly process which should disregard such obvious cleavage.

As the work progressed, however, the chief value of the findings was increasingly felt to lie in illustrations of especially fine and resourceful treatment and in the mental attitude or spirit of the worker revealed by them. Discussion of certain of these illustrations has therefore been given a prominent place in the chapter on Characteristics of Home Service Case Work, and certain implications of these characteristics have been dwelt upon in the chapter entitled Underlying Ideas. This method of treatment has led to special attention's being given to the relations between visitors and clients revealed by the records.

A minor point of method concerns the use of statistics. In the judging of case work, the writer soon became convinced, statistical science can offer no aid; the problems involved are too complex and

---

[1] The reference is to Social Diagnosis, by Mary E. Richmond.

too interrelated and the treatment of them is still more so; spiritual values cannot be weighed or measured—analysis which deals with them can be qualitative only, not quantitative. In the preliminary definition of our field of study and of certain of the problems, however, there has proved to be a function, relatively unimportant, for statistics regarding the cases under review. Such figures as seem pertinent are therefore presented from time to time. We mention the subject here only to emphasize the point that these figures are of altogether minor importance. The real stuff of the study is to be found in the citations from case records which illustrate the methods and manner employed by Home Service visitors in the effort to help people out of their difficulties.[1]

[1] It will of course be understood that throughout the study all names of families have been changed. An index, page 229, gives opposite each family name a list of the pages on which that name is introduced.

Part I
INTERPRETATION

CHAPTER I

THE DEVELOPMENT OF THE HOME SERVICE SECTION

Before the case work done by an organization can be understood, it seems necessary that something should be known of that organization —its history, method of functioning, and personnel. We shall therefore attempt briefly to set forth the leading facts which bear upon the detailed discussion of case work that follows.

It should be made clear, however, that nothing approaching a full history of the Home Service Section for Manhattan and the Bronx will be attempted. Such a history would involve a vast assemblage of details regarding chapter organization, relations with the Atlantic Division of the Red Cross and with National Headquarters, and relations with innumerable outside agencies, governmental and private. This would, we believe, obscure rather than illumine the subject in hand, besides being entirely beyond the scope of the study as originally planned.

The First Year of Home Service

In the summer of 1916 work for the families of men on the Mexican border was organized under the Civilian Relief Committee of the New York County Chapter of the American Red Cross. This work was to serve as prelude to the great work of Home Service, so soon to begin. It was with almost the same membership that, on March 28, 1917, a new Civilian Relief Committee, later to become the Home Service Section, was organized in anticipation of the demands soon to be made upon the Red Cross with our entry into the World War. A temporary secretary and an assistant—a social worker who had been a district secretary of the Charity Organization Society and had served in the relief work following several of the great disasters of recent years, as well as in the Mexican border crisis—

were installed with a stenographer in one room of a private house, 30 East 36th Street, which had been loaned to the Chapter. By the end of April the chairman of the Section had assumed her duties and was embarking on the seemingly endless enterprise of establishing a good basis of understanding and co-operation with the various regimental auxiliaries—organizations composed of the wives of officers and enlisted men—and with the many committees that were springing up on all sides to take a hand in the work of war relief. About the middle of May the first group of volunteers, trained in a special course given by the School of Philanthropy (now the New York School of Social Work), joined the staff—a group of rare women, several of whom continued with the Section through three years of devoted service.

In May, also, the Civilian Relief Committee gathered together a group of the leading social workers of the community to serve as a consultation committee which should advise with the chairman and staff. The weekly meetings in which these outside consultants met with the representatives of the Section were devoted to consideration of family problems involving questions of policy, and served not only to guide the case workers of the Section, but to determine lines of demarcation between its work and that of other agencies and to interpret Home Service to those responsible for the social work of the community with families and individuals.

During the spring and early summer of 1917, reports one of the first volunteers, "We simply sat around, impatiently waiting for cases that came in far too slowly to keep us occupied." In fact, there were but 101 new applications in May and the same number in June, while July and August saw an increase of only a little over 50 per cent. Not until fall did the figures begin to go up by leaps and bounds—two hundred plus, three hundred, four hundred, and then, with a wild spurt, seven hundred in December. The year 1917 closed with over two thousand families under care and with a staff of nearly two hundred workers, chiefly part-time volunteers.

What the rapidly increasing demands of that fall and winter meant to a new organization almost wholly dependent on volunteers, many of whom were almost entirely untrained, may best be left to the imagination of the experienced case worker. Those who survived the experience and stood by the Section look back to this period as one of such difficulty and confusion as to make thorough case work, in all but a small minority of cases, an impossibility; though through it all seems to have run a thread of glory, bound up with the desperate and heroic effort to perform an impossible task.

Two training courses for Home Service volunteers were given by the New York School of Social Work during the fall and early winter, and in December the first of nine eight-week courses within the Section itself was conducted by a volunteer, a former graduate of the School; so that there was a periodic influx of new visitors, some of whom proved invaluable, though many shortly fell away owing to unfitness, ill-health, or other demands upon their time.

Almost from the beginning there had been a tentative districting of the two boroughs, but in November they were definitely divided up into six[1] large districts known as divisions—two in the Bronx, four in Manhattan—while to a seventh division, known as Canada, were referred all families in any part of either borough of men in the British or Canadian service; families which, by agreement with the Recruiting Missions and Patriotic Funds of those countries, were to be cared for by the American Red Cross.[2] Each of these divisions was under the direction of a supervisor, volunteer or paid, and was subdivided

---

[1] Later increased to eight, making, with Canada, as stated in the Introduction, a final total of nine.

[2] The agreement entered into in September, 1917, was that the Red Cross should receive such cases from the organizations named or other sources, should keep in close touch with the British and Canadian Patriotic Fund of New York so as to avoid duplication of effort, should utilize Canadian volunteers as fully as possible, and should submit a statement of money expended in behalf of British and Canadian families so that the Section might be reimbursed for actual money relief.

Later, understandings were arrived at with representatives of other national groups among the Allies, individual families of whose reservists had from time to time applied at the Section and been assisted. In February, 1918, an agreement, attempted as far back as the summer, was reached with the Italian Consul, and from that time on the families of Italian reservists were referred by the Consulate and aided in all the varied ways developed in the care of other families, as well as by relief, where needed to supplement the small allowances of the Italian government and the Italian Relief Committee. About this time a somewhat similar understanding was reached with the Bohemian National Alliance and the Slovak League, and in the spring, one with the Polish Mission and Polish White Cross.

Only the British and Canadian families were, however, cared for by a separate division of the staff, the others coming under the various geographical divisions.

The French had from the beginning assumed full responsibility for their own reservists, and so well developed was their organization that it was felt no help was needed by them.

from time to time as trained workers became available for the post of supervising visitor over these subdivisions. All were housed under one roof, a point of policy felt by the chairman to be vital if the diverse elements in them were to be held together in any sort of unity.

While this study will not attempt to deal in detail with the influence exerted by this districting of the city, no one can even begin to understand the work of the Section without grasping the central fact that from the formation of the divisions there began a separate and semi-autonomous development of each, determined very largely by the personality and previous experience of its supervisor, though also in part colored, no doubt, by the characteristics of the population of the district itself. A certain co-ordinating influence was indeed exerted by the consultation committee, but the chairman and secretary of the Section were far too busily occupied with other aspects of organization, and with the never-ending questions of relations with outside agencies, especially those engaged in war work, to give effective supervision to the case work of the Section. Thus it came about that whatever unifying influence was ultimately exerted was to spring largely from the supervisory group itself, growing out of the supervisors' meetings which were held from the winter of 1917–18 on, and in the second year were reorganized into more effective form.[1]

Before, however, we attempt to trace this later and most interesting development of the supervisory group, there are certain features of the first year of Home Service which must be touched upon.

The fall of 1917 was especially rich in new undertakings organized under the wing of the Section which were to have an important relation to the development of its case work.

Medical Co-operation—The Medical Station.—Naturally the health needs of the families whose menfolk had gone into the service were among the first to be considered. As early as May, 1917, a group of physicians volunteered their services—the first of many who thus placed themselves at the call of the Section. Very early in this first year of the war, also, an understanding was entered into with the Henry Street Settlement, which agreed to care for sick persons in Home Service families at the same rate as that made to the

[1] In 1917 the social staff was relieved of all responsibility for clerical details by the appointment of an office manager, responsible to the chairman.

Metropolitan Life Insurance Company (sixty cents a visit), to be paid by the Section. A little later a committee representing the Academy of Medicine and the County Medical Society drew up an agreement for the guidance of Home Service in its relations with medical practitioners and institutions, appointed a medical adviser for the Section, and helped secure the services of specialists in various fields. In November, 1917, the first of the distinct medical ventures organized in co-operation with Home Service was launched.

This was the Medical Station, which aimed to provide the equivalent of private medical care for families accustomed to such care but no longer able to afford it—for families, to put it another way, unaccustomed to attending dispensaries and especially liable to shrink from the experience. This service was offered by a group of women physicians at the Salvation Army Hospital, which generously gave the use of the necessary rooms. It has been faithfully and devotedly carried on ever since and has met a real and great need in many families of moderate means and in others to whom the Section was giving financial aid. Over four thousand patients came to the Station during two years of service. The care of maternity cases was a specialty; some five hundred were seen, of whom about one hundred and fifty either received prenatal care up to the time of delivery or were delivered in the Salvation Army Hospital (or the Booth Memorial Hospital, as it was later called). Over two hundred men in service were examined, and over three hundred discharged soldiers. Of special interest is the fact that a large proportion of the patients cared for had never attended a public dispensary, and were thus of the type which the physicians who established the Station especially planned to serve.

Vocational Scholarships.—Another need, certain to arise in the families of men in service, was early appreciated by the Henry Street Vocational Scholarship Committee, which offered its co-operation in the spring of 1917. This committee had already been carrying on for eight years the work of helping children of working age to continue their education. Anticipating that many boys and girls in families whose older brothers or fathers had gone to war would be forced to abandon plans for schooling and take the first job that offered, its members were eager to do their utmost to prevent such hardships.

Their offer was cordially accepted by the chairman, and in September they began their work by searching the Home Service records filed to date and interviewing children of about fourteen years of age. The arrangement was that all decisions as to economic need were to be made by Home Service and all school contacts and decisions as to educational plans and vocational questions were to rest with the committee, which went into the homes to secure the co-operation of parents but with the distinct understanding that they should not discuss or permit discussion of the economic condition of the family. Within a few months the number of children which the committee had under care was practically doubled by the addition of over a hundred Home Service children. All administrative expenses were borne by the committee, Home Service paying the scholarships, which were fixed at $3.00 a week until the spring of 1919 when the maximum was advanced to $6.00. Both parties to this co-operative arrangement agree in considering it a remarkable success.

The Employment Bureau.—The fall of 1917 also saw the informal establishment of an employment department intended especially to provide opportunities for women and for men who, because of age or incapacity, were unfitted for regular work. This department continued to fill its place in Home Service until after the armistice, when, as the employment situation began to change with the return of the discharged soldiers, it seemed advisable to discontinue it and to work entirely through the regular employment agencies.

The Legal Committee.—In December, 1917, an important experiment in legal aid was launched. Several young lawyers had, during the summer, offered their services to the Section, but they had been called to military service before the passage of the War Risk Insurance Act in October, and it was with the passage of that Act that the need of legal help began to be most acutely felt by Home Service workers. A volunteer offered himself and, gathering around him a group of other lawyers, assumed the responsibility in this field. At first the presence at the Home Service office of some one of this group for a few hours daily was sufficient to meet all needs; but within a few months the number of clients seeking advice on legal or quasi-legal questions had so greatly increased that a separate office and a constantly increasing staff of lawyers, stenographers, and clerks became necessary. With the rapid piling up of allotment and allowance difficulties the Legal Committee found itself forced to specialize in War Risk Insurance problems, and it was arranged to refer other legal questions demanding more than mere advice to an independent organization, the War Committee of the Bar. The guidance and help of these two committees were of great value to Home Service visitors in solving the miscellaneous legal and business difficulties of their clients. Indeed, without the specialized work of the Legal Committee in the War Risk field it is difficult to see how the supervisors and visitors could have found time to handle at all the stupendous load of case problems they were already staggering under.

The Red Cross Workroom.—From January to March, 1918, no new enterprise for the benefit of Home Service families seems to have been launched. In the last named month, however, the Council of Jewish Women organized in an East Side neighborhood a Red Cross workroom where women relatives of men in service were employed. Those who originated and carried on this work aimed to meet the employment problem of the women engaged as well as to produce hospital supplies for the Red Cross. In addition, they sought to exert an Americanizing influence and to build up ideals of patriotic service among the women of the district in which the workroom was located and from which many of the women naturally came—a district which showed decidedly un-American tendencies. Over a hundred different women worked at the room during the fifteen months it was in operation, their wages of 25 cents an hour being paid by the Red Cross, while all the activities of the workroom were directed by the volunteers of the Council. Lunches, a nursery and a kindergarten for children brought by their mothers, and various other forms of friendly service made this workroom a real boon to the women employed there.

To return from our brief review of these special ventures of the Section to the development of its central service of visiting in the homes of men called to the colors, there are two phases of the situation during this first year which seem to demand attention.

Development of Staff.—Mention has already been made of the training courses for volunteers which contributed so much to the cause of Home Service, without which, indeed, the carrying of the load would have been an impossibility. The methods by which the volunteers themselves were recruited might well fill a separate chapter but do not seem especially pertinent to our theme, though it may be said in passing that no stone seems to have been left unturned in the effort to bring this opportunity to serve before the young women of New York City. Nothing, however, could be more pertinent than the method of handling the volunteers, once secured. This may be briefly summarized. Except that they were generally accepted on part time, they were treated exactly like the paid workers and were expected to give equally faithful service, with the same punctual fulfilment of engagements. The usual weekly minimum of service accepted was five half or three full days, and several volunteers, both office workers and visitors, speedily developed into full-time and to all intents and purposes professional workers. How much these high requirements may have had to do with the rapid falling off of the less enthusiastic and less well-equipped volunteers there is no means of calculating; it is certain that the experience of having their work taken seriously, of being held to high standards and trusted with responsibility, was welcomed by the abler and more devoted volunteers and had much to do with securing their loyal and continuous service.

Parallel to this splendid development of volunteer service must be noted a marked failure, during the first year of Home Service, to develop a strong paid staff. In January, 1918, there were in the entire Section but 17 paid workers, and the ratio of paid to volunteer was approximately one to ten; at the end of the year, in March, it was only a little higher—one to eight. The point of view of the New York County Chapter at the outset seems to have been that expenses for rent and salaries should be kept at the lowest possible figure, hence the effort to get along with a minimum of salaried workers. A hampering condition, also, not only during this first year but throughout the life of the Section, was the chairman's feeling that it was inadvisable to weaken the permanent social agencies that were already having to meet the demands made upon them by various war organizations. For this reason no members of the staffs of these agencies were invited to go over to that of the Section. During a period when so many tempting openings at home and abroad were luring workers away from established grooves, the refusal to have a share in building up the new at the expense of the old is understandable and commands respect. On the other hand it is useless to blink the effect which this policy had upon the new organization, where the number of trained workers was pitifully inadequate to the task of training and assimilating the hordes of new volunteers who kept pouring in.

Office Accommodations.—Reference has already been made to the fact that the first office of Home Service was in one room of a loaned house on East 36th Street. This house it later came to occupy entirely. In November the Section was notified that it would have to vacate and the search for a new home began. The choice was influenced by the feeling of the chairman that a private house would present to the client a more homelike and friendly aspect than would an ordinary business office in an office building; by the expectation, doomed to such sad disappointment, that within a few months the War Risk Insurance Bureau would be paying regular allowances to all soldiers' families entitled thereto, thus relieving Home Service of a large part of the load then being carried; and by the Chapter's policy of economy, already touched upon. A private house at 120 East 19th Street was rented and attractively decorated under the direction of an artist volunteer. Hardly, however, had the Section moved in—at the end of January, 1918—when it began to find its quarters cramped. The numbers of new families coming to it did not diminish but continued to be upwards of seven hundred a month; the Legal Committee was crowded out, fortunately into far more suitable and commodious quarters in the Russell Sage Foundation building at 130 East 22d Street; committees were obliged to seek a meeting place in the gallery of a nearby club; and in the overcrowded rooms of the various divisions there were not enough desks or chairs for the use of visitors. These conditions, as well as the icy atmosphere during the coal shortage of that winter, led to the loss of many volunteers, who seemed, during these trying months, to drop away almost as fast as new ones came in. Those who worked through the winter with Home Service are emphatic in the opinion that the inadequate quarters occupied had a most unfortunate influence on the work of the Section.

The Second Year and After

Both in regard to staff and office accommodations the turn in the tide seems to have come in the spring of 1918, just at the beginning of the second year of the war. A committee of three men, members of the Executive Committee of the Chapter, were appointed in April to look into the situation of the Section. They decided, after conference with the chairman, to make two important recommendations: one for an increase in appropriations for salaries, for which about $3,000 a month was then being used—the statement being made that "if the work expands as indicated, the payroll may have to reach $8,000 a month at the close of the year"; the other for an office with somewhat over four times the floor space of the house then occupied.

In May a payroll increase to $6,000 a month was authorized; and in July the Section moved for the second time, to a floor in the Grand Central Palace, where it was far more comfortably housed than ever before though there was still not room for the Legal Committee, which remained at the Russell Sage Foundation building. Negotiations were opened with the management of the Palace in the hope of securing additional space for this important branch of the work, and it seemed probable that Home Service was at last satisfactorily settled, when in August a bomb burst in the form of an announcement that the building had been taken over by the government as a debarkation hospital and must be vacated.

Thus it came about that the summer of 1918 was a period of great difficulty. For a disheartening stretch of time, during intense heat, the work was thrown into confusion by all the incidents of moving and settling—the noise of partitions being put up or taken down, the shifting of telephones and electric lights, etc.; and this at a time when a large proportion of the staff were on vacation. Moreover, it was in July that there occurred the greatest increase in applications since the previous December—from 903 in June (the maximum to date) to 1,206; and the following months witnessed still further increases. This was the period, the chairman reports, when criticisms of Home Service were most numerous.

In September, 1918, however, the Section finally settled into the commodious and attractive quarters at 353 Fourth Avenue which it was henceforward to occupy.[1] Here, on the same floor, there was ample space for the Legal Committee as well as for the divisions and the office staff and a large, pleasant reception room. During this month, also, a vigorous campaign for volunteers to take the next training course was carried on, and a large group of exceptionally

---

[1] Since September 1, 1920, the office has been at 131 West 38th Street.

well-equipped women was gathered in. The salary roll having now increased practically to the limit set in May ($6,000), the executive committee in September authorized the doubling of this appropriation.

It is evident, therefore, that September, 1918, marked the consummation, in a sense, of the new policies adopted in the preceding May—the policies of ample office provision and an ample paid staff. However, these new policies meant no abandonment of the earlier one regarding development of a large volunteer force. So vigorously was the campaign for volunteers pressed during this fall that the Section was able to boast in January, 1919, a staff of 316 volunteers, in contrast to that of 177 a year before.

During the four months following September, as during the four months preceding, the feat of so increasing the paid staff as practically to double the salary roll was again performed; and once more, in January, a further increase was authorized—to $12,000 a month for the "personal service" staff and to $7,000 for the office staff. By this time the entire paid staff of the Section numbered 177, in contrast to the 17 salaried workers of the same month in the preceding year.

The Dental Clinic and the Health Center.—Going back now a little, it will be worth while to dwell for a moment upon two additional ventures launched under the wing of Home Service in the summer and fall of 1918.

In August a group of physicians who were interested in organizing a pay clinic in which families of moderate means could obtain a high type of medical service had formed a committee, rented a floor in a private house in East 39th Street, and equipped a room for the initial experiment of a dental clinic. At the last moment they found themselves unable to obtain a license, and so offered the rooms and equipment to the Home Service Section. Before the end of the month a dentist was engaged and the clinic was opened.

Already, in July, plans for a third health venture had been talked over with an eminent child specialist; later a group of other specialists were interested, and on November 1st the Health Center was opened in the rooms adjoining the dental clinic. The object was to provide, for children from two to fourteen years of age, the kind of careful medical attention received by children in well conducted homes. Under the supervision of a group of consultant physicians, the work was carried on by a corps of young doctors especially trained in pediatrics, one in attendance each afternoon of the week, who were paid a fair rate for their services. Full physical examination to determine nutrition, weight, height, and the presence of defects that called for attention; weekly visits from children needing constant oversight; reference to clinics and hospitals of those in need of dental care or operations; and monthly reporting to the Center of all kept under supervision, with a careful record and follow-up system to insure such reporting and the carrying out of directions are among the leading features of this valuable work.

The Dietitian.—As far back as the summer of 1917 the need of dietetic guidance for Home Service visitors had been felt, and had been partly met for a few months by a dietitian lent by the Association for Improving the Condition of the Poor, who had met from time to time with a group of volunteers. From the fall of 1917 until the fall of 1918 the Section had been without such service, but in October of this latter year an important addition was made to the staff of the Section: a trained dietitian with a year's experience in social work with families. Under the influence of her careful studies of family budgets and her recommendations as to allowances, a gradual standardization of relief in the several divisions was brought about during the year that followed, with most beneficial effect upon case work. The later addition of two visiting dietitians to the staff made possible direct work in certain of the homes—homes where special dietetic guidance and teaching were needed on account of illness or malnutrition, and others where low standards and ignorance combined to create a different type of problem.

The After Care Department.—The armistice brought new problems which led to the prompt organization, in November, of an After Care Department to meet the needs of discharged soldiers who had no homes in Manhattan or the Bronx. The number of men applying to this department rose rapidly from 62 in November, 1918, to over four hundred in April, 1919, while the number of new family cases coming to the divisions gradually decreased. As, however, this divisional intake still remained through the winter several hundred above that for the corresponding months of the preceding year, there was little diminution in the strain on the supervisors and visitors. Such relief as there was resulted from the changing character of cases, which now were in large proportion inquiries regarding home conditions bearing upon discharge and other military questions. These involved relatively little real case work.

The Psychiatric Clinic.—One other important medical development in connection with Home Service remains to be noted. As the men began to return from overseas it was soon recognized that many among them were suffering from nervous and mental disorders and in need of special psychiatric advice and treatment. The Mental Hygiene Committee of the State Charities Aid Association was interested and eager to work out some plan with the Section. The original project was to establish a clinic in a house where men could be lodged as well as studied, but this had to be abandoned in the spring because of the difficulty in finding a house. A clinic was, however, established in April, 1919, at the Cornell Medical School. A psychiatrist who held regular hours, and two psychiatric workers under the direction of the Mental Hygiene Committee became a part of the staff of the After Care Department, and later conducted a clinic at the office of the Section. Still later, in the fall of 1919, the psychiatric worker of the Mental Hygiene Committee who had been supervising this work was able to arrange to give certain regular hours weekly to consultation with visitors over difficult mental problems in cases under the care of the divisions.

Vacation Work.—A new feature of the work in the summer of 1919 was a seashore cottage home for Jewish women and children, opened in June at Long Branch. This was planned and carried on by the Council of Jewish Women, the expenses being met from an appropriation out of funds turned over to the Section by the Council—the proceeds of a benefit concert by a distinguished Jewish violinist. Fresh-air work had been carried on by the Section during both the preceding summers—to a small extent only in 1917, on a larger scale in 1918, when special arrangements had been made with several existing vacation homes; but the cottage at Long Branch was the only vacation home organized especially for the benefit of Home Service families. It accommodated 33 women and children at a time, usually for periods of two weeks, and proved a most successful venture. A special worker engaged to plan and manage vacation activities, including the parties to the cottage, also helped to make the summer outing work of this year a success.

Work for War Brides.—The work of the Section for War Brides—one of the most distinctive of its activities, inasmuch as only one other Home Service Section in the country was called upon to do such work, and that on a comparatively small scale—dates from December, 1918. At the beginning of that month the Section extended aid for the first time to the wife of a man married overseas. From then until July 1, 1920, when this study came to an end, 4,349 brides who had entered the country at the port of New York came under the care of the Section. Many of them arrived on the same ships with their husbands, but the latter were obliged to go into camp before being discharged, so could not immediately assume their family responsibilities. A number of the wives had babies, and several were accompanied by older children to whom our soldiers had become stepfathers; in all, 323 children were cared for with their mothers. Except when met at the docks by relatives, these young women were generally transported by the Red Cross Motor Corps to the Hostess House of the Young Women's Christian Association in Lexington Avenue, where they were entertained until the Red Cross, which had a desk and a worker on duty there, could get into communication with relatives or with the Home Service Section in the town to which they were going and arrange transportation for them, or until their husbands could make such arrangements themselves. This work was entirely distinct from that of the divisions; it was carried on by a separate staff headed by the secretary of the Section.

Development of the Supervisors' Conference.—We have deliberately run ahead of our story in order to leave to the last what is perhaps the most significant development in Home Service organization. It will be remembered that in telling of the division of Manhattan and the Bronx into districts, in the late fall of 1917, and the appointment of a supervisor over each division, we spoke of the independent and semi-autonomous development of each of the units thus created, there being no general detailed supervision of them all. The reaction of the supervisors to such an arrangement was of course sure to be as varied as their personalities. No written records bearing upon this point exist, but there seems to be no question that among some of the group at least, there was from the outset a consciousness of the need of such supervision which was expressed not only among themselves but to their chairman. With all the difficulties and absorbing problems which beset the path of the Section—problems of co-operation with other agencies and of co-operation between the divisions and the various supplementary services of the Section, problems of office accommodations and management, and problems of staff development—and in view of the very great competition during this period for the services of skilled case workers capable of exercising such large-scale supervision, it is not surprising that this need remained unsupplied; but such was the case, with the divergencies in practice and irregularities in quality of work certain to result.

Meanwhile there had been a gradual development in organization which tended to bring about a rapprochement among the divisions, while at the same time it wrought what amounted to a revolution in the management of the internal affairs of the Section. From the very beginning of Home Service activity conferences of visitors had been held at frequent intervals to discuss case work problems; with the development of the divisions separate divisional conferences took their place, and a general body made up of representatives of both clerical and visiting staffs was formed to discuss matters of interest to the Section as a whole. Another and more significant grouping was that of the supervisors—the one with which we are here especially concerned. At these supervisors' meetings were brought up such varied matters as instructions from Red Cross headquarters; information from military authorities on such points as method of discharge; offers of co-operation from hospitals or social agencies; the location of new offices; vacation schedules; the use of volunteer physicians and how to secure more such physicians in an emergency; the question of uniforms for Home Service workers; interpretations of the Civil Rights Bill; questions directly bearing on case work, such as the extent to which insurance of members of families should be kept up by Home Service; certain office details, such as the turning in of receipts to the treasurer or reporting payment for telegrams received; and the adjustment of relations between the divisions on the one hand and the supplementary services, especially that of the Medical Station, the Legal Committee, and the Scholarships Committee, on the other. Representatives of these separate services were more or less frequently present at the meetings and discussion was general, while occasionally—not frequently—a vote on some point was taken.

Thus from the first the meetings served a valuable purpose as a center for the distribution of information and the adjustment of difficulties, while giving the chairman an opportunity to obtain the views of the supervisory group on any subject on which she might feel the need of advice.

In spite of all efforts, however, a lack of co-ordination and system in the relations of the various divisions to one another and to outside bodies continued to be a source of trouble, as was not surprising in an organization of such rapid growth, forced constantly to readapt itself to new conditions and submit to new regulations. It was primarily with the aim of remedying this difficulty that the supervisors, in the early winter of 1918–19, determined to ask for a larger share in the shaping of policies and for the appointment of one of their number as a general supervisor whose special function should be to work out such co-ordination and system. The situation bears a certain resemblance to that which has arisen in recent years between many employers and employe-groups in industry, in that a thoroughly self-conscious body of workers, knowing that they had contributed largely to the development of the common undertaking, sought to be admitted to a share in its management. The motive, however, differed; desire for the success of the enterprise being, in the case of Home Service, the one predominant element in it.

Equally different from that of the ordinary employer, happily, was the reaction of the chairman of the Section in this instance; for she seems to have arrived simultaneously at the same conclusion as the supervisors and to have welcomed them very cordially into the desired partnership. Thus it came about that the year 1919 opened with an experiment in democratic management.[1] In January the plan was ushered in by two all-day conferences of the group, in which every phase of Home Service policy and practice which the supervisors wished to have discussed was given its place on the program; and in the regular weekly meetings which followed it became the cus-

---

[1] In referring to the plan of management herein outlined as "democratic," we are of course using the term in a relative, not an absolute sense. Obviously a committee made up of supervisors and others appointed by the chairman was not strictly representative, any more than a group of shop foremen would be. There was, however, in the Section, no such natural antagonism of interests as exists between workers and employers in the field of industry.

tom to debate and decide in parliamentary fashion all important and many minor questions of policy and procedure.

The membership of these meetings had already been expanded beyond the chairman, secretary, supervisors, and office manager, who had at first formed the group. The dietitian, a social worker who had been taken on the staff to serve as a liaison officer between the Medical Station and the divisions, and the volunteer who conducted training courses for new workers became members of the group during the fall or early winter; and in the following spring and summer others were added—the chief of the new After Care Department and his assistant, the assistant office manager, and several of the assistant supervisors. The group thus became more truly representative of the whole body of workers in the Section.

At about the same time that this experiment in democratic management was being launched, a member of the supervisory group was selected by the chairman, in accordance with the expressed wish of the group, to be senior case supervisor. Her responsibility was primarily an executive one—the putting into practical effect of many of the decisions arrived at in the supervisors' meetings, together with a wide variety of functions which tended to bring about a better co-ordination and systematization of the various services maintained by the Section. Among these functions, as originally formulated by the chairman, "case work standardization" was included, with the qualification: "Standardization not in any way to hinder the development of individuality in the different divisions." As a matter of fact, while the senior supervisor never systematically read cases from the various divisions and did not impose her views upon the supervisors, she was more or less consulted in difficult cases by them and undoubtedly exerted an influence which, combined with that of the supervisors' meetings and that of the dietitian, gradually brought about a degree of standardization.

The method of functioning of the supervisors' meetings was partly by direct discussion and vote, partly by reference of the larger, more complex problems to committees, and by action upon their reports when presented. One of the earliest questions taken up in committee was that of the salaries of the social staff. Where a question like this, involving financial outlay, was concerned, a report accepted by the supervisors' meeting had, of course, to be submitted to the executive committee of the Chapter, which controls the purse strings, before it could be put into effect. As a matter of fact, both this and a later report on salaries were approved by the executive committee. The chairman states that from the time the new arrangement went into effect she took no question to the executive committee without first bringing it before the supervisors, and that the executive committee never reversed a decision of the supervisors' meeting. Questions involving relations with such government agencies as the War Risk Insurance Bureau and the Federal Board for Vocational Education were worked out between representatives of the Section, representatives of these federal bodies, and representatives of the Atlantic Division of the Red Cross; but the working plans agreed upon by these representatives had to be formally accepted by the supervisory group before being put into effect.

Following the crucial decision that Home Service should go out of existence as soon as its war task was completed,[1] a vast mass of detail as to the way this decision should be carried out had to be considered. The distinction between able-bodied discharged men and the disabled, and between different types of disabled; the conditions under which various classes of cases should be closed or transferred to other agencies; the question of Home Service responsibility for the families of men who have enlisted since the armistice and for men dishonorably discharged; these are among the larger questions that were decided in the supervisors' meetings. Interspersed among such questions of policy and the many problems involved in relations with the War Risk Insurance Bureau and the Federal Board for Vocational Education were a variety of case work problems such as formerly had been considered by the consultation committee.[2]

The chairmanship of the supervisors' meetings was, by express wish of the supervisors themselves, vested in the chairman of the Section,

---

[1] As finally worked out, this decision meant that Home Service discontinued its work for discharged men on July 1, 1920, except for the disabled and those less than six months out of service, with their families. For the disabled, work will come to an end as rapidly as they receive compensation and complete their training under the Federal Board for Vocational Education.

[2] The consultation committee met last in July, 1919. It was felt that Home Service policies were by this time so well established that the calling together for advisory action of busy executives and others with absorbing regular duties was hardly practicable.

and her influence with the group was naturally great. There was, we believe, a sincere effort on her part to maintain an attitude which should leave the members free to express themselves fully upon any and all questions and to come to their own conclusions. Where some peculiarly vital policy was at issue about which she held strong convictions, she expressed these convictions forcibly, sometimes in advance of any expression of opinion by the group, and carried her point. The situation seems to have been much the same as in a manufacturing plant where a shop committee is functioning: the employer's representative, with a broad outlook over the industrial field and access to sources of information closed to the employes, is in a position to present statements and arguments which they, lacking the means to verify or refute, accept. Where such an arrangement proves a success it would seem that it must be because the management is broad-minded and fair enough to win and hold the confidence of its workers. Such was the situation in Home Service. A strong sentiment of loyalty also existed, and where there were differences of opinion doubtless had much to do with the final result.

In closing we may sum up briefly the elements which seem to have been responsible for the strength and for the weaknesses of Home Service.

To take first the darker side of the picture: So far as internal management goes, and leaving aside for this purpose consideration of the appalling volume of the task imposed and the repeated dumping upon the Section of unexpected new burdens resulting from the failure of government agencies to play their allotted rôles, the weaknesses of Home Service seem traceable mainly to three causes. First was the failure to provide at the outset a staff of experienced salaried workers that should keep pace with the growth of the volunteer staff, and so be available to guide and educate this latter body. Second was the failure to provide during the first winter adequate working quarters for the staff. Third was the failure to develop, at an early stage in the history of the Section, such case supervision as would have brought about standardization of the work of all the divisions. As already pointed out, the second of these failures had been retrieved, and the first was in process of being retrieved, by the middle of the second year.

The strength of the Section, on the other hand, lay at first chiefly in its volunteer staff; in the skillful recruiting and excellent training given, in the tireless devotion which animated that staff, from the chairman down, and in the wise policy, heartily urged by the leading volunteers, of holding the members of the group to strict professional standards. Next in chronological order may be counted the later development of a strong salaried staff and the amalgamation of the two, so that each came to partake in large degree of the peculiar strength of the other; and last was the statesmanship shown in developing what was virtually a partnership between the employer's representative and the leading representatives of the working force—a partnership which resulted in utilization for the benefit of the Section of a spirit of solidarity among the workers and of pride in their own democratic organization such as could hardly have been achieved in any other way.

CHAPTER II

CHARACTERISTICS OF HOME SERVICE CASE WORK

One fundamental fact is essential to an understanding of the case work of Home Service in New York City: the fact that the Section never conceived of its activities as limited to dealing with problems springing directly out of the war emergency, but always held itself responsible for meeting any sort of need that might arise in the family of a man in Service. By agreement with the permanent family agencies of the city it assumed at the outset full case work responsibility for all families of service men except such as were already under the active care of one of these agencies—a very small percentage of those coming to the Section.[1] It did not matter, that is to say, whether the young wife and children applying had always been adequately cared for by the soldier-husband and were experiencing since his departure their first period of difficulty, or whether he had been a deserter and non-supporter; it was immaterial whether the mother of a sailor-son had been wholly dependent upon him for support, or whether he had been one of several working children contributing only just enough to cover his board: if difficulties which the family felt itself unable to cope with unaided arose—difficulties either purely financial or due to ill health, unemployment, bad conduct, or any one of a thousand other possible complications—Home Service stood ready to do its utmost to help.

How far that utmost, in the vast total of more than twenty-five thousand families that came to the Section during the three years under review, proved equal to the need is another question. Regarding the quality of Home Service case work no criticisms that we

[1] Of 54 cases (among the 454 cross-section case records read) which had been known to family agencies, only two were, at the time of application, under active care of such agencies. See footnote on page 43.

could frame are half so severe as those made to us by certain of the supervisory group. While all agreed that there had been steady improvement, the general feeling seems to have been that during the first year, and even down to the date of the armistice, conditions were such as to make thorough work in any but a small minority of cases an impossibility.

What these unfavorable conditions were has already been indicated. After the overwhelming volume of new work, perhaps the one most disastrous and most generally emphasized by the supervisors was the inadequate and rapidly changing staff, or to state the difficulty from another angle, the mass of untrained workers to be dealt with. A large share of the energies of all the supervisors went into the training of their visitors, yet in an appalling proportion of cases training was hardly completed when the visitor left. The supervisor of one division summed up her experience as follows: All through the winter of 1918–19 she struggled to train eleven supervising visitors, who in turn were training the visitors in the eleven subdivisions which they headed. In the spring seven of these supervising visitors, three of them volunteer, four paid workers, left. As a result, the subdivisions were reduced to eight, some of which had over them supervising visitors who were "pretty weak." In discussing with this same supervisor a group of family records opened in May, 1918, it was found that of the nine visitors who had worked on them only one was still with the Section some fifteen months later. The supervisor's guess was that 150 different visitors had worked in the division during her year of service.

How many of the lapses in treatment in the cases read are traceable to these constant losses of staff members it is impossible to say, but certainly a very large proportion are so accounted for. When a visitor left there was frequently no one who could take up her cases, every one on the staff being charged to the limit, and it was sometimes months before anyone appeared to whom they could be reassigned; so that unless her clients took the initiative in seeking help they were certain to go unvisited. As supervisors and visitors were habitually working until all hours in the office or field and carrying case records home to be read at night, such disregard cannot be attributed to neglect; yet its effect upon the families under care was of course just as disastrous as though due to this cause.

Another fact has to be borne in mind constantly, in attempting to judge the work of the Section from these family records: the fact that under such rush conditions as prevailed throughout the greater part of the life of Home Service, the most neglected part of the work was sure to be the record keeping. While all the supervisors labored to train their new workers in this as an indispensable part of their technique, it was, perhaps for a majority, the last point to be mastered. It is therefore unsafe to assume, when no visit is entered in a case during a certain period, that no visit was made; or when no attention seems to have been paid to a certain difficulty—as ill health or unemployment—that the disability was not in fact considered and helpful suggestions made. Only in regard to material relief do we have an outside check upon the case record in the form of the cash card kept in the cashier's office, on which all relief is entered beginning with the summer of 1918; but in attempting to judge regarding the wisdom of giving or withholding relief we are as much hampered as in any other matter, since we can never be sure that all the reasons that influenced the visitor or supervisor in her decision are set down in the record.

It is evident, then, that detailed criticism of the treatment of individual families because of things undone rests upon a very uncertain foundation. This point should be borne in mind whenever sins of omission are noted in the case summaries appearing in the chapters that follow. Sins of commission, on the other hand—violations of sound case work principles or of the principles of sound commonsense—will receive individual comment. It is, however, chiefly in positive merits in treatment that we are interested and feel sure that the reader will be interested; and for this reason we propose to begin our case work study by calling attention to certain illustrations of what we believe to be the characteristic excellences of Home Service at its best.

One of these characteristic excellences we have variously phrased as flexibility of technique, freshness and originality, freedom from cut-and-dried conventionality, readiness to experiment.

To give a sound basis of technical training to their large groups of inexperienced visitors, paid and volunteer, was from the outset (as has already been stated) one of the chief objects sought by the supervisors, especially by those who in other positions had given and received intensive training. In weekly study courses and in close personal consultation with supervisors and head visitors, guidance was given in each stage of the process of preliminary study—the first interview, the selection of sources of information and the approach to each, the final summing-up and plan-making. While in the earlier years the overwhelming burden of work and the changing mass of workers made application of such processes in every case an impossibility, the ideal was steadily held and worked toward, with the result that large numbers of records give evidence of as thorough and well-grounded work as any the older societies can boast.

What has interested the writer especially in this connection, however, has been neither the large number of examples of such careful work nor the large number of cases in which emergency pressure and lack of training made such work impossible, but a smaller number of somewhat exceptional cases in which departures from the usual practice were apparently made deliberately for well-considered reasons. Especially in the earlier approaches to certain family situations there is a refreshing freedom from conventional methods, a responsiveness to reality, a following of the dictates of clear common-sense which fully justifies itself by its results. Investigation was, in these cases, omitted or limited deliberately for clear and sufficient reasons and particularly effective treatment followed. Three such cases we propose to cite at some length.

Mrs. Drew with her two children had recently come to New York from the West to be near her mother in the expectation that her husband, who had joined the Canadian forces, was soon to be sent overseas. Her status as a soldier's wife was established by an introduction from the Canadian Society of New York, which referred her as probably in need of financial aid. When called upon she was found with the children in a very neat, bright little apartment of three rooms. She told her story frankly—a simple story of early marriage and life since in various western cities where her husband had held good positions as a proofreader; of recent temporary sojourn in her mother's home and the decision that as the latter did not get on well with the children it would be better to separate. She spoke of her connection with a well-known Protestant church, showed many letters from her husband, and discussed her financial situation fully, exhibiting account books kept for three years past and some fine sewing which she was doing to help out. She was pleasing in appearance and manner and seemed transparently honest. In addition she expressed herself as "glad that Red Cross visitor had come," for "now she felt someone would take a personal interest in her." She had "no one to whom she could go for advice."

The only visit paid in this case before the plan of treatment was launched was one to the mother; she was a woman of German birth and sympathies who kept a furnished-room house of obviously good type. Whether any attempt was made to draw her out as to the facts of her daughter's life does not appear; their statements so far as quoted agree. The church connection was not followed up at this time, nor were any letters of inquiry written to the western cities where the Drews had lived. The situation presented was apparently a simple one: a self-respecting family of high standards not quite able to make ends meet on the government checks received, and with certain health needs calling for attention. The treatment was peculiarly thorough, kindly, and successful, every need as it developed later being met. The young mother herself rose superbly to every situation, working steadily first at one part-time position found for her, then at another, and keeping a model home until she was finally persuaded to undergo a needed operation and take a long rest. Never was there the slightest indication that any misconception regarding the family had resulted from lack of inquiry as to details of its earlier life, or that better results might have been attained if the usual program of investigation had been followed. Had such been the case, the fact would surely have come to light during the nearly three years that the Drews were in contact with the Section; for they were known with peculiar intimacy, Mrs. Drew turning to her visitor for advice in each of her problems as it arose, and relying upon her as upon a sister in the tragedy of her husband's death, while at the same time she herself revealed a truly heroic quality of courage and self-devotion.[1]

[1] A selected record. Family reported by the Social Service Exchange to be unknown to any of the agencies registering with it. (Abbreviated notes giving the information gleaned from the Social Service Exchange will be appended to all citations of any length included in this study. We may note here that of 351 families in what we have called the cross-section group for which Exchange returns were available only 15 per cent (54) had ever been known to any one of the three societies doing family case work (the Charity Organization Society, the Association for Improving the Condition of the Poor, or the United Hebrew Charities), while an additional 10 per cent (36) not known to these societies had

It may be said that the good outcome in this case was a matter of chance merely. To this we cannot agree. The position of the supervisor was simply that the situation was so clear that investigation would be a waste of time. An inquiry would not have led to any difficulty with Mrs. Drew, who evidently had nothing to conceal and furthermore would probably never have heard of letters sent to the West. If neither this Home Service Section nor those in the western cities where the Drews had lived had been overburdened with pressing needs the usual procedure might thus have been followed without ill effect, but as things were, the omission of investigation seems to us a mere common-sense economy of effort.

The question of whether the early history of Mrs. Dutcher should be looked up was a more complex one. This young woman, almost a stranger in New York, had been living on savings up to the time when she became known to Home Service. She was of good education and accustomed to comfortable living standards. Her one child, a little girl, was dangerously ill with influenza and pneumonia when the visitor was called in, and relief was given without question during this crisis. After it was over relations were continued; aid in securing a larger allotment from the husband, help in finding employment, and arrangements for country care for the little girl being among the services rendered. Mrs. Dutcher was decidedly difficult to deal with—inclined to stand on her dignity with regard to the type of work she would accept and to resent suggestions regarding repayment even of the small sum, out of the total given, which had been explicitly called a loan. She had been (apparently) quite frank about her family affairs, but had especially requested that her old parents in another city be not seen, stating that her father had money but was exceedingly close and had repeatedly refused to help her. Her wish was respected, the only attempt to get light on her early history or family situation being a very discreet letter to a clergyman who could not

---

been known to other social agencies in the community. This leaves 75 per cent of the families who, so far as these Social Service Exchange records show, had never been in contact with any social agency. Even allowing for a margin of error, for possible acquaintance with agencies not listed in the Exchange, and for recent comers to New York who may have been known to social agencies elsewhere, probably a large majority of these families turned to a social agency for the first time in turning to Home Service.)

remember her. The few connections she had made in New York during her short residence were followed up, but they knew little about her.

It is our opinion that those handling the case were right in thus respecting Mrs. Dutcher's wishes. Hers was undoubtedly a case the understanding of which might have been aided by information gleaned from earlier associates; but on the other hand, a break with her would certainly have followed an attempt at the usual investigation through another Section and the chance for usefulness would have been lost. She later became exceedingly frank in her revelations regarding her past life; her troubles at this period were in her state of mind, the result partly of natural temperament and marriage with a husband whose love she did not return, partly of unfortunate earlier experiences of such a character that to a great extent her word would have to be taken regarding them. A very able visitor and the psychiatrists who studied her case were able to give some help to her, which clearly they would never have had the opportunity to do had strict investigation at the outset been insisted upon.[1]

Perhaps the best illustration of our point is furnished by the case of Mrs. Marlton. Her need was first brought to the attention of Home Service by an old friend who called to explain her situation. An officer's wife, the assigned pay she received would have been sufficient to keep her even though she was ill and unable to work; but her husband's parents had fallen upon evil days since their son had gone overseas and she had been sending all she received to them. Her husband had been wounded and she was carefully keeping from him the news of his parents' misfortunes and her own self-denial; her friends had helped her to the limit, and past the limit, of their ability. She was a very nervous and sensitive type of highly cultured woman and in a critical state of health, so that approach to her would have to be peculiarly delicate and tactful.

These facts evidently explain the lack of investigation, though there is no discussion in the record of the advisability of deliberately omitting any customary preliminary steps. With the utmost simplicity and quiet good breeding the meeting between Mrs. Marlton and the visitor was managed, just as an introduction might have been arranged by her friend with a possible employer or anyone else. Of

[1] Selected record. Family known only to a diet kitchen and a day nursery.

certain rather intimate facts connected with the health problem which had been revealed to her the visitor showed no knowledge until, in a later talk, they quite naturally came out. It was, so far as Mrs. Marlton knew, solely on the issue of economic need that the two had been brought together, and this they quietly and sensibly took up, working out a tentative budget together. An adequate allowance was given and the efforts of Mrs. Marlton's physician and friends in her behalf were supplemented with remarkable tact and skill. After nearly a year her health had been sufficiently restored so that she could take first part-time work, and then a full-time position with complete economic independence. Before this point was reached the visitor had met other friends of Mrs. Marlton who confirmed in various particulars the story originally told; but never at any time was there anything which could be called an investigation. It seems evident both that it was unnecessary and that had it been attempted the whole delicate fabric of the treatment (which cannot here be gone into as the details would render it identifiable) would have been endangered.[1]

The flexibility of technique which thus revealed itself in omitting unnecessary investigations or investigations which would have done positive harm[2] naturally found expression also in the later stages of treatment.

The giving of relief, for example, was sometimes highly unconventional.

One volunteer visitor was confronted with the old, old problem of an aged parent in need whose irresponsible children were failing to take care of him. Help had been given somewhat irregularly for

---

[1] Selected record. Not known to any social agency.

[2] Many trained case workers will, we believe, agree that in a certain minority of cases investigation may wisely be omitted or curtailed. At the same time they may feel that it is dangerous to admit so much, lest encouragement be given to the untrained and half-trained who are eager to seize upon anything which may seem to justify the easygoing ways to which they are prone. In reply the writer can only say that she thinks the risk should be run in the interest of honesty. Furthermore, she suspects that there is much truth in the comment of one supervisor who felt that acceptance of this point would make things harder for her: The "path of least resistance," she pointed out, was to follow an invariable rule and investigate fully in all cases; the admission that there might be exceptions imposed a heavy burden of discrimination. Our own feeling is that this is a burden which the trained worker should be ready to assume.

months while an effort was being made to solve the problem of the one son at home, a youth of delinquent tendencies. A point had been reached where it was believed essential that the young man should be forced to depend upon himself, yet his irregular earnings clearly could not cover the support of the blind old father who, it was felt, should not be left to suffer. In this dilemma the visitor called upon a neighbor of the old man and arranged with her to give him three meals a day. The plan worked admirably for a month or more, though after the return of his soldier-son the father did try to persuade his hostess to serve instead one meal a day for three, in his rooms. Not this action of his but the fact that he now had two able-bodied sons working or able to work, finally led to the discontinuance of the experiment.[1]

Other unusual relief adjustments were made in certain families under the guise of an educational purpose. One such family,[2] whose pride led them to refuse relief in the customary forms yet whose need was evident, was aided through scholarships for the children so presented that their pride was not hurt. Was this a subterfuge wholly unjustified and certain to work demoralization in the family? We can only say that so far as the record shows, no such result has yet followed; and considering the way in which many better-to-do families and individuals survive such special aids without obvious moral disintegration we are inclined to think the case hopeful at least. Genuinely educational in aim, on the other hand, were the allowances and special grants made in certain cases where exceptionally talented young people suffering under physical handicaps were concerned, and in certain others where deserted wives with children to support were given special training. Another exceptional venture was that made in the case of a young woman who had been helped through many months of valiant struggle to support her two children, and who had received an offer of work which would greatly increase her earning power. She was enabled to take the children home to her mother in Europe so that she might be free to return and pursue her career.[3] And perhaps the most venturesome experiment of all was the lending

---

[1] Cross-section record. Known to a family society and two other agencies.

[2] Selected record. Known only to a health agency.

[3] Selected record. Not known to any social agency.

of $1,500 to a young professional man whose resources had been exhausted during the war and who wished to be enabled to travel, with his wife, half-way round the world so that he might take advantage of a promising opening. This is the only one of the cases cited where we have some doubt as to the wisdom of the action taken; in spite of the fact that the young man's character and professional standing were above reproach and that a life insurance policy to cover the loan was taken out, we are not convinced that it was wise to run the risks involved when other if less alluring prospects were open to him here. However, even were our doubt justified, this would still rank with the other instances cited as evidence of a fresh response to unusual stimuli which helped to keep case work in the Section from becoming stereotyped.[1]

The most striking departures from the conventional and accepted in treatment, however, were not made on questions of relief, though relief was sometimes involved. Two cases in which irregular marital relations formed the crucial problem may be cited as illustrations of the extreme of this tendency.

Young Mrs. Buick was living with her mother and had just given birth to her fourth child when she became known to Home Service. During the months which followed she worked hard and did her best to meet her home responsibilities. Not only was the mother repeatedly seen but relatives of the man were visited; yet it was not until several months later, after Mrs. Buick had suddenly abandoned her family and gone to a town "up state," that rumors of her not being the wife of Buick, and having a legal husband living, reached her visitor; the relatives-in-law, though suspicious and most unfriendly to her, seem not themselves to have known definitely whether the couple were married, and the mother had kept silent as to her knowledge until her discretion relaxed during a period of intoxication. The visitor followed up the young mother through the Home Service Section in the town to which she had gone, then went herself to visit her and persuaded her to return. The temporary desertion had apparently been the result of nervous reaction against the home conditions resulting from the mother's drunkenness and the malicious interference of Buick's people. There had been most suspicious cir-

[1] Selected record. Not known to any social agency.

cumstances attending her absence: she had assumed the name of a man met on her journey, and the room she had occupied was in a house run by a woman of dubious reputation; but the visitor, after very careful investigation, including communication with the man in question through another Home Service Section in his home town, came to the conclusion that Mrs. Buick was innocent of anything worse than bad judgment, and went to work to defend her against Buick's relatives and to get back the children whom the court had taken away on their instigation. This accomplished, there followed vacations for her and the children, the getting of the family furniture out of storage, and the setting up of a new home in the suburban town where her visitor lived, well away from the disturbing relatives on both sides of the family.

The considerations which led to this certainly unusual procedure—for the home was established not to keep mother and children away from Buick, but expressly to be ready for his homecoming—are worth setting forth fully. Chief among them was perhaps the excellent reputation of the young man and his devotion not only to his own children—or the one of them he had known and who died before his return—but to the two older children by the legal husband. Next was the visitor's faith in Mrs. Buick herself. She had been given a sound early training by a grandmother who seems to have been a fine old lady, but after she went to live with her mother, in her teens, she had been led into bad associations, for the mother drank and in a few years had squandered a small fortune with undesirable companions. Just the circumstances of her marriage we are not told, nor yet the circumstances of her husband's leaving her and her acceptance of a home with Buick; but the visitor's faith in her is evidenced not only by the services already mentioned as rendered, but by the determination to secure her freedom for her so that she might marry the man whose name she now bore. The legal husband was hunted up and proved quite ready to avail himself of the opportunity to obtain a divorce, and after much labor this was actually put through. At the date of reading Buick had come home and was supporting his family, and the couple were awaiting the expiration of the prescribed period following the decree to be married; while the visitor, from her home nearby, was continuing the friendly interest and oversight which distinguish the case from the time of her assuming charge.[1]

Our other instance of unconventional action in regard to marital problems involved a question of bigamy. A man in service, Charles Dawson, had married several years before in another city but had lived with his wife only a few weeks; apparently his mother had influenced him to leave her and go home to live. One child had been born of this union, now a boy of eight, for the support of whom the wife received $10 a month through the husband's mother. In 1916 Charles had married Lucy Reilly, a New York girl, without the previous knowledge of his mother, who ever since (as she told the visitor) had been living in terror of the coming out of the truth. Lucy had come to the attention of the New York Section shortly before the birth of her baby in 1918 and had been helped through this crisis; she was living with her mother and sister, very respectable folk, and the news of her husband's previous marriage came as a great shock.

The situation was brought to the attention of the New York Section by the Section in the city where the legal wife lived. She had lately learned of the second marriage, was greatly incensed, and had engaged a lawyer with the avowed intent of putting her husband "behind the bars."

Such was the situation when the man was discharged: a very angry legal wife in another city, and a very sad little second wife, restrained by her religious scruples from joining the man she had loved and who professed love for her. To be out of danger from the law Dawson went to a third city, where he obtained employment, and the Home Service visitor attempted to straighten matters out for her clients.

This involved several days spent in visiting the legal wife and the Home Service Section which had known her, also her lawyer and the theater where she worked—visits which resulted in an exceedingly interesting series of interviews. The wife proved to be a chorus girl in a low music house of particularly bad repute, but no evidence of immorality on her part came to light. Investigation also revealed that the man's mother was the owner of some fairly valuable property,

---

[1] Selected record. Not known to any social agency. The Buicks have since been married in an adjoining state.

and shortly before the date of reading the record she had been prevailed upon to offer a lump sum to the lawyer of the legal wife if he would get the latter a divorce from Charles; the offer of $5.00 a week from Charles and a supplementary $1.00 from his mother had been made to the wife contingent upon the obtaining of the divorce; and an effort was being made to bring her to a state of mind where she would see that it was to her advantage to give up the idea of vengeance and consent to a divorce with the accompanying financial support. All this had involved an immense amount of labor, including the seeing of several lawyers in both cities. One of the most interesting items in the case is the decision obtained from a priest consulted: that if the first marriage had been performed by a non-Catholic later than 1908 it would not be recognized by the church. These conditions proved to have been fulfilled; had it turned out otherwise the effort to obtain the divorce would probably not have been made, since Lucy, as a good Catholic, could never have married Charles while the first wife lived.

It appears that this attempt to save a bigamist from the result of his crime and to obtain a divorce which would enable him to remarry was not regarded as improper by the members of the bar consulted; and it is obvious that the legal wife would be better off with the measure of financial support that would go with a divorce than if she had succeeded in getting her husband locked up. A lurking question as to whether Lucy's best interests were really served by enabling her to marry a man with such a past is not answered by the record, in which little is told us of Dawson; one can only hope that events will justify the decidedly breezy and unconventional espousal of his cause.[1]

Naturally the attitude toward moral and other problems varies with the visitor and supervisor, and it is not possible to assert that the stand taken in the two cases referred to above is any more typical

[1] Selected record. Not known to any social agency.

It should be stated that these comments are based upon a reading of the Dawson case in the early winter of 1919–20, when it was under active care. One of those responsible for the handling of the case, reading the above passage in June, 1920, wrote as follows, evidently referring to developments during the intervening months: "Charles's weaknesses were brought out and it was put up to Lucy that she and only she could decide whether it was best for her to marry Charles. Marriage was never advised but made possible, partly because making legal the separation between Charles and Maude [his legal wife] is in itself considered by some of us a social act and a preventive measure that will work for the good of the community."

of Home Service than that taken in others discussed later in this report where there is no departure from the conventional and accepted. We do think, however, that a tendency to base action on the inner facts of such situations rather than on the more obvious external facts which determine their legal classification is manifest. Such a tendency is probably more or less characteristic of the younger generation of case workers everywhere. Indeed, it is not wholly absent even among the most conservative. In another case we note that an unmarried couple who had lived together many years and had had six children were well known to the priest in their church; he regretted that they could not be married, as the fate of the woman's deserting husband was unknown, but evidently did not feel it his duty to insist that they separate and approved the giving of relief to them by the social worker of his parish.[1]

A second characteristic of Home Service dealings is consideration for the point of view of the family. In our reading a few examples of ultimatum stands and "no-thoroughfare" situations were brought to light, but very few; the usual attitude was one of open-minded willingness to help in any reasonable plan proposed by the family and to listen patiently even to unreasonable ones.

The case of Mrs. Niles is an illustration in point. She had an eight-room apartment for which she paid $45, and rented out four rooms. When all went well she took in $60 a month, but one or more rooms were vacant much of the time. The visitor urged her to find a smaller apartment and to go out to work, leaving her baby in a day nursery. This she refused to do, not being willing to leave the child to the care of others and maintained that in the long run the present arrangement was best, as rent and gas were covered; this view the visitor accepted, giving relief and various forms of service during a long period.[2]

The visitor to the Marx family proposed that they give up their button-making business, sell the machinery and thus offer the son—now, she felt, sacrificed to the family business—a better chance; the Red Cross would stand back of them, she promised. They at

[1] Cross-section record. Known to a family society and to seven other social agencies.

[2] Cross-section record. Known only to a diet kitchen.

first agreed, then changed their minds. A button expert was later sent in to consult with them, but though he found little prospect of growth in the business they clung to it. Their judgment was accepted, friendly relations were continued, and a variety of services were performed involving considerable expenditures from the relief funds.[1]

Consideration for the point of view of sick people is especially marked. Cases of disabled discharged men afford, perhaps, the most striking but by no means the only instances of this. We have in mind a man suffering from tuberculosis; one said by experts to be, in the New York climate, 100 per cent disabled from asthma, and who later developed a venereal infection; and one diagnosed (rather doubtfully) as a victim of shell-shock. No one of these men was devoid of good qualities, but the demands which they made upon the patience and resourcefulness of their visitors were certainly a searching test of the possession of that consideration of which we have been speaking. Karl Sartoris[2] (the mildest instance), writing from the third sanatorium to which he had been sent in six months, that he thought he would like to be transferred to a fourth, may have caused a moment's irritation in the bosom of his faithful friend, but it certainly did not show in any of the wise, kindly letters written him, and we are thankful to say that he finally settled down and at last accounts was gaining. When Morris Sossnitz,[2] returning to New York unbenefited after a brief sojourn in the third place to which he had been sent in the desperate hope of finding a climate that would help him, announced that he was going to use his recently received compensation check to transport himself and his wife to Colorado, without awaiting the adjustments with the Federal Board for his training which his visitor was trying to make or the completion of his treatments for the venereal infection which complicated his case, efforts were indeed made to dissuade him; but on his persisting, his case was explained to the Home Service Section in the city to which he was going and every effort made to obtain the same sympathetic handling for him there. This is, however, the last and most justifiable of the many difficult situations which he and his young wife had "put up"

[1] Selected record. Known only to a health agency.
[2] Selected record. Not known to any social agency.

to their visitor in the course of six months of intensive treatment. As for Leonardis,[1] it is impossible to determine how many of his vagaries were due to a disordered mental or nervous state, since toward the end the physicians of the Federal Board concluded that there was nothing the matter with his mind and gave him up in disgust, and since no information regarding his condition before the war was available; but certainly a more exasperating human being would be hard to find, and we confess ourselves lost in admiration before the inexhaustible patience with which his visitor met each new complication presented by him.

The stories of these men are so long and so interwoven with details which have no significance for our immediate purpose that we refrain from citing them more at length at this stage. The case of little Emilia Vaccaro[1] furnishes a simpler illustration of the same point. This child of thirteen suffered from a bad case of tuberculosis of the hip. She was taken twice to the Hospital Admission Bureau by the Red Cross Motor Corps and was sent away to a sanatorium; but within a few days she had prevailed upon her family to bring her home, and the visitor's best efforts failed to persuade her to go away again or her mother to consent to her going. This "failure to co-operate" was not, however, allowed to put an end to friendly relations; milk was supplied and great pains taken to place and keep Emilia under the best medical care available. All this may seem to the present generation of case workers a mere commonplace of decently considerate treatment. If so, it is welcome evidence that the epoch is definitely past when immediate discontinuance of relief was assumed to follow normally upon the refusal of a mother to leave her only son and enter a hospital, and when the giving of an outfit so that a tuberculous young deserted wife could go to a sanatorium was conditioned upon her consenting first to appear against her husband in court—incidents known to have occurred in a reputable agency less than ten years ago.

Perhaps the most striking illustration of our point is, however, furnished by the Section's dealings with Mrs. Vizet.[2] This fiery Irishwoman had married a French butler in the house where she was

---

[1] Cross-section record. Not known to any social agency.

[2] Selected record. Known to a family society.

working as cook. After a few years he had deserted, leaving her with two small children. By court order he had been forced to pay her a weekly allowance for a year or two until he disappeared. All this was several years before the war began. Mrs. Vizet was alert from the outbreak of the conflict to the probability that her husband would return to France, but it was not until 1917 that she succeeded in unearthing definite proof that he was in the military service of that country. She at once applied for an allotment and received one regularly from some time in 1918 until several months after demobilization.

Meanwhile, during all the years since she had been abandoned, she had been working beyond her strength to all hours of the night, doing an incredible number of washings and ironings weekly. At first she had received a small amount of help from one of the family agencies, but since 1912 had supported herself and children entirely (except for the allotment in the last year). She had, moreover, accumulated savings—$400 invested in Liberty Bonds—and had purchased two suburban lots worth several hundred dollars.

In the course of this struggle she had developed what amounted to a mania against not only her husband but the French government, which she insisted must pay her the full allotment from the date when Vizet was enlisted, in 1915, to the date when her allotment had begun, in 1918, and which she further persisted in holding accountable for returning her husband to this country so that she might force him to support the children. There was also a pending claim against a truck driver who had run over and seriously injured her little girl—now happily almost completely recovered.

Such was the situation when Home Service was called in—a woman on the verge of breakdown who did not at first ask relief but demanded what she felt were her rights.

Treatment was at first along conventional lines. There was a good investigation: Mrs. Vizet's own relatives, her priest, and employers all spoke highly of her, but those who had known her husband as well (including her two sisters) gave him a very fair character and attributed the family troubles to incompatibility and her ungovernable temper.

The French Benevolent Society and French Consulate alike assured the visitor that there could be no exception in this case to the French government's rule that allotments were paid only from the date of the wife's application. Then began a long struggle to convince Mrs. Vizet first, that it was idle to attempt to push this claim; second, that she should submit herself and children to medical examination; third, that she should sell some of her Liberty Bonds and take a needed rest; fourth, that she should place her suit against the truckman in the hands of the Red Cross lawyers who would put it through without charge. All of these propositions alike she rejected—every suggestion regarding her abandonment of her claims against the French or the sale of her bonds throwing her into spasms of rage which from the outset impressed her visitors as maniacal; and for several months the situation was dead-locked, her visitor insisting that the free legal service offered must be accepted and the bonds—which she had partly pledged to pay her lawyer—used for living expenses instead, before the Section could properly be expected to help her.

Then came a reversal of policy, led up to by a violent tirade against her visitor indulged in at the Red Cross office and a telephone conversation between Mrs. Vizet and the supervisor of the district, in which the woman broke down and wept over the effort that was being made to force her to sell her bonds. Her feeling was that they were all she had to leave her children and that she could not part with them. A new visitor was put on the case. Mrs. Vizet was promised that every effort would be made to recover for her from the French government, the fight against the employment of a private lawyer was dropped, together with the question of selling her bonds, and a liberal allowance, planned by the dietitian, was arranged.

It is interesting to note that this allowance was reduced at the outset from the proposed $19 a week to $14, upon Mrs. Vizet's own insistence that she continue to do $5.00 or $6.00 worth of washing weekly; she was thankful to accept help for the children but wished to retain a measure of personal independence. She was entirely reasonable and co-operative about expenditures and account keeping, and very appreciative of the help given—which included milk and eggs, money for coal and other extras, as well as the cash allowance; and gradually she was brought to an equally co-operative attitude in health matters, submitting to examination at the Medical Station for herself, letting her boy go regularly to the Health Center and undergo an operation on his tonsils, and finally even consenting to a similar operation on the daughter (not yet performed at the date of reading). Gradual improvement in the health of all the family had taken place under the improved conditions made possible by regular income and the mother's comparative freedom for the performance of her normal household duties. (She stated on one occasion that "she and the children were talking yesterday about how wonderful it had been to have three meals a day.") All this seems to us quite worth while, even though it had involved acceptance of certain unreasonable demands on the part of an overwrought and probably somewhat mentally unbalanced woman. Moreover, that her original stand on the French allotment question was not quite so insane as it seemed is proved by the efforts made at the Consulate, under pressure from the Section, to secure permission to make a special adjustment with her, and the final offer of one year's back allotments in compromise.[1]

The last three-fourths or so of this record, from the time when the change in visitors was made and the new and more liberal policy inaugurated, is well worth reading. In particular, we enjoyed the following refreshing account of the new visitor's method of meeting the first outbreak of temper to which Mrs. Vizet treated her—a tirade against the Section for its just-abandoned policy of urging her to sell her bonds: "Visitor emphasized the fact that she would not listen to her talk about the Red Cross in such a disrespectful manner. Visitor further explained that she had just as violent a temper as Mrs. Vizet, and it was just as serious for her to aggravate the visitor by ideas that were not in accordance with hers as it was for visitor to disagree in ideas with Mrs. Vizet. It would be necessary for them to discuss matters quietly and calmly, otherwise a serious quarrel might result. This seemed to appeal to Mrs. Vizet and she was much quieter in her attitude toward visitor."

What is here written sounds poor and pale in comparison with the impression made upon our mind by the reading of some of the best of these records. The truth is that brief summaries cannot give any conception of the cumulative effect of thirty or forty pages in which

[1] Whether Mrs. Vizet's condition was really psychopathic had not been finally determined at the date of our reading, the mental specialists who had examined her having disagreed; nor had a final solution of other problems in her case been worked out.

problem after problem is met with the same unvarying patience, the same determination to give the benefit of every doubt and believe the best until the worst is proved. More than once we have thought, "This must be the sort of thing that was meant by that saying about seventy-times-seven."

A third quality which was found to be characteristic of Home Service work at its best is a truly co-operative spirit, a real respect for the work of other agencies with differing points of view. Representatives of the Henry Street Scholarships Committee have stated to the writer that the arrangement between the two organizations was the "most successful piece of co-operation" they knew of, and the members of the Council of Jewish Women who conducted the Red Cross workrooms and seaside home for Jewish women and children are equally enthusiastic. The representative of the St. Vincent de Paul Society from the Bronx, who was a faithful attendant at the consultation committee and most helpful to the case workers in that district, also bears cordial testimony to this co-operative spirit. From the chairman down, the Section seems to have been characterized by an open-minded, generous, and cosmopolitan spirit, a striking lack of racial and religious prejudice. It was a pleasure, also, to note the absence of an attitude sometimes encountered among social workers, which seems to rest on the assumption that the trained case worker is the one person in the community fitted to cope with family problems.

In the nature of things case work testimony to these characteristics is difficult to collect; a record rarely goes into matters of feeling or the spirit which animates its makers. Instances of successful co-operation with a number of medical agencies and physicians, with teachers, with the St. Vincent de Paul, with the Jewish Big Brothers, the Boy Conservation Bureau, and the Children's Court have especially impressed us. These will be found scattered through the citations in the chapters that follow, and seem to belong under the discussion of the various problems there grouped. Three instances will here be cited which bring out especially the spirit of co-operation animating the workers.

The first[1] illustrates especially the tone and temper in which we

[1] Selected record. Not known to any social agency.

believe criticism of another agency's work should be offered and received. The young wife of a discharged man had been in a hospital for some time suffering from severe injuries, the result of a fall. The visitor, calling to see her one day, was surprised to learn that she had gone home against advice and without the Section's being notified. The visitor wrote as follows to the head of the Social Service Department at the hospital:

"Since early in January Mrs. Ella Godonov has been a patient in Ward M suffering from a badly fractured leg. She is the wife of a discharged soldier with whom the Red Cross has worked almost constantly since the time of the woman's admittance to the hospital.

"We have succeeded in putting this man in touch with the Federal Board for Vocational Training and have also hastened for him the payment of his compensation. We have also been able to place the child in a suitable home pending the discharge of the mother from the hospital.

"We have communicated many times by telephone with your office and once by letter. Realizing, however, that these frequent telephone requests for information regarding the woman were not always satisfactory, we requested of your office and also Miss Upham, the nurse in Ward D, if we might be informed of any change of plan for the woman and also of any change in her condition. It was especially important that we should know when Mrs. Godonov was to be discharged from the hospital because we realized how important it was that we should put her in touch with a nurse who could look after the dressing of her ankle.

"When our visitor called at the hospital last Friday she was very much shocked to learn that Mrs. Godonov had been discharged from the hospital on the previous Sunday, June 2d. Upon calling at the woman's home she found the young woman in bed, her ankle having been taken care of by her husband. We have put her in touch at once with a Henry Street Nurse who reports to us today that Mrs. Godonov has a running sore on her ankle which will no doubt take six months to heal and that her condition is quite alarming.

"We realize perfectly how impossible it is for your office to keep in daily touch with all of the patients about whom requests are made, but we feel that in this case a real hardship has resulted from our not having been informed of the woman's discharge. We realize that Mrs. Godonov took this step upon her own initiative and responsibility and that the hospital in no way is responsible for her present condition, but we feel that we ourselves would have been better able to help the young woman had we known on Monday of her discharge from the hospital instead of waiting until Friday to learn this."

In answer, four days later, came the following letter:

"I was away at Atlantic City last week and so heard nothing of Mrs. Godonov's discharge from the hospital. Possibly I would not have known of it had I been here, for it is impossible for our office to keep in daily touch with the fifteen hundred patients who are here. But I am extremely sorry that the slip should have occurred, and that you should not have been notified of her discharge. Upon inquiry, however, I find that neither our visitor to that ward nor Miss Upham, the head nurse, quite appreciated the necessity for letting you know immediately that she had left the hospital, inasmuch as her husband had taken her home and they, supposing you to be in close touch with the family, and he would notify you, did not themselves do so.

"I inquired also about the condition of the ankle: that is serious, and the prognosis doubtful. I am indeed sorry that the lapse of attention should have occurred.

"I appreciate the considerate tone of your protest and repeat that I regret that anything should have gone wrong in this instance, especially as we have always received such splendid co-operation from the Red Cross."

If errors and oversights were always treated in this spirit social work could be carried on upon a higher plane. But this can never be until specialists in different fields form the habit of looking for and appreciating the best in one another's work instead of being ever on the alert for the expected slips and shortcomings.

The story of a woman of refinement, a drug victim, who was cured of her habit while under the care of the Section, furnishes an example of co-operation with a physician which is of especial interest. The visitor, already in full possession of the patient's story, met the doctor first in the sick room, to which she had summoned him on finding her client ill with one of the terrific headaches that had led to the formation of her habit. He, knowing in advance that the visitor was fully informed as to the nature of the trouble but that the patient was unaware of the fact, took occasion to chide the latter for her use of "sleeping medicines," remarking to the visitor that probably she had not been told that such medicines were being taken.

After this the subject was in the open and a frank working together possible. On two later occasions the visitor was with her client in a similar crisis and called in the physician; when a nurse was needed she provided one; and in addition to furnishing the full support needed for many months, found numerous other friendly offices to perform. When at last the combined efforts of all concerned had resulted in what both patient and doctor believed to be a "really permanent cure," a final conversation between case worker and physician took place which is worth noting. Dr. Turner "showed the visitor the full history and record" of the case, expressing his delight in the outcome. And then he offered a suggestion which strikes us as singularly wise and far-seeing. He "advised our not seeking her unless she appeals to us for new contacts," for he "thinks she is now able to stand alone . . . and if she can do so she would probably want to see less and less of us, and this reaction would be natural as she would not want to be self-conscious in the future with regard to our knowledge." The acceptance of this suggestion is shown in the withdrawal of Home Service. To the writer's mind—perhaps because the bare facts of the record are illumined for her by a personal acquaintance with both the social worker and the physician in the case—this episode furnishes an illustration of that fine sincerity and full confidence in the disinterestedness and high-mindedness of a fellow-worker which are characteristic of social case work at its best.

Our third instance of the true co-operative spirit involves a somewhat longer story.

Mrs. Terenska came in person to the Section in the summer of 1918, having been referred by a priest to whom she appealed for advice. The family had been driven from their home in Poland in the early days of the war and after many hardships had settled in Russia. Later Terenska had been drafted into the Russian Army and his wife, with her mother and three little children, made their way to New York. Here their small remaining capital had gone into the furnishing of a four-room apartment in a cheap tenement house. Mrs. Terenska was a woman of education and refinement, accustomed to a high standard of living, as her husband had been a well-paid government official; but in her ignorance of English she had been compelled to accept a position at $9.00 a week and had only been able to manage by the aid of a wonderfully kind friend whom she had made—the office manager at her first place of employment. This woman had helped out with a small allowance to supplement her salary until the total amounted to over $300. Mrs. Terenska insisted upon regarding this aid as a loan, though her friend had given it without any thought of return, and though her small salary, now increased to $18, had not permitted any repayment.

At the time Mrs. Terenska became known to Home Service she had been working steadily without vacation for nearly two years and was pretty well worn out; she was haunted by the fear of what would befall her children if she should be incapacitated by illness. Her little boy, too—a nervous child who had suffered greatly from exposure and fear during their wanderings—was in poor condition. During the first year help consisted chiefly in medical care—regular attendance at the Health Center for the children, the care of a private physician who had offered his services to the Red Cross for the mother—and milk and eggs to aid in building up the child. But before the winter was over Mrs. Terenska's salary had reached the figure set by the dietitian as required to meet the family's needs, and in the spring this help was discontinued.

The visitor, however, kept up her friendly intercourse with the mother and her oversight of the children's health. Early in the following summer she felt so strongly that Mrs. Terenska was in need of a vacation if a serious breakdown in health was to be avoided, that it was decided to assume responsibility for a month in the country for the entire family. With some difficulty the mother was persuaded to accept what she felt was too great a gift. Arrangements were made for the children at pay camps and for the mother and grandmother at a delightful farm which had opened its hospitable doors to many Home Service clients; necessary clothing was furnished and rent and insurance carried for a month; and all the family returned greatly benefited—the children so bursting with health that their cases were promptly closed at the Health Center, and the mother with such a fund of physical and spiritual strength that, as she said to her visitor, "she thought she would never again be in quite such low spirits."

Most of the work which this very inadequate summary records may seem to the reader to be concerned primarily with physical health. Yet the visitor, from her first call on, had kept in mind what she felt was a deeper need. She refers to this again in recording the conversation she had with Mrs. Terenska upon the latter's return from the vacation: "Visitor feels that the spiritual need spoken of in the first interview with Mrs. T. has after almost a year been met. . . . She has made lasting friends of Mr. and Mrs. Howe, at whose house she was a guest and of several other people who were present at the same time." In her letter to Mrs. Howe the visitor is more explicit: "If you could hear some of the things Mrs. T. has said to me about the help you and Mr. Howe have been to her you would feel more than repaid for any effort her entertainment may have cost you. Today she said, 'Miss Taft, I can never again be so fearful of the future as I was before I went to Kent. Mr. Howe said something about courage that I shall never forget.' This is one of many remarks that make me know what her visit to you has meant."

It may be because we have talked both with the visitor and with Mrs. Terenska, and have thus been able roughly to gauge the depth and genuineness of the relation between them, that we are so struck by these passages. What impresses us is that it does not seem to occur to the visitor that she herself may have made a contribution to the mother's spiritual need. Instead she gladly gives full credit for the change she sees to those who have apparently accomplished in a few weeks what she had long realized needed doing. A better illustration of the unselfregardfulness and the generosity which characterize true co-operation would be hard to find.[1]

Still another feature which is characteristic of the best of Home Service work is the insistence upon normal standards. The calculations of the dietitian, for example, rested on a scientific basis which took into account not only differences in sex, age, and type of work performed, but also state of health and the degree of skill available for choice and preparation of foods. Of the three scales (A, B, and C) giving requirements to meet different conditions, the lowest, says the dietitian, was rarely used, for it was seldom that such rare things as perfect health and a high degree of skill were found together, and only exceptional knowledge and skill could produce an adequate diet, even for well people, with these minimum amounts. Any housewife who has experimented knows how much more forethought goes into planning inexpensive meals than expensive ones, how much more art into preparing cheap cuts or meat substitutes than into cooking chops and steaks. Yet it is only comparatively recently that we have ceased demanding of untrained mothers what would be an impossibility for the best equipped member of our own circle of acquaintances.

[1] Selected record. Not known to any social agency.

So science has contributed toward a democratization of relief, emphasizing the common human needs of all classes while taking into account every significant variation in individual requirements. While the men in service were being accustomed to a certain standard dietary, and their families at home, of all grades and living customs, were being subjected to the educational bombardment of the food administration, it was certainly appropriate that Home Service, in its special field, should be transforming its relief giving into a fairer approximation to the democratic ideal.[1]

Last of all, there is, pervading some of these records, a spirit of friendship, of genuine democratic fellowship, which seems to merit comment. Mrs. Drew, saying at the end of her visitor's first call that she was glad she had called and that now someone would take a personal interest in her; Mrs. Tartora, suggesting, when the need of relief was past, that she would like the visitor to call again, that the advice given by the Red Cross is the "only kind she can trust"; Mrs. Zimmerman, presiding at the meeting of the visitor and her soldier son with the statement that the former is her "best friend," "the Red Cross is all right," are only a few among many. There are records—a few of them only in our reading—where relations with a family were abruptly broken off at the family's request, or where some obvious defect of method or temper in the visitor might well have led to such a result; but we feel sure that these failures are more than balanced by the instances in which a fine relation existed though no trace of it appears in the record.

Take, for example, the case of Mrs. Thomas. She had received an allowance of $5.50 from the Canadian Patriotic Fund when staying in Montreal, and came to the Section to see about having it transferred to her here. It is recorded that "she could not see why there was any question about this arrangement." There is a record of three visits to her at the "very good furnished room house" which she kept, and then the statement (in a report to the Fund) that "no assistance was needed by Mrs. Thomas as she has always supported herself and was receiving her pay regularly from Canada." There is no evidence that this decision was explained to Mrs. Thomas, and had the record ended here, we should have had no idea that anything had been

[1] The advantage possessed by Red Cross workers in the ample relief funds at their disposal should be noted.

accomplished beyond arriving at a probably just but unwelcome decision not to assist financially.

Three months later, however, Mrs. Thomas called at the Home Service office. She wanted to show the visitor a picture of her husband and to tell her what a splendid man he was and about his advancement in service; also to relate how she had paid off the debts that had accumulated while she was in Canada through the mismanagement of a friend left in charge of her house. "She especially wanted to thank the visitor for encouragement given her several months ago in talking over plans to pay off debts—and she is justly proud of her success in getting straightened out. It was agreed that Mrs. Thomas should come to see visitor whenever she wished, and that visitor stood ready to help her in any way that in the future might seem to suggest itself."[1]

It was, however, naturally in the families that were longest and most thoroughly known that such friendships reached their fullest development. Several such families have been mentioned—the Drews, the Dutchers, the Buicks, the Terenskas. A few others will be cited.

Several young girls, either quite alone in the world or with families with whom they were living in more or less strained relations, were among those to whom the finest sort of friendship was given. Two such instances may be mentioned, especially noteworthy because no question of relief was involved in either, and because of the very definite influence exerted in bringing about a better understanding between mothers and daughters.

The mother of Rosa Varella appealed to the Section for information about Henry Cutler, a young American sailor whom her daughter declared she was going to marry as soon as his term of service was up. Rosa had resorted to various subterfuges in order to enjoy a measure of that freedom in going out with him to evening entertainments which was regarded as a natural right by her American friends, and her actions had alienated and alarmed her parents with their strict old-world ideas in such matters. The mother herself had hardly met the young man; he seemed to avoid accepting invitations to visit in the family; moreover, he had never given the daughter any presents and his statements about his family and background seemed not to hang together. The visitor had a talk with him, finding him frank enough but inclined

[1] Cross-section record. Not known to any social agency.

to resent the mother's interference; she also wrote to the Home Service Section in the farming district where his family lived and received a favorable report of them and him. This greatly relieved the mother's mind; but it came to light about this time that Cutler, who had been declining invitations from the family on the ground that he was restricted for having been absent without leave in France, had in fact a perfectly clear record; and soon after he wrote to Rosa, breaking the engagement. This caused a terrible scene between mother and daughter, the girl accusing the mother of having caused the breach by her interference.

It was from this point on that the visitor did her most effective work; in talks with the mother she brought her to see the need of giving her daughter more freedom and letting her mingle with American girls from whom she might gain a truer idea of the sort of freedom permitted girls in this country than that she had picked up from her comrades in the place where she worked. With the daughter, whom she took to lunch on several occasions, she labored, on the other hand, to bring about a better understanding of the mother's point of view, pointing out how natural and legitimate was her desire to know something of the man her daughter proposed to marry and assuring the girl that American parents also sought to inform themselves on such points. A reconciliation followed, the girl was permitted to join a club and go out evenings, and at last accounts was handling very wisely a recrudescence of affection on the part of her former fiancé which she confided to her visitor.[1]

The other case is that of Annette Privet, a little French girl who, when deserted in England by her lover, had struggled on for over two years, supporting herself and her child, until finally her mother sent her money to come to the United States.

She was much out of health, due, the doctors said, to "air-raid neurosis," but her family—a mother, brother, and sister, the two latter professional dancers—were quite unappreciative of her condition and resentful of having to support her, and kept urging her to work. They also—or at least the mother—felt keenly the disgrace of her irregular affair, made her unhappy by talk of the past, and seem to have been

---

[1] Selected record. Search for family of girl apparently never requested of Social Service Exchange.

none too kind to the child, a lovely, fairy-like little creature of three years. At the time when the girl first sought the help of the Section (in the hope of getting support from the child's father) she had already found a job in a nursery with Mimi, and she worked until compelled by illness to enter a hospital. It was then that the visitor took occasion to call several times on her family, who at first seemed inclined to shirk the responsibility but ultimately assumed the care of the little girl, and, upon her leaving the hospital, of Annette herself. It was not long after this event that Annette's mother came to the office for the first time. She said that she "wanted to explain to the visitor a long-delayed apology that she had seemed so unmotherly toward her own family. She realized when she knew how much visitor had done for both Annette and Mimi she had fallen short in her duty, and must have seemed very grudging in all that she said about them. . . . She has talked it over with Louise and Pierre, and they have decided that Annette must be adequately cared for for a long time to get well. . . . They will do all in their power to give her a proper home." A few days later the visitor called on the family and noted that the mother "is doing everything for them." Still later Mrs. Privet came to the office bringing some flowers for the visitor's Easter: "She feels that a great deal has been done to make them understand Annette and she is friendly now in her attitude toward them and toward the Red Cross. . . . She believes we have brought her good luck, as the two children are doing splendidly and are happy about Annette."[1]

Young married women probably are more numerous than the unmarried in these records, and certainly have absorbed a larger share of the visitor's time. Naturally wives with babies and little children were on the whole those hardest hit by the war and most in need of sustaining friendship. The story of one may serve as typical of many:

Mrs. Vail, with two little sons three years and one year old, was found living in two rooms very scantily furnished but immaculately clean. The visitor describes her as a "very bright and pretty woman, wonderfully brave and cheerful without realizing she is so." This first visitor, however, does not seem to have got to know her very well. Mrs. Vail was given some financial aid in emergencies when the babies

[1] Selected record. Not known to any social agency.

were ill, but when they were well again was advised (rather casually, it would seem) to put them in a day nursery and go to work as she had done before. This she seems to have done, and it was about two months later when she again appealed for help, one of the children having broken his arm. The dietitian had meanwhile come on the staff and the Vail family was referred to her for budget study. This led to the giving of milk regularly to supplement the young mother's earnings and the irregularly received allotment and allowance from the government, together with a cash allowance and grants as needed. Medical care was also quite persistently given.

It was not, however, until several months after the making of the first budget that evidences begin to appear of a special interest in her client on the part of the latest visitor assigned to Mrs. Vail. She came, it appears, of a family of good traditions, but her home since her marriage had been constantly upset by a drinking husband. He seems, however, to have had his good points; to be sure, Home Service workers know how frequently the worst of husbands wrote home from overseas like reformed characters, but there is a true ring about this young man. "Mrs. Vail received a letter from her husband this week," we read in February, 1919, "in which he states that he is very happy that we are going to get prohibition, for he thinks that they are going to have a happy home." Evidently the visitor became convinced that there was a good chance of this being brought about, and entered into the wife's desire to have a pleasant place to receive him in. Forthwith there is a stocking up with needed furniture and household equipment—a crib and spring, mattresses and pillows, sheets and pillow-cases, cups and saucers, paints and a brush, etc. A chiffonnier and $20 for clothing were given by a friend of the visitor's, a second-hand sewing machine was purchased, and we read that Mrs. Vail is "enjoying housekeeping with the new things."

All this might be, perhaps, without any marked development of a relationship between the visitor and Mrs. Vail, but the former's supervisor, when we talked with her, laughingly supplied the missing link in describing the scene occasioned by Mrs. Vail's arrival one day at the office with the announcement that word had come from her husband that he would be home shortly. The visitor "had no idea how funny she was" as she excitedly discussed the final preparations for his reception with the wife. The last item in the case, at the date of our reading, told of his arrival and his pleasure in the homecoming; and relates that he gave his wife $69, went with her to buy a suit for herself, and promptly went to work.[1]

One other case summary may be given in closing this chapter. It illustrates three of the five points we have been trying to bring out as characteristic of Home Service at its best—the maintenance of normal standards, special consideration for the point of view of the family, and cordial relations of friendship, evidenced here in an unusual and peculiarly touching way.

Miles Gregory[2] had been discharged less than a month when, in January, 1919, his family was referred to Home Service by a society under whose care they had formerly been. The father had a record for drink and desertion but was now at home, not drinking and unable to work on account of diabetes. The mother and little sister were also in poor health and Miles with his salary of $16 a week was the sole reliance of the family. The budget card, dated in March, shows a deficit in income as compared with needed expenditures of $8.85, with the statement that the Red Cross was giving two quarts of milk daily and a weekly allowance of $6.60.

On the health side a vast amount of effort was put into getting the father to submit to medical treatment. He was at last induced to go to a clinic, and a visiting dietitian was sent in to give instruction and encouragement in regard to the special diet ordered by the physician there—a service continued with great tact and fair success for many months. Still later, when his exactions and violent temper had pretty much worn out his delicate wife, he was persuaded to enter a hospital for a time, thus bringing immeasurable relief to the overburdened family. The mother and daughter, meanwhile, had been for months under the care of the Medical Station; and while the former, circumstanced as she was and suffering from heart trouble, could be little helped, the small girl had been completely cured of a serious difficulty.

An especially interesting question arose when Miles' salary was raised to $18. The visitor suggested reducing the allowance by two dollars, whereupon Mrs. Gregory burst into tears and explained that he still gave her only the $11 formerly contributed. The visitor talked

[1] Selected record. Not known to any social agency.

[2] Selected record. Known to a family society.

over the matter with the dietitian and they decided that it "seems unwise to ask Miles to give all of his $2.00 raise as this might discourage him. Thought it best to let him keep this until he has another raise when matter can be taken up." It may be well to add that there was never any occasion to regret the decision thus made. Since the father's death late in 1919 Miles has assumed full responsibility for his family; he has steadily worked up, until now, at twenty, he is earning $30 a week.

Recently he has married—a very fine girl, apparently, who also works and helps him keep up the home. Writing the visitor of his plans, shortly before he launched upon this matrimonial venture, he says: "But one thing you may be sure, that my mother will be with us, also Annie, and they will be taken care of."

It was at about this same time that an episode is recorded which gives us an insight into the exceptional character of this boy and the attitude of himself and his mother toward the Home Service visitors whom they had known. We quote verbatim from the record:

"Mrs. Gregory . . . told visitor Miles was in some department [store] where there was a Red Cross booth selling buttons for one dollar. When he saw someone passing by without giving the dollar he turned to the lady in charge and said: 'If people only knew how much good the Red Cross did they would certainly give that dollar, which they would probably otherwise waste.' He said he knew what he was talking about, because his family had been helped by the Red Cross. The lady asked him if he would like to get up on the platform and make a little speech about it. He said he would be delighted. He then got up on the platform and told exactly what the Red Cross had done for his family after his return; gave the names of everyone he knew in the Red Cross to prove his point and apparently had an ovation. His mother was very much pleased with him and tears came into her eyes as she told visitor about him."

CHAPTER III

UNDERLYING IDEAS

In the preceding chapters we have reviewed the outstanding features of Home Service organization and personnel and have dwelt upon a number of qualities which seem to us characteristic of, and fundamental to, the best work done by the Section. In the present chapter we propose to touch upon certain ideas closely related to these characteristic qualities—old ideas which had to be abandoned before they could emerge, newer ideas which they body forth. The qualities are none of them peculiar to Home Service; any claim to originality on this score would be absurd. The Section did not deliberately go forth to do battle with the old ideas nor did it invent new ones. Probably a somewhat better claim to originality could be made in the matter of organization and personnel developments, but for this view we hold no brief. We do believe, however, that the impromptu pooling of personalities in Home Service—an experimental organization formed to meet an exceptional situation—has found expression in ways that cast a shaft of light on some familiar aspects of case work and lend fresh emphasis to certain current concepts.

It may be well to recapitulate briefly the five qualities to the illustration of which the chapter on Characteristics was mainly devoted.

1. Flexibility in treatment, growing out of freedom from conventionality and responsiveness to the realities in situations met.

2. Consideration for the point of view of the family and the individual dealt with—openmindedness in listening to their plans and so far as possible adopting them.

3. Cordial co-operation with other agencies and individuals, resting upon a genuine appreciation of the special contributions made by them.

4. Emphasis upon maintenance of normal standards in normal and even in some abnormal families.

5. A spirit of genuine democratic fellowship between visitors and clients.

One of the underlying assumptions of an older generation in charitable work, which like most ideas of older generations is still more or less current in our own day, was the assumption that their clients—or "applicants"—were suffering mainly through their own fault; that they were in a sense a peculiar people whose defective characters accounted for their position at the foot of the social scale. Needless to say, reaction against this view had set in some years before the war.

It is perfectly obvious, of course, that many family disasters, in Home Service families as in others, do result from defects of character, as will be amply evidenced in a later chapter of this study. But there has, we believe, come to be a clear recognition that large numbers of families—in the war emergency certainly an ample majority—have come to need help through no fault of their own. Probably there is also in the background, parallel with this recognition, the realization (hardly to be avoided by reading Americans) that quite as serious faults of character frequently coexist with success as with failure; that success, indeed, is frequently traceable to character defects quite as grave in their social consequences as any that lead to failure; and that defects of both sorts are to be found at times even in the households of case workers and their friends. What may perhaps be called the solidarity of the "dependent classes," as it existed in the minds of charitable workers of an earlier day, has thus been quite broken down in the view of the Home Service worker and others of her generation; she has ceased to think of her clients and her own circle of acquaintances (including herself) as mutually exclusive and wholly dissimilar groups. As one Home Service worker put it, "There has been a greater tendency to assume that worker and client are more alike than different." It is this changed conception which has made possible that "genuine democratic fellowship" and that "consideration for the point of view of the family" which are two of the qualities of Home Service on which we have commented.

It has naturally been easier to develop and hold this conception when dealing with families brought to the Section by a special emergency, so large a proportion of whom were previously unknown to social agencies; though, as review of the chapter on Problems of Conduct will show, some of the most difficult situations arose in families of this class. But industrial accidents and tuberculosis—to name only two of the many causes which bring clients to the peace-time family agencies—are no more respecters of persons than the draft and the War Risk Insurance Bureau; and case workers everywhere are more and more coming to see their clients as persons, not as members of any class.

Another age-old assumption in the charitable field (which, like the one already discussed, has been slowly losing ground) was that the receiving of financial aid necessarily destroyed self-respect and undermined the character. A corollary to this was the notion that the less financial aid received the less would be the resulting demoralization.

Home Service workers would never deny that demoralization does sometimes follow relief-giving; but that there is any necessary connection between the two most of them would, we feel confident, emphatically deny. Certainly we, on the basis of our reading of records, are prepared to stand out against any such idea, and still more vigorously against the idea that the danger of demoralization can be minimized by keeping the amount of relief at a minimum. The emphasis laid upon a normal living standard based on budget study, which distinguished the later years of Home Service activity, is of course the very antithesis of the second of these ideas. However much we may revolt against the idea of economic dependence for anyone, there is no blinking the fact that in the present stage of our social evolution the necessity for it must in many cases be accepted if worse evils are to be avoided; and once this necessity is accepted anything which leads to the omission of measures, however costly, which will tend to restore normal conditions is a weakness in our case work.

Three of our five characteristic qualities are thus seen to be linked with certain changes in fundamental ideas regarding the clients of social organizations—changes which have been taking place with varying rates of speed in many parts of the field of social service. The other two characteristics—flexibility of treatment and cordial co-operative relations—are linked rather with certain changes in ideas regarding organization and personnel which we shall now endeavor to point out.

First of all come ideas regarding the make-up of a social work staff. Certain rather exceptional organizations have depended largely upon volunteers, paid secretaries holding responsibilities quite definitely subject to their committees. More commonly in our cities paid workers have carried the main or exclusive responsibility, and volunteers, where used at all, have been trained and directed by these professionals and in the main have filled quite subordinate rôles. Their influence on committees has indeed been considerable and individuals among them have always been highly appreciated for their wisdom and devotion; but it has been only rarely that they have been charged with executive functions or have taken any more active part in case work than that of friendly visitor to a few selected families. Frequently the prevailing idea among professional workers regarding them has been that they were unreliable, sentimental, and not to be taken seriously.

How Home Service has combined and balanced the forces of its paid workers and volunteers has already been described in the first chapter. The eager desire to serve in the war emergency made possible insistence upon the following of training courses, the rejection of the unfit, and the holding of those retained to a regular half-time schedule and the definite fulfilment of engagements. An inner group of those who proved especially fitted for the work labored full time and overtime, assuming responsibilities in case work and supervision equal to any carried by the paid staff and becoming to all intents and purposes as professional as they.

What is the real significance of this development? It is easy to say, as has been frequently said, that only war service enthusiasm made it possible. But this is a very small segment of the truth about the matter; that a large quantity of work was done without pay might have meant nothing but the saving of Red Cross funds. Of far greater interest is the fact, as we see it, that this development of volunteer service meant also an increased flexibility in treatment and a deeper current of co-operation—precisely the two characteristics of Home Service which we began to discuss on page 73.

We do not mean to imply that the volunteers of the Section were wholly responsible for the emergence of these qualities. But in so far as they were drawn into the work from other fields of activity and brought with them a stored-up wealth of experience and personality, they contributed to the freedom and freshness of response to the realities of life of which we have spoken and thus to flexibility in treatment; in so far as they were free from the prejudices and inhibitions which tend to attach themselves like barnacles to professional workers who linger long in any port,[1] they helped to create that atmosphere of cordial goodwill and cosmopolitan open-mindedness toward co-operating agencies and individuals which so many have found characteristic of the Section.

Of course for every Home Service volunteer capable of making such contributions of the spirit there were many to whom financial independence had meant no such heaping up of inner riches, who were merely kindly people ready to do tasks set them to the best of their ability. On the other hand, the paid workers also had been drawn to the Section from diverse fields and not a few of them had lived years as full and varied as their volunteer confrères. Others among them brought the enthusiasm and unhackneyed freshness of youth, its readiness to experiment and run hazardous risks.

In the last analysis it would seem that the question of pay or no pay was not a determining factor in the quality of the contribution made by any Home Service worker. The extent to which she had been free to live and grow—or had lived and grown in spite of restricting conditions—and the extent to which her tastes and opportunities had led her to study people and to live in a world of ideas and fine relationships rather than in one of material things had more to do with the matter. A native, spontaneous helpfulness seems sometimes to

---

[1] In using this barnacle figure the writer wishes to point out that she is referring to a *tendency* only. Every situation in life has implicit in it tendencies that make for deterioration as well as tendencies that make for growth. The advantages to social work of having professional workers who stick to their jobs are obvious and manifold, and a constant flitting leads to progress neither in work nor in worker. None the less, special measures are, we believe, necessary to counteract the tendency to develop the prejudices and inhibitions referred to. Among such measures are the payment of salaries that measure up to those paid for equally responsible work in the business world, so that the tension which grips those who struggle to live on a bare subsistence wage may be relaxed and ampler opportunities for recreation may be available; the granting of exceptional vacations to balance periods of exceptional strain; and encouragement to study under inspiring leadership—such encouragement to include the setting aside of regular hours or days for the purpose. Under the conditions which prevail at present in most family agencies—conditions which lead the underpaid worker continually to pour herself out in overtime service (as purely "volunteer" as that contributed by any woman of leisure) the wonder is not that some grow cramped and set but that so many retain their spontaneity and freshness of outlook.

lie back of such an interest in people and to be the deeper motive force. Thus a professional said of a certain volunteer worker that she "had really been doing case work for years before she knew that there was any such thing."

It was this same volunteer who, when telling of a rather radical stand she had taken on a certain question, added with a laugh, "And for weeks afterward I went about in mortal terror of losing my job." It is not often, we imagine, that just that attitude is taken by an unpaid worker. And this is perhaps as good a place as any to record one fact which stands out with peculiar prominence in our recollections of many talks with the volunteers of the Section. Never once did we get the impression by direct word or indirect implication that any one of them regarded herself as having done anything in the least remarkable, self-sacrificing, or even admirable in giving her services; not only was there none of the spread-eagle "all-that-I-have-and-am-belongs-to-the-Red-Cross" type of talk which we have chanced to hear in other quarters, but there was nothing at all—unless in response to some comment or inquiry of our own—to show that the volunteer was conscious of a different status from that of her salaried fellow-workers.

A feature of Home Service work which helped both to increase flexibility of treatment and to strengthen co-operative relations was the ample funds available. Supervisors have been practically unrestricted in their planning by questions as to the material means of carrying through proposed measures. Yet our reading of cases has produced only a few exceptional instances in which an over-liberal policy seems to have been pursued, and the chairman of the Section tells us that at no time were the funds made available by the executive committee of the chapter drawn upon up to the limit.

This experience would seem to run directly counter to what has long been a prevailing conviction among a large group of charitable agencies—the conviction that the existence of a large relief fund leads to extravagance and loose giving, and that in order to hold workers in check the money to carry out plans for families must be raised by individual appeals. Many agencies carry this idea still further, holding the district secretaries themselves responsible for raising the funds needed for their families.

We were interested in the views upon this point stated by one thoughtful Home Service supervisor, who had worked with two charity organization societies and who expressed a strong personal distaste for relief-giving. She was convinced, she said, that supervisors should never be hampered by the necessity of raising money to carry out plans, a necessity which made them "hesitate to do what should be done." Our own observation of the working of the two plans inclines us to the same view. Sound training and sound character together should be sufficient to prevent the raiding of the treasury and insure the wise use of funds. This, however, is not an argument against the use of individual appeals, which unquestionably have great educational value and may reach givers who have remained impervious to other efforts to interest them.

Another point in which Home Service experience seems to run counter to prevailing custom is one of organization. Most social case work agencies are directed, as we all know, by a board on which persons with case work experience are in a decided minority, if indeed they are represented at all. Even the general secretary in many large agencies has never been a case worker, or his experience in such work dates back so far that he is out of touch with modern methods. There are, of course, case committees on which board members sometimes sit, but only rarely does the professional staff, whose work with individual families forms the raison d'être of the organization, have representation in its management and the formulation of its larger policies.

As related in the first chapter, this traditional arrangement was modified in the Home Service Section when, at the beginning of 1919, the supervisory group was recognized by the chairman as a legislative body with power to determine questions of policy. The types of question with which it has since dealt are there indicated[1] and will be seen to include many which would usually be decided by a general secretary or board without consultation with case workers, or after purely voluntary consultation with the general case work supervisor; as well as other problems which would ordinarily come before a case committee.

---

[1] See pages 35–36.

That this plan has, on the whole, worked harmoniously and efficiently no one connected with the Section would, we believe, question. Its exact results, as compared with those which would have followed the usual scheme of organization, we cannot pretend to trace. But it does seem clear that those who are capable of guiding wisely the destinies of multitudes of families at critical junctures in their lives, as experienced case workers are presumed to be, must have something of value to contribute to the guidance of the organization of which they are such an essential part; and that, conversely, they will be strengthened in their contacts with those families if they are given the opportunity to see their case work job in relation to all the larger community questions which come before the executives of a society.

In the foregoing discussion all the specific points in the prevailing or earlier thinking of social case workers which have impressed us as bearing a significant relation to Home Service practice have been covered. Nothing said, however, whether in this and earlier chapters or in the more detailed analysis of Part II, has half indicated the glow of enthusiasm with which the best of these Home Service records were read. Previous reading of selected cases from a variety of agencies had brought a number which roused similar feelings; but the total of such has certainly been more than quadrupled in the past year, and the writer emerges from this season of browsing with a sense that she has at last sounded the depths and heights of the possible in case work. More patience and goodwill, more open-mindedness and tolerance, more generosity in judging and giving, more ingenuity and resourcefulness, more persistence, a freer outpouring of mind and heart in a genuine labor of love one could hardly hope to find.

In closing this attempt at an interpretation, it may be well to dwell at some length on one or two additional points in connection with this review of Home Service, although they do not belong in any recognized category of ideas on social case work.

It has long been a conviction of the writer, for example, that the sincerity and real depth of enthusiasm for service in case work possessed by any worker was to be measured not by relations with clients alone but by those with fellow-workers and subordinates as well, and indeed primarily; for the one set of relations may be governed more or less strictly by a professional code, while the other is sure to be a direct expression of personality.

It has chanced that in numerous contacts with social workers during the past twenty years we have several times been impressed by an hiatus between theory and practice in this regard. That anyone committed to the principle of close study of the individual in need and the lifting of him out of his slough of despond into new vigor and hopefulness and forward-looking activity could consciously or negligently exert a depressive influence upon a younger worker may seem inconceivable, yet we have more than once known this to happen. Sometimes persistent underpay has disheartened and stifled growth; sometimes there has been a seeming indifference to the way in which the work might be affecting the individual, while it was assumed that every ounce of the individual's devotion would go into the work; occasionally there has even been a tendency in a superior to "take it out on" subordinates when things went wrong. Such treatment would be objectionable in any mere business office—how much more so when meted out by those regarded as exponents of the finest sort of human relationships! Again and again a phrase has gone through our mind as we meditated on this topic (one that for years has recurred at intervals to trouble our serenity as a social worker): "If you love not your helper, with whom you associate intimately from day to day, how shall you love your client? . . . "

During our year with the Home Service Section we were naturally witness to only a minute fraction of the human interchange within the office; but a good deal of positive evidence to the particularly happy relations among supervisors and visitors came to our attention, and we believe that in this respect life within the Section measured up to the finest traditions in the social work field. Here—as doubtless in many other offices within that field—supervisors took as deep and vital an interest in helping their visitors to overcome difficulties and develop latent powers as they did in straightening out the tangled affairs of any client. Here, too, they made as definite an effort to secure a scale of pay for their subordinates which should make possible a normal life as they did to obtain allowances which should ensure a normal scale of living for dependent families. To them—as to the true social worker everywhere, whether so-called or not—a human being frustrated, or disappointed, or ill-adapted, or struggling under burdens too heavy for her strength, was a fellow-being in need, however she came to be known, and the same head and heart responded to that need. Somehow this type of evidence to a genuine interest in the welfare of others is more convincing to us than almost any other.

Thus far this study has aimed chiefly at setting forth and interpreting what was finest in the work of Home Service. It is perhaps unduly easy to feel optimistic about case work when one has recently read so many illustrations of it at its best; but Part II will, we believe, bear witness that we have not aimed to deceive ourself, or others, either as to the hard facts of life revealed in the records read or as to the inadequacy of many of the efforts to deal with those facts. Bitter disappointment following her most valiant struggles seems sometimes to be the case worker's almost daily bread;

> " . . the half of a broken hope for a pillow at night
> That somehow the right is the right
> And the smooth shall bloom from the rough. . . ."

of which Stevenson writes, is about all the consolation she can often gather to herself. This being so we have asked ourself seriously what is the charm that holds so many fine spirits to this work? Perhaps the answer may be expressed in the closing lines of a poem by John Masefield. It is one of the lovely lyrical outbursts in which his feeling for the sea finds expression—the sea, which "leads me, lures me, calls me," he writes,

> "To add more miles to the tally
> Of gray miles left behind,
> In quest of that one beauty
> God put me here to find."

One may find the most exquisite beauty in the world—the beauty of human character brought out in human relationships—anywhere in the world; and there is perhaps no work that reveals more of the ugly and sordid in human nature than social case work; yet—perhaps because shadow emphasizes sunshine and adversity brings out strength and devotion as well as meanness and weakness—there is hardly any road one can follow, we believe, that will give one in a year's time so many poignant glimpses of inner loveliness as this road.

PART II
ANALYSIS

CHAPTER IV

PRELIMINARY STATEMENT

In the foregoing pages the attempt was made—after tracing the development of the Section in its more important aspects—to bring out the qualities which, in the light of our review of Home Service case work, seemed to characterize that work at its best and to comment briefly on certain ideas implicit in those qualities.

The pages which follow, on the other hand, aim at an impartial and as nearly as possible a complete analysis of our findings. We began work without any preconceived notions as to what it would disclose, merely jotting down, for each record read, all the problems brought to light and the steps taken to solve them.[1] Later we classified these problems, and finally selected for comment those which either occurred most frequently or seemed most significant socially. It is now our purpose to present, for each of these groups of problems, citations or brief stories which shall make clear the nature of the problem under discussion in the special form it takes in the particular case, and shall relate what was done to solve it. This will be done without any attempt at a general summing-up of the good and evil in the methods pursued, leaving the reader free to judge for himself, after review of each chapter, how adequately or inadequately the problems under discussion were met by Home Service.

In approaching this detailed consideration of work done, certain distinctions among the case records read should be recognized. No reference is made here to the distinction between "cross-section" and "selected" records, which is fully explained in the Introduction,[2] but to a more fundamental division of these records into two classes: those presenting only inquiries or other problems peculiar to war-

[1] For methods pursued in choosing cases for examination see Introduction, page 13.

[2] See page 13.

time, and those in which there emerge, often in addition to one or more war problems, the kinds of problems usually met by family agencies in peace times—health problems, relief problems, problems of conduct, and the like. The latter class includes 245,[1] or 54 per cent of the total 454 cross-section records read, as well as all the selected records. As elsewhere explained (see page 13), 217 of the total 454 cross-section records originated in May, 1918, and are believed to be representative of the work of the war period, while 237 originated in May, 1919, and may be accepted as representative of the post-armistice period. The proportion of cases involving what we shall call "peace-time problems" in the two periods differed greatly, 168, or 77 per cent, in the earlier period falling in this class, while only 77, or 32 per cent, in the later period did so. The great increase of mere inquiry cases, which began with the armistice and is traceable largely to the need of commanding officers for information regarding home conditions of men seeking discharge or men imprisoned for military offenses, largely explains the decrease in the proportion of cases in which the more fundamental types of family problems, such as are met by the permanent family agencies, came to light.

For the purpose of this study, inquiry or other work done to meet problems peculiar to wartime is of entirely secondary interest, since such work is not comparable with the work of the permanent family agency. For this reason our discussion in the chapters which follow relates almost entirely to the essentially peace-time problems with which Home Service wrestled[2]—problems arising very largely out of the same physical, mental, moral, and industrial causes which operate in ordinary times, though accentuated and distorted, and sometimes entirely caused, by the war emergency.

The two types of peace-time problem which were of most frequent occurrence in the cases read were those arising from ill-health, physical or mental, and those involving questions of financial aid. In

[1] Among the remaining 209 cross-section cases 194 presented only problems classified by us as "war problems"; ten either presented no problem at all for Home Service or were immediately referred to another agency; five were never taken up, there being no record of any visit paid to the family. These five date from May, 1918, when the Section was struggling, in desperately cramped quarters, with an overwhelming volume of work, and it is not difficult to imagine how the oversight may have occurred.

[2] See Chapter V, Allotment and Allowance Problems, for the one exceptional case in which it has seemed worth while to give special attention to a war problem.

approximately two-thirds of the 245 cases in which peace-time problems occurred one or more members of the family were known to be suffering from ill-health of one sort or another, including many instances of quite minor ailments; and in almost exactly the same number of cases there arose some question of financial need, though only 44 per cent of the 245 families actually received grants or loans. Employment problems stand next in point of frequency; in approximately one-third of the cases some member of the family was out of a job or in need of one for the first time, or was conspicuously ill-paid or suffering from some form of industrial maladjustment. Some sort of problem growing out of conduct—intemperance, desertion, non-support, sex irregularity or other—came to light in about one-fifth of the families;[1] though in a number of these the problem belonged to the past rather than to the present or was quiescent at the time the family was under care. And there are a few additional problems, arising out of bad housing, need of further education for children or adults, low standards of housekeeping or ignorance of cooking, as well as a miscellany of other causes too numerous to mention.

Work on nearly every type of problem often so involves the use of relief that no clear line of demarcation between the relief problem and the other is possible, and there is a frequent intertwining in families of difficulties classifiable under several different heads. While fully recognizing the disadvantages following the use of the analytical method in dealing with such material we have still pursued it, aiming to make the citations in each chapter full enough to be comprehensible without resort to cross-references, which are, however, employed in some instances. The same family, therefore, frequently reappears in successive chapters. For whatever annoyance this may cause the reader we can only express our regret. Anyone wishing to trace a family through the various passages in which it appears will be aided by the index on page 229. The names used are of course in all cases fictitious.

One other point should be borne in mind in reading the citations in

[1] The actual figures are: 160 cases in which one or more members of the family were suffering in health; 162 in which there was a question of giving relief (108 in which a grant or loan was made); 82 cases in which some employment problem arose; 48 cases in which there emerged what we have called a problem of conduct.

the chapters which follow. The records from which they were made were read between July, 1919, and January, 1920, so that many families whose stories are told in them were still under care when we ceased our reading, a care that in a number of instances was to continue for six months or more. Grave injustice would be done Home Service if we lost sight of this fact, since during the year from the summer of 1919 to the summer of 1920 the Section did some of its best work.

CHAPTER V

ALLOTMENT AND ALLOWANCE PROBLEMS

Of all the types of difficulty brought to Home Service by its clients, that involving the payment of allotments and allowances by the Federal War Risk Insurance Bureau was the commonest, if we may trust the indications in the cases read. In 178, or 39 per cent, of the 454 cross-section cases there is some report of such difficulties; among the 77 selected cases they were found in 46, or 60 per cent. They are naturally much more numerous during the war period than during the post-armistice period, occurring in 66 per cent[1] of the cases which dated from 1918 and in only 14 per cent[2] of those originating in 1919. Every one who was at all intimately associated with soldiers' families during the war is aware of the hardships to which great numbers of them were subjected through the unsatisfactory working of the famous Act which had created the War Risk Insurance Bureau and had outlined the most liberal scheme of governmental aid to the dependents of men called to the colors that had ever been devised.[3] Into the details of the plan and the reasons for the administrative breakdown in its application it is impossible to enter here.

Not all the difficulties with allotments and allowances brought to the attention of the Section were such as to cause a serious problem.

[1] 145 out of 217.

[2] 33 out of 237.

[3] To a man's compulsory allotment to wife or children of $15 a month the government added $15 for a wife, $10 for a first child, $7.50 for a second child, and $5.00 for each additional child until the total allowance should reach $50, the limit set. The man was at liberty to allot, through the Quartermaster's Department, an additional $5.00 or $10, and sometimes did so. The total income for a wife and six children would thus be from $65 to $75. Provisions were the same for non-commissioned officers as for privates; commissioned officers were entirely outside the scope of these provisions. An allotment to parents and brothers and sisters was purely voluntary, and if dependency existed, a government allowance was upon application added to the allotment. The regulations under which said allowances were granted were changed from time to time so that it is not possible to give a brief summary.

In a sprinkling of the cases in which families came to Home Service for aid in such difficulties the man had been in service so short a time that it would not be reasonable to expect payments to have begun, and in a number of other instances the first check arrived between the application and the visit to the home or within a few days thereafter. In the great bulk of cases, however, there was either serious delay in the starting of the payments or a later interruption in their receipt. These delays and interruptions were due to a variety of causes: to failure on the part of the man in service to make allotment from his pay to the wife, mother, or other relative for whom he was responsible, his failure to apply for the government allowance which should accompany that allotment, or his error in filling out the necessary application papers; to discontinuance of his allotment by the man; to the cutting off of his pay during imprisonment, or by disciplinary fines; to change of allottee, as, in case of the man's marriage while in service, from mother to wife; to death of an allottee—checks not being payable to other members of the family; to changes of address; to wrong spellings of names; and—last but not least—to changes in rulings by the War Risk Bureau[1] and clerical or other errors in its office.

---

[1] The following quotation from the report of the chairman of the legal committee, under date of March 30, 1919, gives a notion of what some of the rulings referred to involved:

"In June, 1918, the War Risk Insurance Act was amended in several important particulars. At the same time a most unfortunate ruling was made. This was that in Class B cases [father, mother, brother, sister, etc.] where an allotment had been made but no allowance was payable (either because it was not applied for, or because the man had not stated a sufficient prior monthly habitual contribution), the Bureau would not pay even the allotment. The case was simply suspended. The argument was that the Bureau was overburdened with cases involving both allotment and allowance, that allotments alone were properly payable by the Quartermaster's Office in the army and other offices in other service Departments, and that the Bureau should not be encumbered by such cases which could be handled by other offices. In connection with this ruling a notice was sent to all Commanding Officers on June 26th, 1918, that in such cases the man should be instructed to fill out Quartermaster Form 38 if he was in the army, and other appropriate forms if it was in some other branch. This notice of June 26th, was effective from July 1st. It was, of course, impossible for this message to accomplish anything in the cases of the millions of men then in Europe by July 1st (four days later) nor in many months, where the man was perhaps in the battle area, or in a hospital, or missing or on detached service. Besides this a Commanding Officer could hardly know whether the man's form was sufficient to carry an allowance, or, if it was originally sufficient, that the allowance had not been cut off in Washington after an investigation. Nor, in countless cases, did the commanding officer or personnel officer, or other officer or man assigned to this work,

In not far from a third of the cases read in which there were allowance and allotment difficulties—certainly in more than one-fourth—there appears to have been in the minds of the family some doubt as to whether the man in service had made allotment and applied for an allowance, or, in a smaller number of cases, a certainty that he had not. A few husbands—habitual deserters and non-supporters for the most part—had enlisted as single; others had gone off declaring they would make no allotment; still others deliberately or negligently failed to do so; while many of the less dutiful sons, or those who had been unduly imposed upon by their families in the past, also failed to take such action.

In a large proportion of these cases the initial effort to meet the difficulty was made by the visitor in the division, who, when there was doubt whether the son or husband had made out the necessary papers, commonly wrote him inquiring and advising regarding the action to take. This step was, however, occasionally omitted when it seemed unfair to ask support from a son, as in one instance where a non-supporting stepfather was living on the mother's earnings. Such letters were usually informal, friendly communications, telling of a recent call and giving some item of family news, together with the assurance of continued interest and helpfulness toward the family. Very frequently they elicited prompt and cordial answers from the men, with the statement that the required papers had been filed.

---

have time in the stress of other more pressing work to bother about such matters. This Committee immediately protested against this ruling, but without effect. In a vast number of cases the mother who had received, at any rate, $15 monthly prior to July 1st, 1918, received nothing thereafter for many months and in many cases to this day. A partial remedy was provided recently, when in February, 1919 (after seven months of damage done), Congress passed an Act to compel the reinstatement of the allotment, under certain conditions.

"Another ruling which was vigorously opposed was one that payments on account of insurance should be considered as mitigating the condition of dependency in compensation cases of a "dependent parent." By the ruling the parents of a man who had taken out say $5,000 insurance and who received $28.75 per month insurance upon his death were not entitled to the $30.00 a month compensation which they might have obtained as "dependent parents," if he had taken out no insurance. In other words, the man who took out insurance (which had been held forth, so glowingly) accomplished nothing more for his dependent parents, in the event of his death, than the man who had not taken out any such insurance. This situation was remedied by a Treasury decision (40) in December, 1918."

[To the foregoing paragraph the following note was appended: "It is not the purpose of this report to criticize the Bureau of War Risk Insurance. The matters mentioned herein are only referred to, incidentally, to throw some light on our Committee's work."]

Commonly, at the same time that the man was written to, or later, a letter was sent to his commanding officer asking that he be urged or aided to take the desired action. A fair proportion of these letters also were answered; but naturally during the moving of troops from camp to camp letters went astray, and once the regiment had gone overseas answers from both men and officers were comparatively rare as well as much delayed. Follow-up letters were frequent. Where satisfactory answers were not received, or time dragged on without the arrival of the looked-for check, the family was commonly referred, or its representative personally taken, to the legal committee, which handled the great majority of all these cases.

In the main the work of this committee consisted of correspondence with the War Risk Insurance Bureau—or the Red Cross office in Washington which acted as intermediary—and the passing on of replies received from that Bureau to the relatives of the man in service. In a large proportion of the cases no particular cause was ever discovered to explain the delay or interruption in the allowance. The often interminable delays on the part of the Bureau in the sending of replies as well as checks, and the frequent failure to reply at all, meant the indefinite prolongation of much of this correspondence with Washington and brought about a state of extreme exasperation on the part of the representatives of the legal committee which not infrequently found expression in the letters sent, and even in the filling out of the form letters upon the use of which the Bureau insisted.

When special reasons for non-receipt of checks were discovered they were of course met by special measures. If a husband ignored his wife and children, help was given in preparing the applications which the law permits the wife to make and in obtaining the necessary certificates of marriage and birth and the affidavits required. If the husband made seemingly unjustified charges against his wife in the effort to support a claim for exemption from allotment the wife was aided to present her version properly. When an original allottee died the man was written to in regard to making out a new form. Many wrong addresses and spellings of names were corrected. In the case of illegitimate children of men in service, every effort was made to induce the father to acknowledge and allot to his child; and when babies were born to wives of men in service, help was given to the mothers in preparing the new applications for additional allowances required.

In the great majority of cases every possible helpful action seems to have been taken both by the divisions and by the legal committee. The correspondence of the committee was carried on with especial thoroughness and persistence. Occasional failures on the part of visitors to refer clients to the committee, or unexplained delays in referring, occur; and there are instances of promises by a visitor to write a son or his commanding officer which were apparently not kept, and cases where, when a letter was returned with word that a man had been sent to another camp, no further effort to reach him was made. Only one defect in service seems, however, to call for special mention: a lack of free interchange of information between the Home Service divisions and the legal committee, resulting, in certain instances, in unnecessary work done by the committee and occasionally in serious misunderstandings and errors.

In order to meet the desire of visitors for information regarding allotment and allowance developments in the families under their care, the legal committee early adopted the custom of sending to the various divisions carbons of letters written in the interest of families assigned to those divisions. These letters are filed as part of the case record. There are of course gaps in these files, but on the whole they seem to have been fairly complete. The visitor, however, appears almost invariably to have learned from the family of the receipt of a delayed government check before the legal committee had been notified by the authorities in Washington of its having been sent. Indeed, so much in arrears was the correspondence of the War Risk Bureau that unless notified by the visitor the committee was likely to remain indefinitely in ignorance of such receipt and to continue sending letters to Washington urging payment of sums already paid. To meet this difficulty a request for regular notification by the divisions when families under their care received delayed checks was made by the legal committee. Copies of a few such notifications were found among cases read, but the sending of them seems never to have become an established habit. Naturally, the training of an overworked and rapidly changing staff of visitors to send a special notice in all such cases was a quite different matter from training stenographers in the legal committee to make extra carbons of letters and send them to the divisions. The committee, however, unquestionably labored under a grave disadvantage from lack of the information thus inadvertently withheld.

In other cases the ignorance of the legal committee of social facts known to the division having the family under care led to work at cross-purposes.

Here, for example, is a woman commonly known as the wife of a soldier, and with two small babies by him as well as an older child said to be the daughter of a former husband. The fact that she had no legal claim on the man in service was known to the division from the outset, and the letter which the visitor promptly sent to him urged that he make allotment to his children but did not press any claim for their mother. Some six weeks later a statement appears in the record to the effect that Mrs. Treimer is receiving an allotment, amount not stated. Shortly afterward Mrs. Treimer appears to have applied to the legal committee and a correspondence was started by the committee to obtain her allowance as a wife. Carbons of the original letter to Washington making this demand and of later correspondence are filed with the case record, but it was not until several months after this correspondence was started that the legal committee got wind from some source of an irregularity in the situation and wrote asking the division for the facts. Meanwhile the woman had received several months' full allowance from the government, as legal wife.[1] (Cross-section record. Known to a family agency.)

Most of the defects in the conduct of cases are obviously traceable to the appalling pressure of new applications which has been mentioned as chiefly responsible for the errors of omission of Home Service.

From time to time an allotment and allowance problem of more or less unusual character called for correspondingly exceptional treatment on the part either of the division visitor or the legal committee.

Thus in one case a visitor succeeded in persuading a man home on furlough to double his allotment to his wife (he was a machinist's mate receiving almost twice the pay of a common soldier).
(Selected record. Known to a diet kitchen and to a day nursery.)

In another, the legal committee fought a long and resourceful battle in the cause of a wife who had been browbeaten by her husband in signing a paper declaring herself to be his sister. Inquiry of the

[1] We do not mean to imply that receipt of full allowance by a woman not legally married is necessarily a disaster, but it is clearly not desirable that the Red Cross urge any claim on a false basis. In this case the woman soon after went to live with a third man.

War Risk Insurance Bureau disclosed the fact that he had married a second wife to whom he had made the usual allotment and for whom he had secured the regular government allowance. Vigorous correspondence with the Home Service Section in the town where the second wife lived, with her family, with the man's attorney, and with the Adjutant General of the Army followed. While the legal committee did not succeed in its effort to have the man punished for bigamy instead of being discharged, it did finally establish the wife's status with the War Risk Insurance Bureau. (Selected record. Known to a family agency.)

With the return of the discharged men to their homes a new type of allotment and allowance problem began to appear. Not a few found that while the sums allotted by them had been regularly deducted from their pay, payments to their allottees had been by no means so regular. In some such cases allowances from the government were also due. The men were aided to file applications both for the arrears of pay due them because of unpaid allotments and for allowances due. The results in these cases were not recorded at the date of our reading.[1]

Help of a similar sort was given to relatives of men in the Canadian forces in securing their government allowances. Eleven instances where such help was needed came to our attention—10 among the 33 cross-section cases read in which the families were Canadians or British subjects, one among the selected cases. In two the only help extended was in supplying separation allowance forms; in the others, aid was given in filling out the statutory declaration forms and these were forwarded to the Canadian government, or other correspondence aiming to secure various adjustments was carried on. Replies were almost always promptly received from the authorities in Canada and satisfactory arrangements completed within a reasonable time.

[1] Practically no legal committee cases were read after the end of 1919. We are informed that many allotment and allowance payments have since been secured.

CHAPTER VI

HEALTH PROBLEMS

Obviously it would be impossible to take up in detail every one of the numberless types of disease with which Home Service came into contact in these cases. Only those which seem to have social significance will be touched upon. The care given women in pregnancy and confinement may not be generally regarded as a socially interesting medical problem, but in connection with the wives of men absent in the service of their country it has seemed to call for mention. Tuberculosis, venereal disease, mental and nervous disorders and defects, and drug addiction naturally are the most important topics to be discussed, while dental treatment and the treatment of the defects of children seem also, in view of the widespread interest in these topics, to claim a place.

Pregnancy and Confinement

In 40 cases read—22 among the cross-section, 18 among the selected records—a woman was pregnant or had just been confined at the time she became known to Home Service. Thirty-one of these women were the wives of men in service or recently discharged, but in two instances another man was the father of the child. Two of the women were the mothers of men in the service, and one a sister. Three women had no legal status as wives, though they were commonly known under the name of the man in service, and three were unmarried mothers in the ordinary meaning of the term.

In two cases a decision was almost immediately reached that the families were not responsibilities of Home Service.

The husband in one family had enlisted in the regular army before the war, and the son in the other had enlisted since the armistice. The wife, in the first of these cases, was expecting to be confined within a few days; her husband, discharged months before, was at home out of work. She was given temporary relief and a card to a maternity center, and was referred to the district office of the Charity Organization Society. The mother in the second case had just been confined in a wretchedly poor home; prompt and generous emergency relief was given and the Charity Organization Society, which had previously known the family, was consulted and agreed to take charge, an arrangement entirely satisfactory to the mother. (Cross-section records. One family unknown to any social agency, the other known to a family society.)

Still another of these women was not properly a client of the Section as she lived in Brooklyn. She was brought to the office on one occasion by her sister-in-law, a resident of Manhattan. She was referred to a medical agency, but there is no record of her going. (Cross-section record. Not known to any social agency.)

Among the other 37 women who were properly Home Service cases, not all were given definite care in pregnancy or confinement. With several acquaintance was very brief and little or no action was called for.

One young woman whom the Section had been asked to visit was surprised at the call as she was well, at work, and in no need. Later, when difficulties arose, her parents-in-law were ready to assume all responsibility. (Cross-section record. Not known to any social agency.)

Another wife stated that she did not care to place herself under a physician's care yet, and soon after returned to her family in Brooklyn. (Cross-section record. Not known to any social agency.)

Two women were already under medical care when referred. One of them, who was lonely and forlorn, received much friendly help of various kinds, but moved without leaving an address before the time for her confinement. The other was living with a married sister to whom she was attached and who was in fair circumstances. No special care was given her. (Cross-section records. Not known to any social agency.)

In two cases there was a definite failure on the part of the visitor to live up to an obligation explicitly assumed—though in neither is there reason to suppose that any great harm resulted.

In one of these cases a little Italian wife, living with her family, was seen when only two months pregnant; the visitor "promised to see her again and advise regarding confinement" but the record contains no entry of a later call. In the other, the visitor, after arranging with a friend of the wife's to accompany her to the Medical Station for examination, and after writing to the man's commanding officer that she would "continue to keep in touch with Mrs. Nadel and advise her of the service she can receive in her confinement," never called again. The wife in this case was reported as having a private physician to whom she paid $2.00 a visit. The family seemed in fair circumstances, had become known to Home Service only when a report was asked for by the husband's commanding officer regarding his request for discharge, and never were in receipt of relief. (Cross-section records. Not known to any social agency.)

In yet another case, where no medical care had been arranged up to the date of our reading for an unmarried prospective mother, this lack of attention to health conditions was clearly due to the fact that she was working as attendant in a hospital where her condition was known and it was to be presumed that she would receive any care needed. (Selected record. Not known to any social agency.)

In two other cases, though some effort was made to arrange for medical care, there is no evidence of any result.

Mrs. Norton was given a card to a hospital and arrangements for her care were made with a maternity center nurse but contact was not continued; her husband was at home and things were going well with the couple at last accounts. (Cross-section record. Known to the Bureau of Domestic Relations and a diet kitchen.)

Mrs. Cantor was living with her family in very crowded quarters and was nervous and anxious to get away to a quiet place, but when an opportunity to go to a convalescent home in the country was offered her, declined it; nor is it recorded that she ever took the advice of the visitor to go to a prenatal clinic. (Cross-section record. Not known to any social agency.)

Mrs. Vail, who had been known to the Section for some months, receiving a little help from time to time, had reported in October that she had been to the prenatal clinic at Bellevue and was to go again in January. She was out of touch with Home Service in February when her baby was born, but was soon after brought to attention again by another agency to which she had applied for clothing. When visited she stated that the last government money received by her was not yet exhausted and that she had understood she was to apply to the Section if in need. (Selected record. Not known to any social agency.)

All thirteen cases thus far cited, including the three which were not properly charges upon the Section, have this one point in common, that whether or not advice as to ways of obtaining needed care was offered there is no record of any such care having been given as a result.

In three additional cases some other health need of the prospective mother had claimed first attention and had received it at the hands of Home Service; but the ordinary requirements of women in pregnancy and confinement had either not yet been met or had been met by the women themselves.

Thus Mrs. Unger was suffering from chronic bronchitis and needed a change of air. The visitor offered a chance for convalescent care at the seaside, but the doctor had recommended the mountains and when she arranged to stay with friends at Liberty the necessary funds were supplied to enable her to go. She said she must return in two weeks on account of the Jewish holidays and did so, her cough having disappeared. It was only about a week later that the record was read, and though the plan had been made to place her under prenatal care, this had not yet been done. (Selected record. Not known to any social agency.)

The fact that Mrs. Kurz had tuberculosis was discovered when she was four months pregnant, and Home Service, which had insisted on her being examined, backed the treatment which followed, making it possible for her to stay in the country till shortly before the time of her confinement. For this event she seems to have arranged at a hospital herself; when visited at her mother-in-law's soon after, she reported herself "cured" and the baby "fine." (Selected record. Not known to any social agency.)

Mrs. Sullivan was syphilitic as well as pregnant. After most persistent effort she was taken to the Medical Station and kept under treatment there until the nurse in charge reported that the last Wassermann was negative, that she was in "good condition" and "the coming child has every chance of being perfectly normal." How soon the baby was expected was not stated, but three weeks later, upon the occasion of the visitor's next recorded call, it was learned that it had been born dead, at home, that the mother had soon after become very ill and on the advice of the attending midwife had been taken to a hospital. Here she had been operated on and after about two weeks had been sent home, still wretchedly ill. She expressed regret that she had not taken the visitor's advice and gone to a hospital for her confinement, consented to return for treatment as soon as arrangements could be made, and did so. (Selected record. Not known to any social agency.)

In the remaining 24 cases some definite treatment directly bearing upon the woman's condition as mother or prospective mother was given; that is to say, contact with a medical agency or convalescent care was arranged, or if arrangements for such care had been made by the client or another agency supplementary help of some sort was given.

With a number of these women prenatal care was given, but the time for confinement had not arrived or contact had been lost before it came, or a miscarriage occurred—the last contingency intervening in the case of Mrs. Hartmann some time after she had gone to a maternity center on the recommendation of the visitor.

Mrs. Nobel was sent to a maternity center and continued to go regularly. She was living with an aunt who though kind was very poor, and the center reported on at least two occasions that she was not receiving proper food. Milk was ordered, and after nearly a month's delay it was arranged to give her an allowance. Immediately thereafter her long-delayed government check arrived and contact with her lapsed. (Cross-section record. Not known to any social agency.)

Mrs. Bellaro went regularly to the Medical Station for examination and was supplied with the clothing needed for herself and the coming child; the time for her confinement, which was arranged to take place at the Booth Memorial Hospital, had not yet arrived at the date of reading this record. (Cross-section record. Not known to any social agency.)

A very young girl, Linda Antokolsky, was still in the early stages of pregnancy when her family's record was read, but had been sent to a prenatal clinic promptly upon the discovery of her condition. (Selected record. Known to seven social agencies, but not to a family society.)

Mrs. Emmet had been examined at the Medical Station and given a layette, but suddenly moved, giving no clue to her whereabouts. Not till several months later did she again come to the attention of the Section. She was then living in the Bronx and her baby had been born during the interval. (Selected record. Not known to any social agency.)

Of eighteen women confined while under the care of the Section, six seem to have gone through the experience at home.

Mrs. Tartora, when urged to go to the Medical Station for examination refused, but after much persuasion went to a woman's infirmary and was greatly pleased with the attention received. She was confined at home, where she lived with a very devoted father and sister, the visitor giving a layette and all needed help during her illness. (Cross-section record. Not known to any social agency.)

Two other women, Mrs. Tierney and Mrs. Kendall, first became known to Home Service shortly before confinement and made their own arrangements to be cared for at home, one of them refusing the hospital care urged upon her. Both were supplied with material necessities until well again. (Cross-section records. Known to family societies.)

Mrs. Neary had been referred to the Medical Station for examination. It does not appear whether she went. She made her own arrangements for confinement, the visitor assisting by persuading her mother-in-law to care for the little boy during this period, one in which she was apparently in receipt of government funds. Certainly there was not a shadow of neglect in the case, which was most persistently and devotedly cared for. (Selected record. Not known to any social agency.)

Mrs. Carter and Mrs. Scanlon both decided, after their visitors had made all arrangements for confinement in a hospital—and, in Mrs. Scanlon's case, after arrangements for the placing of the four children had been made—that they preferred to stay at home. Mrs. Scanlon was cared for by a devoted friend who was a trained nurse's aid; Mrs. Carter by a Metropolitan social service nurse; in both cases Home Service maintaining friendly relations and giving help—financial included in the case of Mrs. Scanlon but not in that of Mrs. Carter, who had just received a large government check. (Selected records. Mrs. Carter was known to the Board of Child Welfare and to a medical agency; Mrs. Scanlon not to any agency.)

Twelve women in all were confined in hospitals while under the care of the Section. The following notes cover seven of these cases:

Mrs. Isaacs went to the Medical Station once for examination, but made her own arrangements for her confinement in another hospital. (Cross-section record. Not known to any social agency.)

Mrs. Young had made her own arrangements at a hospital, but it was the visitor who called the ambulance to take her there and the visitor who arranged for the care of the children in her absence, sending one to the country, bringing in a friend of the mother to care for the others at home, and supplying food. (Selected record. Not known to any New York agency, but known to a family society in another city.)

Mrs. Noonan was brought by her visitor under the care first of a maternity center, then of a hospital where she was confined. Baby clothing was given and relief supplied, and later a country outing for mother and children was arranged. (Selected record. Not known to any social agency.)

Mrs. Shea was referred and finally went to a maternity center. After the baby's arrival she was sent, apparently by the authorities at the hospital, to a nurses' home for two weeks. Home Service supplied needed clothing and relief. (Selected record. Known to a family society and two other agencies.)

The Medical Station found Mrs. Larkin in a condition calling for special diet, which was prescribed. Later she was given a letter of introduction to a maternity hospital where she was confined. After her return she was referred to a diet kitchen.

Soon afterward it became necessary for her to return to the hospital for an emergency operation and the visitor, after repeated efforts, succeeded in placing the baby where it was well cared for. Following her return home mother and baby were sent to a convalescent home in the country. Many friendly offices to this especially co-operative young mother were accompanied by adequate relief during the entire period. (Selected record. Not known to any social agency.)

A decided contrast is represented by Mrs. Meadows. She was, indeed, got to a maternity hospital several times for examination, but after her confinement there, all efforts to persuade her to accept convalescent care proved unavailing. (Selected record. Known to a family society and four other agencies.)

Amy Tulliver, one of the unmarried mothers cared for, a girl of pleasing personality and good reputation, was found living in rather untidy and dubious quarters. As her confinement for which she had arranged was very near, the visitor did not attempt to move her, devoting herself to aiding in preparations for the coming event by giving a baby outfit and much needed clothing for the girl herself. Convalescent care was afterward arranged for her, first by Home Service, then, when an outbreak of contagious disease in the house selected made a change necessary, by the social worker in the hospital where she had been confined. At the date of reading she had not yet returned to town, but arrangements were being made (again by the hospital social worker) for her and the baby at a Shelter until she could be placed at service, and the visitor was planning to meet and conduct her thither. (Selected record. Known only to a medical social service department.)

Care by the Medical Station has been mentioned in several of the foregoing citations. Nine of the 40 women mentioned in this chapter were, as a matter of fact, examined or treated there, and of these nine, five were confined at the Booth Memorial Hospital in which the Station is situated. Notes on these five cases follow:

Mrs. Hilton came to the Section simply for guidance in finding a hospital where she could be cared for at the least expense; she was an officer's wife, in good circumstances. Arrangements were made for her at the Booth Memorial Hospital, she paying expenses herself; no further need of Home Service attention ever appeared. (Selected record. Not known to any social agency.)

For Mrs. Doyle the hospital care given (paid for by the Section) was also the only service rendered, the husband soon after his wife went home writing a letter of thanks in which he stated she would continue to live with her sister and would need no further assistance. (Cross-section record. Not known to any social agency.)

Comparatively little help was needed by Mrs. Dawson. She was given a card to the Medical Station and evidently went, as she was later confined at the Booth Memorial Hospital. She had a good home with her family and soon returned to work. (Selected record. Not known to any social agency.)

Mrs. Ide, a very attractive colored woman, gave birth at this hospital to a premature baby that died. When ready to leave, she was taken home by the visitor and put to bed, after which financial help was given till she felt strong enough to go to work. (Selected record. Not known to any social agency.)

Mrs. Bauman had already been helped on several occasions, but her case had been closed in August, 1918, after she had taken a place at service with her child. In the following March she appeared again, stating she was suffering from a growth in her abdomen. She was sent to the Medical Station, where she was found to be on the verge of confinement, having concealed her pregnancy up to the last moment as the child was not her husband's. During the period of confinement she made such a favorable impression that she was kept on to work in the hospital, and was still there when we read the record several months later. (Cross-section record. Known to a family society, the Bureau of Domestic Relations, and another agency.)

Only one case remains to be mentioned, that of a young wife who was referred to Home Service by a hospital shortly before her return home with her new-born baby. She and her family were very independent and unwilling to accept relief, but she did avail herself of an offer of convalescent care in the country and returned to town enthusiastic about her experience. (Cross-section record. Not known to any social agency.)

Tuberculosis

Among the cases read there were 37 in which tuberculosis or a suspicion of its existence was recorded—25 in the cross-section and 12 in the selected group. Two cross-section cases, however, did not belong to the Section; we give the circumstances of these to clear the ground.

One, an emergency case, referred by a tuberculosis clinic, was that of a father who had come home from the tuberculosis hospital where he was under care to be with his wife in her confinement. As already explained under pregnancy and confinement cases, this was not properly a Home Service family, the son in the Army having enlisted since the armistice; and so, after emergency relief had been given, was returned to the care of the society which had previously known it. (Cross-section record. Known to a family society.)

Mrs. Reed, with her baby, came from New Jersey, where she had long been known to a Home Service Section, and was staying with relatives in New York. She was referred for placement to the State Charities Aid Association, which found a job for her at service. Later the agency's physician discovered that she was tuberculous and advised her to return to her place of legal residence. This she presumably did; at all events, after this diagnosis she did not again come under the care of the Section. (Cross-section record. Not known to any New York agency.)

The task of getting suspicious cases examined is of course quite as important a responsibility of the social case worker as is that of arranging for care or persuading clients to accept care once they have been found to be infected. For this reason we shall begin our survey by noting the circumstances of the cases in which there is ground for suspecting that tuberculosis existed in members of a family under care, yet in which positive proof of the presence of the disease is lacking.

A man one day appeared at the Home Service office, accompanied by a woman who he said was his wife, and, asserting that he had quick consumption, demanded to be sent to California at once. He would not permit his wife to be spoken to, refused all information as to his personal background, and when urged to see a doctor declined to do so unless the supervisor interviewing him would promise to send him to California if he were found to be tuberculous. Failing to extract such a promise and refusing to listen to any plan but his own, he left the office and was never seen again. Who shall say whether his was a case of tuberculosis or not? (Cross-section record. Not known to any social agency.)

In one family there was a sister said to be an arrested case. No action was taken—probably none was needed—on this point, though care was given her in another illness. (Cross-section record. Not known to any social agency.)

A wife reported that her husband in service was an arrested case. Part of the plan made for the family called for examination of him following discharge, but on his return he appeared in good health and promptly secured an outdoor job, and nothing more was ever said about an examination. (Selected record. Not known to any social agency.)

In three families the only member known to be infected was away from home; but, as always in such cases, the health of other members of the household was of course more or less subject to suspicion.

In one the absent member was the father; the soldier son, home on furlough, fell ill with grippe and a series of complications that rendered his case a critical one. Home Service wrote to ask extension of his furlough, and later, when he was ordered back to camp before he was fit to go, succeeded after much telephoning in arranging to have certain army medical officers call on him to make an examination. Doubtless these activities on the young man's behalf would have been carried on just the same if there had been no ground for suspecting a possible pre-existing infection; and the case contains no evidence of efforts to have other members of the family examined. (Cross-section record. Not known to any social agency.)

In the second of these families a brother had come down with tuberculosis, leaving three young sisters to struggle on alone. So great was their pride and independence that they would never have appealed for help, but Home Service was brought into the family situation by a request from the commanding officer of an older brother in service for report on his application for discharge. The family physician, seen, stated that the girls were in physical need of the support of this brother. To pass on to the commanding officer this report, backed by her own observations, was all that the visitor could do to help, since aid was declined. (Cross-section record. Not known to any social agency.)

In the Meyer household there were three adults—father, mother, and daughter. Another daughter had been sent to California several years before with tuberculosis. The girl at home presented an acute mental problem which absorbed the visitor's attention, and it is not till toward the close of the record that there is mention of an encounter with the father in which he is described as exceedingly delicate-appearing and emaciated. No suggestion of examination for him had been made up to the date of our reading. (Selected record. Known to a family society and a health agency.)

In one family the only evidence of tuberculous condition is a note on the face-card opposite the name of the father. No mention of the condition occurs in the history, though the son reports the father not strong and unable to work regularly; and one can only wonder whether the solitary entry was a clerical error or whether there was a failure in follow-up due to the visitor's oversight. (Cross-section record. Not known to any social agency.)

In another case the school record of a young girl contained the words "infected lungs." A hospital where she had been under care reported only "grippe and sciatica." It is recorded that "arrangements were made" with her mother to send the girl to the country—after which no further entry appears. It is quite likely that she went, despite this lapse—but we shall never know. (Cross-section record. Not known to any social agency.)

The twenty-year-old sister in yet another family is reported as in need of lighter and better paying work; she has been out, sick—is said to have had a "weak lung." Efforts to get her suitable employment were made, but there is no evidence that the state of her health was ever inquired into or an examination urged. (Cross-section record. Known only to a church.)

One mother was suffering from chronic bronchitis which it was feared might involve something worse. Examination, however, gave negative results as to tuberculosis, and the woman was sent to a seaside home for a vacation. (Selected record. Known to a family society.)

The mother of three children still at home had died of tuberculosis. The father, described as "delicate looking and very neat," was urged to go to a hospital for examination, and when the report was received that his only trouble was with his teeth, was sent to a dental college where an estimate of the needed work was made. Unfortunately the work seems never to have been done; when last seen the man was on his way to seek work at a certain factory and was told to call again in regard to the dental work if he failed to get a position. There is no evidence in the record that any effort was made to have the children examined. (Cross-section record. Known to a family society and four other agencies.)

In another case where there were no children at home the father was found recovering from grippe and pneumonia. His physician feared tuberculosis. The visitor urged examination at a certain clinic, which advised country care. While efforts were made to find a place in the country for him, the mother had him examined at another clinic, where the doctor advised against sending him to the country till it was certain whether he was tuberculous, and recommended plenty of nourishing food. Contact with the family was lost soon after, before final diagnosis was reported. Help had included the payment of rent for a month and a half and the finding of several additional days' work a week for the mother. (Cross-section record. Not known to any social agency.)

Little Alan Carnegie, who had had grippe and was badly run down, was taken under care by a certain clinic quite independent of any action by the visitor, and was being kept there "on the roof" every day; on inquiry the visitor was told there was no definite diagnosis of his case yet. As long before as nine months the visitor had recorded that she believed the "grandmother and the child undernourished," and had labored with the old lady to get her to accept relief, finally inducing her to let a daily quart of milk for Alan be sent in with some other help in food and clothing. More recently, when the government checks were again delayed, a regular allowance of $8 a week had been given for five weeks, until after the father of the boys had returned and gone to work. (Cross-section record. Known to a family society and one other agency.)

A young girl of nineteen was living alone with her mother in the absence of the brother in service. Her father had died many years before of tuberculosis. She was described as "tall, refined, sweet looking, quiet in manner," with a "pretty color" which to the visitor's mind indicated health. She said she was willing to work hard for her mother and herself, had not had a day off in six years—a statement one can only hope to be exaggerated. Her reputation was excellent. During the following fall or early winter, at a time when the only contact of Home Service with the family was through the legal committee, which was endeavoring to get the mother's allotment and allowance for her, the girl came down with influenza. A month or so later the mother appealed for relief and a visitor called. The girl, who had returned to work, had a slight cough and was advised to go to a doctor for examination, advice which she seems not to have followed. Relief was not given: there was an abundant meal on the table at the time of the visit; it was found that the mother as well as the daughter was working, and it was felt they "could get along" if the government checks due came. This was in January. Contact was then lost for several months, during which there is no record of events except that the checks did not come. In July a new visitor called. She reports as follows regarding the girl: "She is a tall, slender, hollow-cheeked, anemic looking young girl . . . had not felt well since having influenza early last winter, which left her with a tickling cough in her throat. Visitor told her that it was probably nothing serious, but that it would be a very good idea to have an examination at the clinic. She said she would take time off and go for the examination next Thursday." However, there is no record that she did so on that or any other day, though the desirability of an examination was again suggested. At the end of August she was sent away for a week's vacation in the country, her board and her wages for the week being given her. About the time of her return, after what she reported was a very pleasant time, the long-delayed check (for $275) arrived, and contact with the family was again broken, they stating that they were going to relatives in another city. (Cross-section record. Not known to any social agency.)

Two more cases in the suspect class remain. In one a sister was in a tuberculosis hospital and a brother, said to be weak and to have an infected lung, was at home. Unavailing efforts were made to induce this brother and another sister to go to clinics for examination. They had a comfortable home—six well lighted and well kept rooms—and "the standard of living seemed high." (Cross-section record. Known to the Department of Public Charities and a diet kitchen.)

In the remaining case the brother-in-law of the man in service, who though crippled was giving a home to the latter's mother, was reported ill, with symptoms that aroused the visitor's suspicions. Examination was advised, but he returned to work shortly and his physician when seen refused to give a diagnosis. It is interesting to note that this man's wife wanted home work but that the visitor felt she should not be encouraged to take any until the condition of the husband was known. (Cross-section record. Known to a family society and the Bureau of Domestic Relations.)

In one case there was practical certainty that tuberculosis existed, though no definite diagnosis seems to have been received from a medical agency while the family was under care.

Mrs. Tullio is reported by the visitor of a family agency formerly in charge to have been "at one time considered tuberculous," and a child was, at the time Home Service knew the family, under care on a day-boat. No attention whatever seems to have been paid to the health problems in this family. The only possible explanation we can think of is that so far as tuberculosis is concerned, it may have been considered that the clinic which had the child under care was looking out for the other members of the family—though there is no indication that such was the case. (Cross-section record. Known to a family society and two other agencies.)

In another instance doctors disagreed, somewhat to the embarrassment of the Section.

Twelve-year-old Tony Carillo was suspected of being tuberculous and when taken by the Home Service visitor to a certain hospital tuberculosis clinic was declared to have "tuberculosis of the lymph and enlargement of the heart." Later, at the same hospital, another physician told the visitor "it was a great mistake to rubber-stamp Tony as tubercular. . . . The Von Pirquet test was negative and there is no active tuberculosis in his case." He added that the boy "can be sent anywhere . . . without running a risk to anyone. Maintains it was a mistake to send him to the tuberculosis clinic." On the basis of this second opinion the boy was got away to the country, first for three weeks, then (as he showed marked improvement) for a protracted stay, which had only begun when we read the record. (Selected record. Known to a family society.)

In the cases which remain to be mentioned there was a definite diagnosis of tuberculosis in some form.

Michael Dimattia, twelve years old, in an incipient stage, was at a hospital when his family became known to Home Service. A letter of inquiry to the hospital brought the reply that he was improved and ready to go home. After his return there is no mention in the record of his health, though help in various difficulties was given the family. (Cross-section record. Known to a family society.)

In one family visited with the object of making a report regarding discharge to the son's commanding officer, the mother was found to be tuberculous. Living conditions were good, a private physician had charge of the case, and the family were hoping to send her away for her health soon. No action was taken. (Cross-section record. Known to a family society and two other agencies.)

An elderly woman, mother-in-law of a man in service, was said to be a second-stage case of tuberculosis. She absolutely refused to be sent away, and her daughter would not insist upon her going though she was irritable and difficult to care for. Apparently she had no physician in New York; there was talk of consulting the one who had attended her when she lived in Brooklyn, but no record that this was done or that any action was taken. Like the preceding case, this was one visited in order to make a discharge report, and no request for help of any sort ever came from the family. (Cross-section record. Not known to any social agency.)

After the Robinowitz family had been under care for some time the mother's physician stated that she had tuberculosis and should go to the country. The visitor urged hospital care and sent in a visiting nurse to try to induce the mother to accept it, all to no avail. Finally a married daughter carried her off to the country, where she stayed most of the summer. The visitor meanwhile placed the two children at a seaside sanatorium where they were kept about six weeks. In the fall efforts were renewed to induce the mother to be examined and let her children be examined—all to no avail; appointments made were not kept, and the effort was finally given up in despair. (Cross-section record. Not known to any social agency.)

In one family, the Marxes, much other good work was done but the question of tuberculosis was hardly touched upon.

The father died in a hospital of the disease soon after the family came to the attention of the Section. One of the first acts of the visitor was to urge moving from the dark rooms occupied, all interior except for the front room used as a shop, and this was accomplished very soon. Hospital records of a year or two previous showed the children to have been negative; new examinations were advised but never were made, the supervisor's explanation being that the mother could not be brought to consent. The closest and friendliest relations with the family were maintained, scholarships being given first to one and ultimately to three children, but this one vital point remains uncovered. It would seem as though care of the children's health might have been made a preliminary condition to the granting of the scholarships. (Selected record. Known only to a clinic.)

Her visitor insisted on the examination of young Mrs. Kurz, but when she had been pronounced tuberculous it was her mother-in-law who found a place in Sullivan County where she could go. As her allotment and allowance were delayed, Home Service paid her board for over a month and during the fall sent money again as needed. She remained away about five months, returning just in time for her confinement, soon after which she stated that she had been pronounced cured. Her husband was now at home and they soon went to housekeeping again. When last seen, some months later, she was again having trouble with her lungs and was receiving tuberculin treatment. No later contact is recorded. (Selected record. Not known to any social agency.)

The sister of a man in service was found to have what her physician called "lingering consumption." She was taken to a board of health clinic and the diagnosis of tuberculosis confirmed. She belonged to a Jewish family which occupied six good light rooms, well furnished and immaculately clean; but they were not able to stretch their resources to cover the full cost of boarding her at the place recommended by her physician, and as she was in need of an immediate change and could not bear the idea of a sanatorium, Home Service gave a weekly allowance sufficient to enable the family to meet the extra expense involved. This arrangement was still in force at the date of reading five months later. (Selected record. Not known to any social agency.)

Mrs. Zimmerman, said by her physician to have "chronic tuberculosis," was declared at the board of health clinic to which she was taken by the visitor to be an advanced case. The family promptly borrowed money and sent her to a farm in the Catskills. As the father was a sufferer from asthma and out of work a great deal, the earnings of the two working children were small and the allotment and allowance from the son in service was in arrears, a good deal of financial aid was given the family, while at the same time the father and daughter were taken to clinics and the other children urged to go. The only diagnosis recorded is one of the father: pulmonary trouble "probably not tuberculosis." Much trouble was taken to find an outdoor job for him, which he did not take, as he had something else in view; and the youngest child was got away to the country for a vacation. (Selected record. Known to a family society and a clinic.)

Mrs. Limburg's case was handled by two different divisions. The visitor in the first had her several times at the Medical Station, where no traces of tuberculosis were found "except positive sputum." Efforts were made to have her put herself under care at a certain tuberculosis clinic; she went occasionally but was not co-operative. Finally she moved, coming under the care of another division, and the new visitor immediately got her to a hospital where she was found to have both pneumonia and tuberculosis. Before she was well her husband came home, and she left against the advice of the hospital authorities. It was not until three months later that she could be prevailed upon to enter a sanatorium; at last accounts she was at a seaside hospital and had taken her little daughter with her, thus crowning with at least temporary success a long uphill struggle on the part of the visitor to induce her to place herself and the child under suitable care. (Selected record. Not known to any social agency.)

In three cases tuberculosis had assumed other than the pulmonary form.

The little daughter of eleven, in one family, had a trouble diagnosed at the Medical Station as "tubercular boils." As it is never mentioned again one hopes that it turned out to be not so serious as this sounds and soon disappeared, for there was no lapse in treatment in this case. Both this child and her little sister were sent to the country in the summer of 1919, and upon their return were reported in good condition by the mother. (Selected record. Known to two social agencies.)

A wife who in May had applied for help in getting work was in August reported ill in a public hospital. She was visited, and it was learned that the diagnosis was tuberculosis of the kidney. Later she was sent, apparently by the hospital social service, to the country for convalescent care. Meanwhile various services not directly related to the woman's health (except as they affected her peace of mind) had been performed, such as obtaining special permission for her husband, who was in a military hospital, to visit her, and the attempt (unsuccessful) to secure better care for the baby; but just about the time that the woman was coming home occurs one of those unexplained and regretable lapses already referred to as resulting from pressure of work and the frequent loss of visitors, and we have no further record of any contact with the family. (Cross-section record. Not known to any social agency.)

The story of little Emilia Vaccaro, who insisted upon being taken home from the sanatorium to which Home Service had sent her and could never again be induced to go away, has already been told (see page 54). The home was immaculately clean and the family of rather high grade though very poor. At the date of reading, the visitor, who had taken great pains to secure the best care available for the child in the city, was still endeavoring to convince the family that she should be sent away. (Cross-section record. Not known to any social agency.)

Two cases, each of exceptional interest in its own way, are as unlike as possible except for the one fact that the member of the family who had been in service was in a government tuberculosis hospital while his family was being cared for by Home Service.

The mother of Tom Hume had died of the disease. The father, also a victim, refused for some time to go to a hospital, finally went, and returned in three weeks. A nurse sent in by the Section reported that he should be in a hospital for the sake of the children, but he died at home a few days later.

Efforts were now concentrated on care for the three small children of the second wife. Taken to the Health Center, the two run-abouts tested positive and the advice was given to register them at a tuberculosis clinic and to report there regularly. At the tuberculosis clinic of a nearby hospital to which they were taken a week later they tested negative. Advice as to their diet and care seems to have been more or less followed, and on later examination the Health Center found them improved.

The case of the baby, which was taken with the other children for examination, must be traced separately. On April 4th the Health Center found it suffering from "advanced bronchitis and laryngitis" and ordered hospital care which the mother refused to permit. On April 12th, at the hospital clinic mentioned above, the little thing was said to have whooping cough. On May 16th the doctor at the Health Center found its lungs partly solidified and advised calling in a Henry Street nurse. The nurse next day reported that she had advised the mother's taking the baby to the board of health clinic, and on the 22nd it was there declared to be suffering from "acute bronchitis, nephritis, and tubercular meningitis." Four days later it died, two and a half months after the death of the father.

No mention was found in the record of examination of the mother.

This family was receiving an allowance from Home Service during the period under discussion, while efforts were being made to secure the widow's pension due the mother. (Selected record. Known only to a medical agency.)

The second case, as already intimated in another chapter (see page 42), is inspiring reading because of the heroic qualities of the mother and the ideal care given the family. The Drews had been known to Home Service for some time when the news came that the father, who was about to be discharged, was tuberculous and would be sent for treatment to a sanatorium. Beginning the next month the two children were taken to the Health Center regularly by the mother, and though one at first tested positive, a month later, in May, the mother and both children were declared negative. In June came the news of the father's sudden death—a terrible blow from which his wife rallied superbly. A two months' stay in the country was arranged for the children at the end of that month, and the mother also took a short vacation to visit relatives, declaring on her return she had had a good rest. In September the children, taken again to the Health Center, were found to have gained, but were still below par. Treatment was continued, with attention to diet, care of teeth, etc., and by midwinter both were in good condition, actually overweight. The mother throughout did her utmost, as wage-earner and otherwise, and every possible help was given her. (Selected record. Not known to any social agency.)

There remain five cases in which the patient was a man discharged from service.

Walker, a Canadian ex-soldier, had left the tuberculosis hospital in Canada where he had been under care, partly, it appeared, because he had come under the influence of Christian Science, partly because he wanted to be with his wife and child. His wife, however, refused all overtures, a fact not at all surprising when it was learned that he had been abusive and had a criminal record. He was induced to enter a hospital, which he left in a day or two. At this time he was receiving Christian Science treatment and was taking a cough medicine containing cocaine. Finally, when offered the alternatives of hospital treatment in this country or return to Canada, he chose the latter, and was put upon a northward-bound train, promising to place himself under treatment upon his arrival. (Cross-section record. Known only to a settlement.)

Joe, the fourth son to be taken into service from the Murphy family, was discharged as tuberculous. He refused absolutely, however, to place himself under care, as did other members of the family to submit to examination, the efforts of the visitor producing no result. The mother's indignation at being refused a loan doubtless had something to do with this attitude of obstinate refusal. The family were of rather high grade, living in a very nicely furnished $25 apartment, and though they felt keenly the absence of the three sons and the depletion of income following their departure, were not in desperate straits. (Cross-section record. Not known to any social agency.)

The son of a Bohemian family when discharged with tuberculosis acted promptly on the visitor's advice to go to the Bureau of War Risk Insurance, and was sent from there to a sanatorium in the South. Later, when his mother was in great distress over bad reports received of his condition, her transportation was paid and she made him a long visit. (Cross-section record. No report from Social Service Exchange in record.)

Karl Sartoris, a clerk of twenty-three, living with his mother and younger brother in a "scrupulously clean" apartment, had been drafted and sent to camp, to be discharged after three days as tuberculous. He was advised to go to the Tuberculosis Hospital Admission Bureau, by which he was sent to a sanatorium at the seashore. He was not satisfied and left five days later, at the end of January.

A relief allowance on the basis of a budget study was now arranged, sufficient to meet the deficit caused by the expense of boarding the sick man at home. Early in February he went off to the country on his own account, a married sister paying his expenses; but this experiment did not last long, and the allowance was continued till the end of March, when he was finally induced to go to another hospital not far from the city. Here he improved, but in July came home and refused to return. Again, physicians at the Admission Bureau, and those at the War Risk Bureau as well, were consulted, and in August he was again sent away, this time to a sanatorium in a higher altitude where many other ex-service men were being cared for. He was at first dissatisfied and begged for a transfer; and many letters were written him by the visitor, all in the friendliest spirit, full of encouragement and good counsel. A complete outfit of warm clothing was also sent. Finally he settled down quite contentedly, and at the date of reading the record, in October, was doing well. (Selected record. Not known to any social agency.)

Bernard Aronson, a young man of unusually fine type, after his discharge for tuberculosis had gone to work without a physician's permission. He was urged to go to the War Risk Bureau and very soon went, through a clinic, to a tuberculosis sanatorium. Friendly intercourse was kept up with him by letter, warm clothing was sent, and efforts made to relieve his anxiety about his family, on whom much friendly service and relief were expended. Especial effort was made to insure examination for all five of the younger brothers and sisters—the three of school age being personally conducted to a clinic where applications for admission to a preventorium were filed for them. Whether the two of working age had been examined at the time we read the record we are not sure; much pains had been taken to inform them of clinics where they could go in the evening, but before they had availed themselves of the opportunity, apparently, the mother fell ill with appendicitis and in the excitement over her operation less urgent matters seem to have been lost sight of. Her lungs, at least, were pronounced sound. Efforts were also made to arrange for moving to a better apartment, the one occupied being dark though always scrupulously clean; but a suitable one had not been found at the date of reading. (Selected record. Known to a family society and three other agencies.)

Nervous and Mental Troubles

In approaching this topic the writer would frankly record her sensation of setting sail upon an uncharted sea, inasmuch as she is entirely without psychiatric training.

Our interest, as social workers, in persons suffering from nervous or mental disorders would seem to be twofold: interest in getting those suspected of being thus abnormal under suitable medical examination and care, and interest in social measures taken as part of or supplementary to such care. We have therefore included, in the cases reviewed under this heading, all in which there seemed reason to suspect the existence of troubles of this sort, whether or not any effective action was taken by Home Service and whether or not a definite medical diagnosis was ever made. We have, however, entirely omitted mention of a number of cases in which persons suspected of being feeble-minded were examined and found to be normal, and of two in which extreme nervousness was associated with diabetes.

Twenty-nine different case records in all are mentioned under this head. It is of interest to note that 17 of these, including all in which there is a case of actual insanity and most of those in which severe neuroses are reported, come from among the selected records. The very serious and urgent, as well as interesting, nature of these cases, and the large amount of intensive work involved, naturally account for the inclusion of so large a number in the small group of 77 selected records. The 12 cross-section records present, on the other hand, problems which are for the most part of minor interest and much less thoroughly handled.

In seven of the 29 case records we shall be concerned solely with an ex-service man; in 19, with a member of such a man's family; while in three instances both the man and a member of his family will call for mention under this head.

Two of the 29 cases, for which no clear diagnoses appear in the record, should be mentioned; definite action was taken in both:

In a family referred because of illness the father was found at home—a man apparently about fifty but who stated he was thirty-four. He was pale and very nervous, and suffered from excessive trembling of the hands and head; had some sort of stomach trouble, he stated, and had spent a large part of the past ten years in hospitals. One of these hospitals was visited and an effort was made to find the physician who had treated the man, but who was no longer there. The man was then induced to go to the hospital to see another physician, who promised the visitor a diagnosis. Inquired of a few days later, this physician stated that the man was suffering from a "disease of the brain" and that he was treating him. The visitor records her inability to draw forth a more precise definition of the trouble, and no further action was taken.

Obviously both on the inquiry and treatment side this represents very incomplete action, though the sick man was placed under treatment. (Cross-section record. Known to a family society and three other social agencies.)

An elderly couple, the Meixners, were allowanced and otherwise cared for during many months while efforts were being made to obtain the allotment and allowance due them from the two sons in service. The father, a "confirmed invalid" who "had not worked in years," was said to be "feeble-minded" and "subject to spasms." The family, though unwilling to have him placed in a public institution, gave their consent to having him enter a Jewish Home and he was finally placed in one through the efforts of the Home Service visitor; but within a month he insisted on going home again against the advice of the institution authorities. (Cross-section record. Not known to any social agency.)

Of cases involving definitely feeble-minded persons there are three in our collection, in all of which some action was taken. In a fourth, the mental deficiency is evidently very slight, while in a fifth the existence of such defect seems merely to have been suspected.

In one, a sergeant in the army, a widower with two small children of his own, had informally adopted a little girl of eleven whose dreadful home conditions had aroused his sympathy. Correspondence with the Home Service Section in the town from which she came confirmed his story of her family, a hopelessly degenerate tribe. Much sympathetic work was done by the visitor and the visiting dietitian to help this simple-hearted, kindly man in the management of his brood, and the records of the frequent visits made contain no evidence that the adopted child was thought deficient mentally or morally. When, however, the children were taken to the Health Center (after being bathed and dressed by the visitor) the little girl was declared by the examining physician to be mentally backward and a masturbator; "a very difficult case, needs constant watching." At a mental clinic some days later she was said to be a high-grade defective measuring seven years by the intelligence test; it was suggested that she might be admitted to an institution for the feeble-minded in the state where her family lived. The visitor carefully explained the situation to the father, especially pointing out the need of separating the little girl from the other children. She also wrote to the institution suggested, which replied that it could not take the child, that application must be made through the state authorities. Sergeant Ritchie about this time found that he was to be ordered away and that he must give up the personal care of the children. He asked the visitor to assume charge of them, offering to pay $50 a month, and upon her explaining that she could not accept the responsibility, made arrangements on his own account with a Home. As this arrangement included the adopted child with the others, the visitor felt it her duty to inform the head of the institution of the diagnosis recently made. Whether the child would have been admitted or not does not appear, for meanwhile the adoptive father had written the real father of his plan and the latter had objected, sending a sister to take the child back. So the little girl passed out of reach of the Section. Whether a letter to some agency in her home community suggesting the advisability of taking her from her family and placing her in an institution would have brought any result one can only surmise. (Cross-section record. Not known to any social agency.)

A girl of fourteen, one of five children at home in another family, was in an ungraded class and acknowledged by her family to be exceptionally stupid. When taken to the Health Center with the other children she was found mentally deficient as well as suffering from a very serious condition of eyes and teeth. These physical troubles, with those of other members of the family, so absorbed the visitor that up to the time we read the record, less than two months after the date of filing, the mental examination planned had not been made; but when it is recorded that during this period an operation on the girl's eyes had been arranged which probably saved her from blindness, and an operation on a horribly abscessed mouth, those familiar with the small results usually following a mental test will probably agree that the more helpful action was rightly taken first. (Selected record. Known only to a visiting teacher.)

In our third case very nearly every person dealt with was suspected of mental deficiency. Tom Glynn, a private still in service but who had never been abroad, had ruined one girl and then hastily married another, blinding her by assuming for the occasion the triple glory of alleged wealth, overseas service, and the insignia of a second lieutenant. He was evidently excessively immoral, giving as a reason for not recalling the times and places of his cohabitation with the girl in question that he "had been going with so many of them." He began to abuse his wife within a few weeks after the wedding; and when the subject of divorce or annulment of his marriage was broached, expressed the wish that things should be fixed so that nobody could ever marry him again. Many observers expressed the opinion that he was mentally deficient, but the examination which the Section urged upon the army authorities was apparently never made. His commanding officer when interviewed was sure that he was not a mental case, and that he was responsible. There is a good deal of talk about a wound which the authorities suspected him of having inflicted upon himself, though this was never proved.

His wife, on the other hand, and wife's sister, were examined. The former was said to be "mentally irresponsible," and in need of close watching; it was also asserted by the examiner that because of her mental condition her marriage was not legal. She was to return for other tests, but had not done so up to the date of reading. The examination followed a long struggle to place her industrially in which no effort or money had been spared. At last accounts she was working in a hospital.

Her sister was apparently normal mentally, though her examiner commented upon her bad heredity and upbringing and said she was undeveloped, little development being possible, and needed oversight. She had already been given a vacation in the country and placed on her return in a home for girls. She later found a job for herself; how long she kept it, we do not know.

A definite effort was made to obtain a background of family history for both husband and wife. The man came from the South. Two letters were written to the Home Service Section in his locality asking for information regarding his family; in reply little information was received beyond the fact that his father owned his own farm. According to the wife, her father and both paternal grandparents had died of tuberculosis, while her father, mother, and one grandparent had been addicted to drink.

Some inquiry regarding her family was also made of the unmarried mother in the case, Annie Sheehan, who appears to be much the most normal individual of the group, of good reputation, and an efficient worker in the hospital, where she acted as nurse-attendant throughout the period recorded. She stated that her mother had been "weak-minded," so that when five years old she herself had been taken and placed in a convent. (Selected record. Not known to any social agency.)

A young mother, Mrs. Wood, who had been unfaithful to her husband in his absence, was later said by a psychiatrist who examined her to be slightly deficient mentally. Her husband was one of the sufferers from shell-shock mentioned later in this chapter, and their story is more fully told in later citations. (Selected record. Known to health agencies only.)

A little Italian-American girl of fifteen, working as a waist packer, was said by her mother to be very nervous and to have terrible fits of temper. The visitor arranged for her examination at a mental clinic, where she is reported to have appeared "a very sweet, pretty, quiet girl who was more than willing to do anything that was suggested to her." She was given a Binet test (of which we can find no report in the record) and examined by a physician who gave her medicine and told her to return in three weeks. At the date of the next entry this time had more than elapsed; the child, however, had not returned on account of illness. Our reading of the record came about a month later, but there was no further note on the subject. (Selected record. Known to a family society.)

In only two cases read is the word epilepsy mentioned, and in only one of these is there definite evidence of the existence of the trouble or definite action regarding it.

An epileptic child had been in an institution but had been taken home by its mother. On account of changed circumstances the mother now felt that she must return the child to the institution, but was experiencing some difficulty in getting it accepted. At her request a letter was written by Home Service which accomplished the desired result. (Selected record. Not known to any social agency.)

In another case the word "epileptic" stands on the face card opposite the name of the twenty-four-year-old sister of a man in service. The record, however, contains no other evidence regarding the "fainting spells" that she was said to suffer from. She was advised to go to the Medical Station, but seems not to have done so and there is no evidence of follow-up. (Cross-section record. Parents known to two family societies.)

Four records reveal the struggles of visitors with very difficult young people apparently in more or less unstable nervous condition.

Jim Quirk, who though not yet twenty had been in service over a year, was disabled on account of heart disease. He received compensation and was started in a training course in wireless telegraphy by the Federal Board, but was unable to follow it because of his nervous condition. The Federal Board suggested a mental examination. Some attention was also given by the visitor to his general health, for he was twice at the Medical Station, where an adenoid operation was advised. Apparently neither piece of advice had been acted on when he went off abruptly to Washington. There, judging from reports received from the local Red Cross, he showed a disposition to "live on" the organization. His mother reported him lazy and he wrote home queer, foolish letters which led his family and the visitor to suspect that his mind was affected. At the date of reading no more definite information regarding his condition was available. (Cross-section record. Not known to any social agency.)

Karl Tausig, who had two brothers in service, was said by different visitors on two occasions to have "talked like a maniac." He appeared intelligent and had earned fair pay as a salesman, but seemed possessed of the idea that he was being unjustly discriminated against as a Jew. He began the study of accountancy in which he was reported to be making fair progress, then abandoned it as "too easy," declaring his intention to study law instead. Whether he was really mentally unbalanced is of course uncertain; at the date of reading, while those working on the case were fully alive to the desirability of a mental examination, the probability of ever inducing the young man to submit to one seemed slight. (Cross-section record. Not known to any social agency.)

Another brother of a man in service, Sam Hoffman, presented a variety of health and character problems on which an immense amount of work was done. Confining ourselves with some difficulty to the health problem (since all are very much intertwined), we note that he was sent to the Medical Station several times and was thoroughly examined; glasses were provided and a salve given for the eczema from which he suffered; a Wassermann test made, result negative; and dental treatment and a mental examination were recommended but seem not to have been put through. (Cross-section record. Known to a family society and two other agencies.)

In the fourth of this quartet of cases it was the sister of a man in service who provided the problem. She was a member of a "refined and respectable" family but was not living at home, apparently because her excessive ill-temper and selfishness had been too much for all concerned. Her problem was first thrust upon the visitor in the case by her appearing in the office homeless, having quarreled with the sister-in-law with whom she had been staying. She was placed in a Home for the night and given a dollar for her meals; next day she was taken back to the home of the sister-in-law, who consented to give her another chance, though she said if she could afford it she would like to put her in a sanatorium. A few days later the visitor took the girl to see a doctor, who advised quiet and rest but did not favor a sanatorium; the visitor then arranged with the girl's family for her to stay with them until a convalescent home could be found. A friend of the family with whom the girl had stayed was also consulted. She said the girl was bold, talkative, lazy, a spoiled child, nervous; and expressed the opinion that she should be examined mentally. The girl refused to go to the country—had been there before she said, and it made her nervous. Finally the visitor made an appointment with her for a mental and physical examination; this she broke, telephoning later that she had work. Dental care was also arranged for her; whether she took advantage of this opportunity does not appear.

The last recorded effort to help, at the date of reading, was the passing on to the girl, via a married sister, of information regarding a new Home for girls which might be suited to her needs. It is worth noting that both this married sister and the mother, as well as the girl in question, presented symptoms described by the visitor as "hysterical." (Cross-section record. Not known to any social agency.)

Four other women who came under the care of Home Service in the records read are said to have been hysterical. The cases of two are worth citing at some length; the few facts known regarding the other two we also give briefly.

Mrs. Nordova, whose son was in service, complained of ill-health and was advised to go to the Medical Station. She went instead to a private physician, who reported that so far as he could tell she was "hysterical only." She was later advised to see the doctor again. Whether she did so does not appear. (Cross-section record. Known to a family society.)

Young Mrs. Tully, who had married a man whom she scarcely knew and had separated from him, told a shocking story of his perversions. Her physician advised against the husband's return. No symptoms of hysteria seem to have been observed by the visitor, but the woman reported that she was subject to convulsions at her menstrual period; and a physician to whom she was later taken said the attacks were "probably hysterical." She seems to have been angered at this examination for some unexplained reason, and a few days later became so insulting to the visitor—who was doing her best to help her secure a divorce—that the latter withdrew from all contact. This of course represents a failure, the source of which we are unable to trace. (Cross-section record. Not known to any social agency.)

One record presents a most detailed study of dealings with an extraordinarily difficult type of woman. Mrs. Cohen made a good appearance upon her personal application, and was found living with a young son and daughter in three well lighted and heated rooms described as clean and neat. She suffered from "attacks" which were having a very bad effect on the little daughter whom they terrified. She expressed willingness to go to the Medical Station but put off going, and when finally got there left before examination and declared herself too ill to return. Meanwhile inquiry of a woman physician at a hospital clinic which Mrs. Cohen had attended brought a rather unprofessional report, accompanied by bursts of laughter, to the effect that she was "not ill," was "crazy as a loon" and "could work." Some time later she did start work at a former job (not apparently urged thereto by the visitor) but gave up in a few days, saying she had been obliged to do so on account of "attacks." An appointment with a specialist in mental diseases was now made, a neighbor being taken along to describe the mysterious "attacks," and after several periods of study the examining physician pronounced the case one of "major hysteria." He was impressed with the bad effect produced upon the child, and advised sending the mother away for three or four weeks to a certain convalescent home for observation. The home named, however, declined to take the case, and a desperate search for one that would do so began.

The family had meanwhile, almost from the beginning, been supported by the Section, while efforts were being made to secure an allotment and allowance from the son in service.

After a month of fruitless effort to place Mrs. Cohen, the specialist was consulted again. This time he examined the mother—and, separately, the child—before a large group of physicians. He gave a prescription and again most emphatically advised sending the woman away, as she was not fit to have charge of home and children.

All hope of finding a place where Mrs. Cohen could be cared for free of charge seems now to have been temporarily abandoned; and after consultation with her father and a brother, who promised to help in the plan, she was placed in an attractive private home out of town; the little girl went to an uncle, while the Big Brother who had been called in to help with the problem of the boy—a refractory lad of sixteen—found him a home.

Within two weeks, however, the woman with whom Mrs. Cohen had been placed reported that she could keep her no longer; endless complaints and gossip started among neighbors were two of the counts against her. So the search for a suitable place was renewed, and two days later she was transferred to a boarding place in the Catskills where she was placed in charge of the local Home Service Section. Again, in less than two weeks, came a message that she would have to return; she was having "fits." This time she was placed at a regular sanatorium, which would apparently have kept her indefinitely; but it was unduly high-priced, and the efforts of the Section to find an institution which would care for her free of charge seeming at last successful, the woman was transferred two or three months later to a sanatorium where she was paid for temporarily by a hospital organization which expected soon to open a free home where she could be accommodated. However, a month later word was received that she could no longer be paid for and apparently the opening of the free home was still in the indefinite future. Meanwhile the relatives had failed to keep their promises of financial help and the woman herself continued to show the most supreme selfishness in all her relations; so it was finally decided to take her to the home of her father, who had a business of his own and owned the building in which he worked, and leave the responsibility with the family. The one good that seemed certainly to have been accomplished at the date of reading was the relief of the little daughter from the fearful burden that she had been struggling under; for she had gone with her uncle's family to the country for a long, restful summer. Whether the benefit was to prove more than temporary only later developments could prove; it was too probable that the mother would shortly regain possession of the child—though all the relatives were pledged to prevent this—and that the old round of emotional self-indulgence would recommence.

The relatives of the family gave information which supplements the portrait of this mother as a selfish neurotic; she had been spoiled by an overindulgent husband, they said, and had driven her own mother to her death by her outrageous behavior. (Selected record. Known only to a settlement.)

The remaining case involving hysteria is more cheerful reading. It is in fact one of those rare and delightful cases in which complete success was achieved.

Lincoln Israel, a young man who had been recently discharged and was living with his wife in another city, wrote to the Section asking that it interest itself in one of his sisters who had suffered a nervous breakdown. The letter was that of an educated man, and the family proved to be one of those in which a great gap had opened between the foreign-born elders and their American-bred children. The girl in question, nineteen years old and the oldest at home, was attractive and intelligent as was also her much better-balanced sister two years younger. To the cure which happily followed, this younger sister and the absent brother largely contributed. This should be freely acknowledged before the measures taken by the visitors are reviewed.

Rachel, the older sister, had stopped work three weeks before the first visit; she was much depressed and suffered from hysterical attacks or "fainting spells." She had before this time been examined at a hospital specializing in nervous troubles, which on being inquired of advised a period of restraint in an institution. The visitor, however, had an interview with the physician who had examined the girl at this hospital, and he gave quite different advice. Elements in the situation brought out by him were the unfortunate home environment, the ignorant mother, and the girl's habit of masturbation, "the only outlet of an hysterical type of adolescent girl"; her needs were to be taken out of the home, relieved of financial responsibility, and given mental stimulus. He advised definitely against institutional care. The girl was also taken to see another physician who gave similar advice, expressing in addition his disapproval of any "long mental examination."

Arrangements were then made for Rachel's admission to a convalescent home in the country. The girl's letters during the four weeks she spent there are evidence of the helpful personal relations established by the visitor with her. Soon after her return to the city the brother reached the point toward which he had all along been working where he could take his sister into his home, and she was sent to him. There she found congenial work, and her happy letters, confirmed by those of her brother, gave evidence of a complete cure, also of the heartiest appreciation of the help given by the visitor toward that end. (Selected record. Not known to any social agency.)

Six ex-soldiers, in cases read by us, were suffering from a nervous condition resulting from some form of shock or illness.

Isaac Tanzer was seen only once, for the purpose of passing on certain information which the Section had been asked by another Red Cross bureau to communicate to him. It appeared that he was suffering from "shell-shock"; could not bear noise, broke down and wept at trifles, etc. He had already been examined and instructed to report at the Marine Hospital. This the visitor urged him to do, and also to apply to the War Risk Insurance Bureau. The outcome is not recorded. (Cross-section record. Not known to any social agency.)

The disability of Albert Cassel showed itself in excessive nervousness and ill-temper. Struggles to get him to the Federal Board and to hasten his compensation were at last crowned with partial success and he was got away to the country with money advanced by Home Service in July. He returned, however, in a week; was apparently sent to another place in August; was again in town in September, no better; was finally, after persistent refusal, persuaded to go to the Federal Board again, and left once more for the country next day. The record, a very fragmentary one, was read soon after this event and later developments are not known. (Cross-section record. Not known to any social agency.)

Tom Eagan, a fine, strong-looking fellow, came to the office with a request from the Federal Board that he be sent to the country; he was reported to be in a neurasthenic condition as a result of influenza. A place was found which proved satisfactory. A month later, when he left it and came to New York very much upset because he felt he should be working to support his mother who was living in another state, he was persuaded to return for the further rest he very evidently needed; and there he still was at the date the record was read. (Selected record. Known to a family society.)

Another ex-service man, Louis Leonardis, was apparently suffering from some mental difficulty. On first contact the visitor's impression had been that he was feeble-minded; and the first answer received from the nerve clinic to which he had been sent for mental and physical examination said merely that the case could not be fully gone into on "such brief observation." Not satisfied with this, the worker sent the man back to the clinic with a note saying, "We believe he is suffering from shell-shock," and word then came from the doctor, "I think you will be justified in considering his condition due to shell-shock." Leonardis was sent soon after to the country, but returned in a few days because worried, he said, about his wife, and the two were then sent together back to the farm where he had been. Within two weeks he was in New York again, reported by those in charge at the farm to have made a murderous attack on his wife and thought by them to be insane. After consultation with the War Risk Bureau he was sent to the Marine Hospital. Some ten days later he left the hospital without permission and in another man's clothes; but being refused the money he asked for, and fearing he would lose his compensation, he returned a day or two later. A physician of the War Risk Bureau about this time came to the conclusion that there was nothing the matter with the man's mind, and the Federal Board announced it was stopping his training pay. This was not actually done until several months later. He had meanwhile left the hospital a second time, been sent back by the visitor and left a third time, refusing absolutely to return; and had been placed for training in a machine-shop where, after fair trial, he was regarded as feeble-minded.

One difficulty in this case was that the man was a foreigner and a stranger in the city, so that there was no way of finding out about his mental condition prior to service. This probably largely accounts for what was certainly rather a loose medical diagnosis. (Selected record. Not known to a social agency.)

Robert Wood was suffering from shell-shock when he returned to America to meet what was apparently an even greater shock in learning of the infidelity of his wife and a whole train of dreadful consequences involved. An effort was made to induce the Army to keep him under treatment for awhile but without success and he went home and to work. At last reading, the break-up of the family was imminent. The man had been urged to accept convalescent care, but in all the dreadful tragedy of the situation had been unwilling to consider leaving home. (The case of man's wife has been already mentioned in this chapter; see page 117.)

Last of this group of shell-shock cases is that of Morris Neuman. He had been gassed and severely wounded, and the physicians of the War Risk Bureau said he needed an oculist's care and six months' rest. His family consisted of a mother and sister, who lived in a "beautifully furnished" three-room apartment in an elevator apartment house; the sister worked as a clerk, and the mother assured the visitor that they wanted no help for themselves (though she later very gratefully accepted the care of the Medical Station). The son, examined at the Medical Station, was said to be suffering from "infection of teeth, tonsils, thyroiditis." He was fitted with glasses and his teeth X-rayed. At this time convalescent care in the country was advised at once, the tonsil operation and work on teeth to come later when he was stronger; but another physician reversed the order, insisting that the tonsils must come out at once. About this time a loan allowance to cover the young man's board until he could be sent away was started, to be repaid when he should receive the government checks due. The tonsils operation was performed at the Booth Memorial Hospital the following month; meanwhile the dental work was going on. A little later a period of examination in a hospital was arranged at the instigation of the War Risk Bureau to determine whether anything in the way of an operation would better the condition of the boy's wound, a bad head injury. The decision was in the negative. Finally, after months of devoted care, a quiet place on a farm was found by the visitor for him, carefully adapted to his peculiar needs. Thither he was sent (the War Risk Bureau paying his board) and there he had stayed, well satisfied up to the date of reading. Co-operation with the family had been perfect, with the friendliest relations all around. (Selected record. Known to a family society.)

One case involving a woman is rather similar to some of those of shell-shocked soldiers which have gone before.

A young girl born in France had been at service in London during part of the war and had suffered from what the hospital authorities under whose care she had been prior to coming to Home Service called "air-raid neurosis." Later she was obliged to return to this hospital for further treatment. Some very interesting work done by the visitor in leading her family to realize her condition and need of a long period of rest has already been dwelt upon in another connection. (See page 66. Selected record. Not known to any social agency.)

Six cases in this large and miscellaneous group remain to be considered: one of a definite psychoneurosis, five of insanity, or probable insanity.

The O'Neil family, with two sons in service, had been known to the Home Service Section six months before the existence of the daughter of the family was discovered. The father was a drunkard, the mother a slatternly, lazy creature, the small boy a truant. The record of the family agency which had previously known the family, summarized at the beginning of the Home Service record, had indeed mentioned a daughter, but no inquiry seems to have been made regarding her, and the visitor who later came on the case was first led to suspect her existence by the talk of certain family connections visited. Then came a day when she boldly invaded the rear room where her aroused suspicions told her the girl was lurking. The story of this and a subsequent interview is best told in the words of the visitor:

"July 1. Asked to see Hannah. Mrs. O'Neil said that the girl never saw anyone, and it was useless to ask her. Told Mrs. O'Neil to try. She went out of the room and came back saying that Hannah was too dirty to see anyone. Asked Mrs. O'Neil to try again, which she did without success, so visitor went into the kitchen to talk with the girl. Passed from the front room, which was in a fairly neat condition, through a side room which was very dirty, and so into a filthy kitchen. There was a kerosene stove burning which smoked, and the room was black. The foul odor was overpowering. Hannah when she heard the visitor coming had hidden herself, so visitor stepped back into the side room and began to talk to Mrs. O'Neil so that Hannah could hear her, thinking perhaps if the girl got accustomed to the sound of her voice she might possibly be persuaded to come out of her hiding place. Gradually visitor began to speak to Hannah, saying that she need not be afraid, and to come out into the room, and that it made no difference if her clothes were dirty, etc. Slowly, the girl came into sight, and by talking gently to her and taking her by the hand, persuaded her to come and sit down. She sat down in a chair but turned her back in such a manner that it was impossible to see her face. The girl was a most pitiful object, ragged, filthy and unkempt. Her hair looked as if it had not been washed in years. Her complexion was gray and she had a fugitive look, like that of some animal who expected to be kicked.

"Visitor asked if she did not want to get well and get out into the sunshine and be the Hannah that she was seven years ago. She said yes, but there was no one to help her. She wanted to get well and she wanted to be herself again but she had no one to help her. Had no clothes to go away, and did not like to have people look at her. She was afraid to go out on the street.

"Told her that all these things would be looked after and clothes provided if she would consent to go away and have care. She said that she would go with the visitor but with no one else.

"Hannah asked if she had to go out into the street. Told her that it would be impossible to get away without crossing over the sidewalk, but possibly some way might be found whereby she could go in an automobile.

"The girl acts very strangely. She slouches over in her chair and pushes her knees up until they meet her chin, and sits there perfectly impassive. When visitor asked the mother some question, Hannah volunteered the information directly, giving dates and places, showing that she is more intelligent than she looks.

"July 11. Asked Mrs. O'Neil if she would give her consent to have Hannah taken away and treated. She replied that she would be very glad to have anything done for the girl which would help her.

"Called at the workrooms of the Bronx Chapter in Tremont Avenue and obtained the following clothes for Hannah O'Neil:

"Two gingham dresses, two gingham aprons, one suit, one thin dress, one extra house dress, three towels.

"Bought for Hannah O'Neil two sets of underclothes, one underskirt, one corset, one pair of shoes. Visitor took her from her own clothes two white shirtwaists, two night dresses, two pairs of stockings, and a hat.

"Called at——. As soon as visitor came to the house Hannah came into the room of her own accord and sat down, drawing a chair next to visitor but turned her back so that her face was hidden. Talked with Mrs. O'Neil and gradually brought Hannah into conversation. Asked her to look at the clothes which were in bundles, and she seemed very much interested in them. She sat with the three towels on her lap and patted them saying to herself at the same time, 'Once I used to have nice clothes. I had hats with flowers and feathers on them. I had thin dresses and I used to have a good time, but I am never going to have a good time again.' Visitor assured her that the good times would come just as soon as she was better. Hannah asked repeatedly, 'Do you think they can make me better in a sanatorium?'

"As the visitor was leaving, Hannah asked if a doctor would come up to the house and examine her as she was afraid to go out into the street. Promised to see what could be done. Hannah said, 'Let me know before he comes, so I can be dressed up in my new clothes.' Visitor talked for a few minutes with the girl and told her to be clean always, not just to use the clothes to dress up in. As soon as these clothes wore out, she would see that she had others, but never wanted to see her in such a dirty condition as she was at present. Hannah promised to take a bath and put on her clean clothes."

This promising beginning was followed by consultation with a hospital for nervous diseases and an arrangement whereby one of the specialists attached to it went with the visitor to call on the girl—a long trip by taxi. He pronounced the case one of psychoneurosis, and traced its beginning to a period seven years before when she had been run down and had dosed herself with medicines recommended by a druggist. At this time she overheard someone commenting upon her queerness and saying that if she was not insane already she was going to be so. This preyed upon her mind and she became morbid. Then came an attack of influenza which affected menstruation; she was confined to her bed for several months and from that time on imagined that she was doomed to become insane. Her family had taken advantage of her state to make of her a household drudge. The physician who examined her found her very intelligent and well informed—she was in the habit of reading the newspapers. He also believed her innocent. In later confidences to her visitor the girl related various events preceding the illness referred to above: her father's excessive drinking and interference with all her youthful pleasures, and finally his violent opposition to her proposed marriage to a prosperous man ten years her senior, a friend of his. For many years she had not stirred from the house or talked with one of her former friends.

At the hospital for nerve cases, to which she was taken on the advice of the examining physician, the girl remained nearly two months, and in that time was wonderfully built up physically and restored to a comparatively normal state. Then the experiment was tried of placing her for three months with a couple, recommended by the hospital, who were running a small school for atypical children. The understanding was that she was to be treated as a member of the family, was to receive certain treatment, and do her share of the housework under the training of the mistress of the house. A contract for the period was signed by her, the Section paying a stipulated sum in advance. Unfortunately rank exploitation was practised on the girl, who was made to do the heavy work of the house, including washing for the entire school, and was never given the treatment promised; in the end she was also unkindly treated, and ran away before her term was up, going home to the parents she had hoped never to live with again. While this was a terrible blow to her visitor, the loss of influence proved to be only temporary; later examination by a mental specialist showed that the gain made had not been lost, as feared, by the weeks at home, and that there was every hope "that with supervision she could be made a self-supporting member of the community." At last accounts she had again been sent to the country. The record shows rare ability in dealing not only with the girl but with her most difficult mother, who at times did her utmost to frustrate the visitor's efforts. The payment of a lump sum in advance for so long a period of treatment as three months was undoubtedly a blunder; as was the failure, in visiting the girl during her stay in the school, to achieve a private conversation in which questioning might have brought to light the breach of contract involved in the work loaded upon her. (Selected record. Known to a family society.)

The first of the four insanity cases to be considered is that of a non-supporting husband with a record of abuse of his wife.

Maurice Meadows had apparently been devoted to two children who had died, and his great grievance against his wife was that she had neglected them, being, he maintained, responsible for their death. His wife had been under the care of the Section before his return from service, and from then on the two were separately looked out for. He was most untruthful and contradictory in his statements. After much effort and special arrangements with his employer the visitor succeeded in having him examined by a specialist who pronounced him a "paranoid," but not bad enough to be confined. He was later taken into court and ordered to make weekly payments to his wife. Shortly after he re-enlisted as a single man. (Selected record. Known to a family society, the Domestic Relations Bureau and Court, a church, and the Department of Public Charities.)

The story of Mrs. Vizet's relations with Home Service has been told at some length in an earlier chapter. (See page 54.) Her outbursts of temper and threats were so terrible as to make the workers in contact with her suspect mental derangement. Up to the time when we last consulted the record, however, there had been no agreement among the psychiatrists who examined her. The first stated: "There is nothing actually psychotic in this case—just pugnacity raised to a high degree appears to explain the woman." The second, some months later, came to the conclusion that she was dangerously insane and recommended that she be immediately committed. When, however, her case was brought to court by the Society for the Prevention of Cruelty to Children the mental expert would not accept this view, and the court arranged for the Catholic Big Sisters to take charge of the family. (Selected record. Known to a family society.)

Mrs. Yeager, the stepmother of a young man just called to service, appealed by letter for help. She was found living alone and in bed, from which she insisted that she could not stir although the doctor who had been called expressed doubt as to whether anything was the matter. A fortnight later he had begun to suspect mental trouble. Efforts were made to persuade her to go to a hospital at once but to no avail; he reported that she declared that she would stay in bed until her stepson came home. After the young man's discharge, however, no change for the better occurred. For months regular relief was helplessly given while one effort after another was made to induce the woman to change her mind. At one time a visitor from a mental clinic was called and made a study of the case, but nothing helpful resulted unless we count as helpful the increased certainty that the case was a mental one. A mental specialist was taken to see Mrs. Yeager and made a diagnosis of "psychoneurosis, neurasthenic type." He advised against hospital care and urged the woman to go out walking and to come to see him at his clinic. This she did not do. Nine months after the first contact, nearly six after the return of the son, the existence of immoral relations between stepson and stepmother is suggested by the original doctor in the case, who affirmed his conviction that her difficulty was mental. Still no progress was made until a new visitor was put on the case—a nurse. She at once noticed symptoms of hyperthyroidism, and consulted a physician known to her in one of the large hospitals who made a diagnosis to that effect, tracing the psychoneurosis from which Mrs. Yeager was suffering to this cause. Then came the effort to persuade the woman to enter the hospital where this physician worked. At first refusing, she did consent to enter another and then, discontented there, herself requested transfer to the one where the visitor had first desired to place her. Here she remained only over one night, leaving next day in a fit of anger. By this time evidence had accumulated as a result of her behavior both in the hospitals and at home which sufficiently indicated insanity, and after an endless amount of work the visitor succeeded in having her forcibly removed and committed to a hospital for the insane. The diagnosis made by the alienist at this time reads: "Depression, undifferentiated toxic psychosis (hyperthyroidism)."

Criticism in this case is easy; but it is not strange that, surrounded as she was by sympathetic neighbors and with relatives who when first consulted expressed only sympathy and concern for her, the woman should have succeeded in imposing her view of her needs. It was only as evidence gradually accumulated that the outlines of the situation became clear. Yet there can be little doubt that had the visitor with a nurse's training been available earlier a solution would have been more quickly worked out and an immense saving in time, money, and energy effected. (Selected record. Not known to any social agency.)

In the Meyer family the insanity of the daughter seemed to be but one phase of a general family breakdown whose ultimate causes are not revealed. The family had been in comfortable circumstances and still occupied six rooms in a good steam-heated house. About two years before they came to the attention of the Red Cross the eldest son had died, and the eldest daughter and chief earner had developed tuberculosis and been sent, with the aid of one of the family agencies, to California. The other son had already joined the Army, and with his allotment and allowance, the earnings of the daughter who remained at home, and what the failing father could make when he was able to follow his trade of tailoring the family had continued to get along. Three or four months ago, however, word had come that the daughter in California, following an attack of influenza, had suffered a hemorrhage and had been sent to a sanatorium. This news seemed to cause the collapse of the girl at home, who stopped work, declared she was ill, and became more and more irritable and disagreeable. Then the son's term of service came to an end and with it the government checks upon which the family had come to depend; and Home Service was called in.

Financial help was given from the outset and the girl was examined, first at a general clinic where she was said to be in a "run down condition" and then at a neurological clinic, where she was said to be suffering from a "fatigue neurosis" and the country was advised. Within a few days after this diagnosis she was sent away to a convalescent home. She was dissatisfied and stayed but six days. Efforts were made to arrange for care in another convalescent home, but she refused to go and became so violent that the mother consented to her commitment. The diagnosis at the hospital for the insane to which she was sent was "manic depression" psychosis.

Hardly was the girl safely in the institution when the mother, influenced by her letters insisting that she was *not* insane, began to urge the visitor to try to get her out. This pressure the visitor resisted, refusing to act against the advice of the physician in charge. Up to the date of reading, however, the mother appeared unreconciled; and, worse still, she had begun to develop symptoms similar to some of her daughter's, sitting for long periods idle, staring blankly into vacancy. Reports from the Home Service Section in the West which was trying to help the discharged brother also suggested possible mental abnormality in him. (Selected record. Known to a family society and a health agency.)

In the last of the families to be discussed under this head there were two cases of insanity. The father, so his wife stated, had had syphilis before she married him, but was supposed to have been cured until it came on again about two years before the family became known to Home Service. He had been confined at a hospital for the insane (diagnosis not stated) and while there made several attempts to drown himself. Later he was discharged and was now living at home, working irregularly (he was a barber) but sleeping most of his time away. Still later he was, through the efforts of another family agency already interested, again placed in the hospital.

The son Orlando, when the family first became known, was in service, but was soon discharged "on account of a disordered mind," so the other interested agency reported; there was also a report from a hospital where he had been examined that he was feeble-minded. The hospital where he had been under care had stated that he was able to work and, though liable to suicide, was dangerous only to himself. His family was troubled by his laziness—for, like the father, he spent most of his time sleeping—and believed him insane. After several attempts to find him work the visitor went with him to the hospital from which he was paroled. The doctor who examined him found him not at the time insane, but said he would probably develop dementia præcox "in a couple of years;" the best work the visitor could do, he said, would be to uphold the man's morale by making him feel he could be self-supporting and rational.

Returning home with the man the visitor did her best to carry out this program. She explained to the family that Orlando was not insane, and enlisted his brother's co-operation in getting him up and to work in the morning. For awhile he did work; then stayed in bed more and more of his time. The visitor herself tried her hand at awakening him and urged him to work with little result. Then she consulted a physician of the War Risk Insurance Bureau, who promised to hail the man to his office and, if he found him sufficiently feeble-minded, send him to a home for feeble-minded soldiers; but upon examination Orlando promised to go to work and was allowed to return home, the examining physician considering him not feeble-minded but a præcox case, and advising that his commitment be left to the appropriate city hospital. Finally after a hard struggle, he was got to this hospital. The visitor's account of the last day's labors are worth quoting.

"Visitor called at the home at quarter of nine in the morning. Orlando was asleep. She told him to get up and dress as she was going to take him to the hospital and have the doctors examine him and see if he could not be made to feel in better condition and able to work. He said that he felt fine and there was no use of his going to see the doctor. All he needed was a little rest as it was too early just now for him to get up. Visitor urged upon him that he must get up and dress immediately and that she would wait for him in the kitchen. He sat upon the edge of the bed and began to put on his shoes. Visitor then left him. After waiting for about one-half hour Orlando did not appear. Visitor returned to the front room and found that he had crept into the bed. With assistance of his mother he was again pulled out and he promised that he would be dressed in a few minutes; that he was going to work. Another hour passed and Orlando appeared in the kitchen all dressed except for his collar and shoes unlaced. He leaned up against the tubs and undertook to discuss at length why he should not go to the hospital. Said he was in perfect condition and that the kind of a fellow he was needed only to go to work. He asked visitor to give him a few days more to make some plans and find a job. His mother shouted and screamed at him a great deal in Italian to which he replied with a few grunts. During her talk with him, visitor understood her to say something about Bellevue. This was like a red rag in the face of a bull. Orlando said there was no use, he was not going with visitor; he was going to go out and find a job. Visitor told him that it was not at all certain that he was going to Bellevue, that he would just go out and see the doctor and see what he had to say. He said he had to eat his breakfast anyway. By twelve o'clock he had finished his breakfast consisting of a great deal of bread and butter and a couple of cups of coffee. During all this time he was perfectly silent while his mother and visitor talked in general about the family's financial situation. When he finished his breakfast . . . he said he had to go in the front room and arrange his collar. He took a great deal of time deciding which tie he would wear. He first looked at one, a long green one very much worn, and then a new polka-dot one. He tried one on and then the other. Finally he decided on the worn-out green tie. Visitor assured him he was all dressed and it was time to start. He darted back into the front room and after a few minutes he was followed by the visitor and his mother, but he had disappeared. After a search it was found that he had escaped through the front door of the flat which had been closed and had a bed against it. When visitor and mother got down to the front stoop he was a couple of steps away from the house. He very kindly returned and said there was no use talking, he was sick of the doctors. They could not do any good. All he needed to do was to put his mind on work and he would be as good as any other fellow. First he would have to harden himself to heavy work.

"After a lengthy discussion on the front stoop, during which Orlando stolidly refused to move and said that visitor was to give him three days in which to get to work and show that he was a good fellow, visitor said all right, she would go and give him the three days.

"Visitor then went to the telephone at the corner drug store and left Orlando in charge of his brother Carlo. After visitor had come from the telephone booth, having spoken to Miss Dale in the office about the advisability of communicating with Bellevue and securing an ambulance, she found that Orlando had escaped. His mother and brother ran in one direction looking for him and visitor in the other, but he could not be found. His mother then said that she was sure that he had gone over to the river on Cherry Street to commit suicide, as he had been previously taken with that idea when on Ward's Island, but she thought perhaps he might forget about Bellevue and return that night as he had no money in his pockets.

"Visitor returned to the home in the afternoon to find out if any news had been heard from Orlando. His mother said that he had returned about fifteen minutes after the visitor had left, asked for the key to the rooms and said he wanted to go to bed. Visitor then explained to the mother that it was necessary to get him to the hospital that afternoon and that she would secure a policeman who would assist. Visitor got the policeman on the beat and stationed him outside the home. Mrs. Elvarado asked visitor that he not go upstairs until it was necessary as she did not want the neighbors to know about the difficulty with Orlando. Visitor then went upstairs and awakened

Orlando. He was very much surprised to see her the second time and said he thought she had gone away. He said that he would not go to the hospital and there was no use of talking to him about it. Visitor then took him to the window and showed him the policeman stationed on the other side. She told him that if he refused to go with her the policeman would take him. He said it was all right, he would go right along.

"En route to the hospital while riding on a Second Avenue car, which was going at top speed, Orlando attempted to jump off. Visitor grabbed him by the collar and threw him across the bench. He said nothing, but remained quiet for awhile after that and when visitor took her eyes off him for a moment he made another attempt to jump off. On this occasion his mother let out a scream and grabbed him. On arriving at 26th Street and getting off the car, Orlando had no sooner put his foot on the street than he started to run down Second Avenue. Visitor pursued him at top speed, followed by a number of youngsters and caught him. He made no attempt to free himself, but stood perfectly still in evident amazement at having been caught. Visitor then told him that it was absurd for him to attempt to run away as police force would find him within half an hour. He was very pathetic in his desire to keep his freedom and insisted that he would go to work the next day. He argued in a childish fashion to the effect that there was no use of his being in an institution and that he wanted to be a regular 'guy' and go to work.

"On arriving at the psychopathic ward at Bellevue Hospital Orlando became very much depressed and said it was all up with him. The first thing he began to tell the doctor in charge was that he was going to work shortly and there was no use of his coming there at all, and that the visitor could fix it up for him if she only would. The doctor told the visitor that he was a case of dementia præcox in the infantile stage. He said his mind acted like that of a child. When visitor told him that the diagnosis at —— Hospital was feeble-mindedness with episodes of excitement he was very much surprised and said that he recalled the patient when he came into the office before he was committed to Ward's Island the last time and that he had diagnosed the case as 'manic depression insanity,' but he said his acquaintance with the boy was too short to discover the dementia præcox symptoms which had since become so evident.

"When Mrs. Elvarado was asked to sign the commitment papers she said she did not think she ought to do it as she had not consulted with the boy's sister, Rosa, in Brooklyn. She cried a great deal and visitor tried to make her understand that Orlando would be better cared for in the hospital than she had been able to care for him. She signed the papers and said she would write Rosa that night." (Selected record. Known to a family society and two other social agencies.)

Whatever we may think of the ethics of promising an insane man "to give him three days more" and then returning to the attack the same afternoon, there can be no question as to the resourcefulness of the methods or the vividness of the account.

Venereal Disease

Among the cross-section cases read four contained evidence of the existence of syphilis in one or more members of a family; among the selected records there were five instances of syphilis and two of gonorrhea.

In one of the four cross-section cases mentioned the father and mother in an Italian family had been declared syphilitic by their own physician, but the Wassermann applied at the Medical Station gave negative results. They insisted that their four visits to the Medical Station had not benefited them and when urged to go to another hospital refused to promise. Later, however, they seem to have gone, for it is recorded that they had waited six hours and then been "too late for treatment." There was talk of a new appointment but no recorded result. Case workers will be able to represent to themselves the labor involved in getting a couple—especially a couple who were receiving no financial aid—to go five times for treatment, and will not be surprised at the outcome. (Cross-section record. Not known to any social agency.)

Whether in the above case the result of the Wassermann is to be accepted as disproof of the family doctor's diagnosis is not indicated. In two instances (not included among those mentioned in the first paragraph) announcement of a negative Wassermann was accompanied by a definite medical opinion that syphilis did not exist. In one of these cases the first diagnosis of "blood infection" had perhaps been tentative, and was at all events changed to the later one, "acid in the system," by the same physician. In the other the original diagnosis was apparently simply a bad blunder: a physician in the country had sent a girl in from a convalescent home with the statement that an eruption on her back was due to "second stage syphilis"; a physician at the Medical Station disagreed on first examination, and when announcing the result of the Wassermann said she thought the sores due to a burn only. (Some sort of plaster had been applied to the girl's back by well-meaning friends.)

With these preliminary observations—meant only to suggest the advisability of reasonable caution in accepting offhand diagnoses—we may turn to the cases in which there seems to have been no question as to the existence of the disease named.

We may say at once that in the three remaining cases of the cross-section group and in two of the five selected cases of syphilis, no action regarding treatment was taken by Home Service beyond that of inquiry. The reasons for such inaction are indicated in the brief notes which follow:

Mrs. Otis was visited in connection with a report on her son's request for discharge. The statement that she was under care for a venereal condition at a certain hospital was verified by consulting the hospital, which reported a positive Wassermann. The family appeared in no need of any kind, and nothing further was done except to make the report asked promptly. (Cross-section record. Not known to any social agency.)

The Tullio family had been long known to one of the family agencies whose visitor reported that a Wassermann test of the mother had been made in 1916 with positive results and that she had been allowed to continue her work of finishing. It is not stated whether she had been treated at that time or since, and no evidence appears in the record that treatment or examination was urged while the family were under Home Service care. This is one of the poorest and most fragmentary records read. (Cross-section record. Known to a family society and two other agencies.)

The Barker family consisted, at the time Home Service made its acquaintance, of only a grandmother and granddaughter—one grandson being in the Navy and the other in an institution. They had been known to eight different agencies, among them one doing family case work whose record revealed earlier conditions. The brother now in an institution was blind and deaf, and previous to his placing had been in a stage of syphilis which made him a "menace." Efforts had been made to keep the girl, also diseased, under medical care, and had been partly successful—she was said to be "improved," not cured. There is no evidence that any action was taken by the Home Service visitor regarding her condition. She was twenty-one, a "very pretty girl," and supported her grandmother by her work in a publishing house. (Cross-section record. Known to a family society and seven other agencies.)

The father of the Marx family died in a hospital shortly after the first visit from Home Service. He had suffered both from tuberculosis and from syphilis. Inquiry of a hospital where the children had been examined brought a report of negative Wassermanns, and the record does not mention the subject again. (Selected record. Known only to a health agency.)

The father of Orlando Elvarado, as was mentioned earlier in this chapter (page 131), was reported by his wife to have had syphilis before their marriage and to have suffered a return of it some two years ago. The only treatment recorded was the placing of the man in a hospital for the insane, which seems to have been accomplished by the family agency which had previously had the family under care and which continued relations during the period of Home Service activity. (Selected record. Known to a family society.)

The other three sufferers from syphilis, all women, received careful attention.

Mrs. Auerbach, twenty-one years old, came of an apparently respectable and prosperous family living in a comfortable private house. She had acquired the disease before her marriage and displayed a total unconcern regarding it which is astounding. While she was willing and even eager to be cured of her taste for drugs, and submitted to hospital treatment for it, she refused treatment for syphilis, even when in the institution. Her physician, early in the record, expresses to the visitor the horror he felt when, shortly after he had impressed upon the woman the need of care so as not to infect others, he saw her eating in a restaurant. The Home Service visitor was no more successful in her efforts at influence. Nor did the young husband show any greater sensitiveness; when first warned of his wife's condition, through the associate field director of his camp, he was reported as planning to have his marriage annulled and as grateful to the Red Cross; later, however, when interviewed by the supervisor, he insisted upon having his wife leave the hospital where it was desired she should remain for treatment, declaring that he himself was "immune"—a statement supported by the negative result of the Wassermann taken in camp. (Selected record. Not known to any social agency.)

Mrs. Sullivan (as stated elsewhere—see page 97) was treated very persistently at the Medical Station during her pregnancy and was finally reported to have had a negative test and to be in "good condition." Her child was, however, born dead. (Selected record. Not known to any social agency.)

Mrs. Salerno, whose husband was in the Italian Army, was said by her physician to be syphilitic. The visitor took her to the board of health where a Wassermann gave positive results, then got her to a hospital and placed her under treatment. She stated that her husband had been heartbroken when he discovered that he had the disease and had infected her, and had gone into the Army with the idea that they should be independently treated and cured before going on with their life together. (Selected record. Not known to any social agency.)

There remain for mention under this heading the two families one or more of whose members were suffering from gonorrhea:

The fact that not only Mrs. Wood but her two little daughters of four and eight were infected with the disease was not discovered until the mother had been sent to a hospital and the children boarded out. The little girls were at once placed in a different hospital for treatment. After their return home arrangements were made with a private physician for continued care and he finally pronounced them cured. The mother meanwhile was urged to keep up her treatments, but in spite of all efforts let them lapse and at last accounts was worse. This is a case where devoted service was backed by ample relief, but the prospect at the date of reading was dark indeed. (Selected record. Known to two health agencies. See Index, page 232, for other pages where this family is mentioned.)

The discovery that young Sossnitz had gonorrhea was made rather late in a long course of treatment, aimed largely at finding a place where he could live free from the asthma which he had acquired while in service. As elsewhere related (see page 53), he had been sent to place after place in Connecticut and New York, only to suffer a repetition of his attacks; and serious consideration was being given his plan to be sent to Colorado, when the physician of the War Risk Insurance Bureau discovered that since his last examination a gonorrheal infection had occurred, and lost all patience, refusing to believe his assertion that it had been innocently acquired. How, when the man insisted contrary to all advice on using a compensation check to transport himself and his wife to a western city, his visitor entered into correspondence with the Home Service Section there to insure medical and other care, has been already told. At the last report he was better in health; whether this statement has reference to the asthma only, or to the other trouble as well, does not appear.

An effort was also made, after the discovery of Sossnitz's condition, to have his wife examined. She refused to go to the Medical Station but did finally go to another hospital. The result of her examination —if one was made—is not stated. (Selected record. Not known to any social agency.)

Drug Addiction

The cross-section reading of 454 cases brought to light not a single instance of a drug addict. Among the 77 selected cases there were two in which victims of the habit appeared—both wives of men in service. There is no doubt that many ex-soldiers who were drug addicts were known to the Section, but no supervisor selected any such case for our reading.

When Mrs. Auerbach's habit of drug-taking was discovered, along with a record of immorality and disease, the visitor joined forces with the girl's father and succeeded within a fortnight of the first acquaintance in inducing her to enter a certain hospital for special treatment. This result was achieved only after a consultation with the police, the board of health, a judge, and the legal committee of the Section; but within a few days the girl was turned loose on the world again because of an error in the commitment papers. No time was lost in dealing with this new complication, for the very next day she was recommitted, this time to another hospital which likewise gave a drug treatment. There she remained for over a month, coming out cured and enthusiastic over the treatment. How long she stayed cured we have no means of knowing, for she refused treatment along other lines, was soon after turned out by her family, and seemed at the date of reading the record to be rapidly drifting beyond the reach of Home Service. (See Index, page 229, for other pages on which this case is discussed. Selected record. Not known to any social agency.)

A greater contrast could hardly exist than that presented by the other victim of the drug habit—a gentle, refined woman, devoted to her soldier husband. Torturing headaches had led her into taking too often a medicine prescribed for her relief, and she was saddled with a habit especially dangerous to one with her weak heart. Fortunately she had friends, and a rarely high-minded and devoted physician was already in attendance. On three different occasions the visitor was with her client when it was necessary to call in this physician, and the records of these visits are of great interest. The successful outcome in this case has been related elsewhere. (See page 61. Selected record. Unknown to any social agency.)

Dental Defects

The cross-section case records furnish 21 examples of families in which need of dental work is noted; the selected records, 27 such examples. When we recall the large number of cross-section records read (454), and the small number of selected records (77), we cannot but be struck by these figures. The proportion of instances of illness of each type studied has, of course, been far greater among the selected than among the cross-section cases; but while a supervisor might, and apparently sometimes did, select certain cases for reading largely because of the especially careful, thorough work done with a tuberculous man, or an expectant mother, or a patient suffering from mental disease, we doubt whether any were selected because they were good examples of dental care. Since there is no reason to assume that there was greater need of such care among the selected than among the cross-section families, we would almost venture the suggestion that the proportions of families in which dental needs are noted in the two groups are an index to the thoroughness with which the families were studied.

It is our strong impression that less has been accomplished in correction of dental defects than in any of the other types of physical defect or illness regarding which data have been assembled. We are inclined to distribute responsibility for the very small results recorded to three conditions: the especially inadequate facilities for free care afforded in the city; the widespread and intense antipathy toward the dentist's chair, by no means peculiar to Red Cross clients; and the fact that toothache is traditionally a thing to be endured, while the relation between bad mouth conditions and other manifestations of ill-health is little appreciated.

We shall summarize first, briefly, the action taken in regard to dental needs recorded in the cross-section cases.

In 13 cases an adult was the sufferer. One man, said to have trouble both with teeth and stomach, had a "prejudice against going to a doctor" from which we gather that an offer of medical, and (probably) of dental care was made but not accepted. Five persons were referred to the dental clinic once or oftener, but whether they went is not stated. For one, arrangements with a private dentist, for another arrangements with a dental college were made, but no statement appears as to whether the work was actually done. In three instances the Medical Station made the diagnosis, and no action of any kind is recorded; one of these diagnoses, however, had only just been made when the record was read, so action may have been taken later. In two remaining cases the men were sent, one to a dental college, one to a private dentist, for estimates; the first estimate was for the modest sum of $13, and this would apparently have been approved and acted upon had the man returned once more to the office, but he seems to have got work and stayed away; the second was for $96, and the ex-soldier who asked a loan of this amount was refused, and thereupon requested that the Red Cross cease its interest in his affairs.

The children, in all but one of the eight cases where record of dental defect in children was made, were attending the Red Cross Health Center, which means that they were surely referred to a dental clinic, usually that maintained by the Section in the same offices. In five of these seven cases there is no record of the children's having gone to the dental clinic; in the other two the child went once but seems never to have returned. One of these children is said to have acquired a toothbrush and powder and to be caring for her teeth; the other, when at the end of the first fifteen-minute appointment it was suggested that she remain for another similar period, fled screaming—tactics which she renewed on a later occasion when urged to return. In the one case where a child had apparently not been to the Health Center, it was from her school health record that the need of dental care was learned; no action is recorded in this case.

It must of course be realized that in many cases where no action is recorded it is probable that the visitor did actually refer the person needing attention to a clinic; and it is quite likely that a number of those referred actually went—though these facts never got into the record.

The selected cases of course show more in the way of results. Among the 14 where adults were concerned there is only one which contains no evidence that an attempt was made to provide treatment. In this the mother of a family stated that she needed a new set of teeth and wanted to spend certain money that had come in—a brother's allotment—for that purpose; but whether she did so we are not told. In three instances a woman was urged to go to the dental clinic; two at last accounts were said to be going, the third went once, but "lost her nerve" and left without having had any work done. In one case an ex-service man was given a dental clinic card; whether he used it does not appear. In the other nine instances some work was actually done.

Mrs. Vail went once to the dental clinic but was afraid to go again. Later, when suffering acutely, she did go but her face was too swollen to admit of any work being done. The record was read soon after and as the case was under active care more may have been accomplished later. (Not known to any social agency.)

Mrs. Litchitifski went to the dental clinic, and when referred from there to a private dentist was given $2.00 to pay for his services. Just what was needed or accomplished does not appear. (Not known to any social agency.)

Mrs. Landgren went to the dental clinic and to a dentist to whom it referred her, and had several teeth extracted. Because of her weakened condition the dentist refused to finish the job although her physician urged its completion. (Not known to any social agency.)

A colored woman, Mrs. Downer, underwent a long course of treatment involving several extractions and fillings, apparently not at the dental clinic as there is record of an approved estimate for $9.00 worth of work (seemingly for only part of the whole). (Not known to any social agency.)

A much disabled ex-soldier, Neuman, was sent to a private dentist, who did about $15 worth of work. It was said that more was needed, but he was sent to the country for convalescent care, apparently, before it was done. (Known to a family society.)

Two women, after going to the dental clinic several times, were sent to a dental college for estimates, but in neither case had the work yet been done as at the date of reading the records, in midsummer, the college was closed. (One was known to a family agency, the other to a health agency only.)

Mrs. Terenska, examined by the dentist at the Red Cross clinic, was told she needed a plate which he offered to make for $18. This offer was accepted, an old friend of Mrs. Terenska's providing the needed sum. (Not known to any social agency.)

Mrs. Drew, with her two children, constitute the prize dental case of our reading, as all of them appear to have had all the work needed on their mouths done. (Not known to any social agency.)

In all but four of the 18 selected cases[1] where need of dental care for children is recorded the children in question—often several in a family —were under the care of the Health Center. The children, in one of the four exceptional families, were said to be in need of attention and planning to go to a certain dental clinic, but the matter is not men-

[1] In five selected cases both adults and children needed dental care.

tioned again; for another child work was authorized but whether done or not does not appear; in the third family a boy was got to the Red Cross dental clinic and three extractions made, but he afterward absolutely refused to return and would not even go to a dentist who would give gas, though the obtaining of his working papers hung on the completion of the work. In the fourth, the visitor learned from the school records that three of the children were in need of dental care; but while she did most faithful and devoted work in getting several members of the family to clinics for other troubles, the following up of this point seems to have been overlooked.

For the children in five families there is no record of action beyond the reference from the Health Center to a dental clinic. (In one of these cases, however, the examination had been made only a short time before the record was read.) In one instance three youngsters were personally conducted to the Red Cross clinic by a visitor, but when summoned by the dentist marched in with locked jaws, so that treatment was impossible. In another, two children went at least once to the dental clinic, where the boy had a tooth filled; but a day or two later he was in such pain with another tooth that he cried all night; and in the morning his mother sent him—the dental clinic being closed that day—to a neighboring dentist who pulled the offending molar. Whether anything further was accomplished our reading does not reveal. Children in two families were got to a clinic once and a few extractions were made; in two others they went several times; in one a girl was taken to the dental clinic and later to a private dentist who is said to have performed an important operation on a badly abscessed mouth. Regarding another little girl the Health Center physician is reported as saying, when she went back for examination, that the dental work in her case was "O.K." The one remaining case is that already mentioned in which mother and children had all needed work done.

Physical Defects of Children

As with the problem of defective teeth in children, so with the other common defects of childhood—adenoids and enlarged tonsils and malnutrition—it would have been possible to pursue the course followed in the preceding sections of this chapter, gathering together from the records read a statement of what had been accomplished up to the date of our reading. In this case it has, however, seemed advisable to follow a different procedure and avail ourselves of a summary of results attained by the Red Cross Health Centers with the much larger group of families—724—one or more of whose children came under their care during a year and eight months of activity.[1] A statement regarding results reported by the Centers in cases of dental defect is also included.

The total number of children who came to the Health Centers was 1,518, 112 of whom were under two, 410 between two and six, and 996 between six and fourteen years of age. Of course a number did not return a second time, so that the total of 5,464 visits to the Centers reported means an average of considerably more than three visits for those children whose parents did avail themselves of the care offered.

The commonest defect found was that of carious teeth, present in 837, or 55 per cent, of the children. In all, 419 of these children—50 per cent—had their teeth attended to; "dentistry finished," the report words it. This result would probably have been impossible of attainment had it not been for the dental clinic maintained in connection with the original Center.

Yet almost as good a record was made in the case of enlarged tonsils and adenoids. Defects coming under this head were noted in 436 of the children—28 per cent—and 213 of these children, or 45 per cent, had the recommended operation performed.

Very different is the record in the case of malnutrition. A total of 407 children—26 per cent—were found to be 10 per cent or more below normal in weight, and hence were placed in this group. Of these only 30—7 per cent—were pronounced cured. Does this mean that home conditions in our overcrowded city, and the high cost of living, proved too much for the doctors? Or are heredity and parental ignorance equally serious factors? Certainly the Centers, together with the visiting staff of the Section, made a most determined assault upon this ignorance, supplementing diet lists with oral explanations, and explanations, wherever it was possible to make use of the visiting dietitians, with demonstrations.

[1] The original Health Center, at 219 East 39th Street, opened November 6, 1918. A second Center was established in the Bronx on March 1, 1920. The figures given combine the records for the two Centers to July 1, 1920.

CHAPTER VII

PROBLEMS OF CONDUCT

Conduct has, of course, played a large part in many of the problems discussed under the various health headings and will play a part under other headings, as that of unemployment; if human beings who were sick or out of work always gave evidence of good-will and good judgment, case workers would lead a comparatively easy life. The problems which we propose to group in the present chapter are, however, those of conduct primarily—of vicious or anti-social conduct chiefly, though there are among them instances that can hardly be so characterized and we have therefore refrained from making these condemnatory words a part of our heading.

Intemperance and Non-support

First of all we may take up problems of intemperance. From one point of view these are of course health problems. They are by no means numerous among the cases read and the victims are largely women. Investigation, of course, frequently revealed that a husband in service had been a drinking man, but no account is here taken of these or other absent members of the family.

Taking first the cases where the drink problem is not complicated with that of non-support, we find that we have record of ten—four cross-section, six selected cases. Three mothers of men in service, one mother-in-law, four wives, and two discharged men make up the list.

Of the three mothers two were helped with relief and in other ways, while the third was referred to the St. Vincent de Paul Society, which confirmed the visitor's impression that she was in no need. None of them was very long under care, and no direct attack upon the drink problem seems to have been made in any one of them; the situations involved were not so urgent as to compel action, in a period of many pressing claims. (Cross-section record. One known to a family society. Other two unknown to any social agency.)

Mrs. Dick, the mother-in-law of young Buick, who was in the Army, created a very serious situation in the home of her daughter: For a time entrusted with the care of the children while the young mother worked outside the home, she drank to excess and fell down badly on the job. After the breaking up of the home which resulted, she was referred to a hospital for work, was taken on and kept, and months afterward was reported to be keeping straight and doing well. (See page 48 for the story of the Buicks. Selected record. Not known to any social agency.)

The wife of Richard Gibson, a soldier in the Canadian forces, is said early in the record to have been drinking. At that time she was helped in various ways, but there is no mention of action on this particular problem. Several months later it was learned that she had been arrested for disorderly conduct, that a neighbor had been caring for her child, and the case had been already referred to the Society for the Prevention of Cruelty to Children, which later took the little girl. When the woman came out after a ten days' sentence she was most penitent, and on her promise not to touch drink again she was helped to get her child back. Consultation was sought at this time with a church worker who had known her for a long time and felt sure that this particular affair was the first of its kind, and who promised to keep in close touch with her. It is recorded that the judge talked to Mrs. Gibson "very wisely." Several calls were paid after this, and apparently all went well. (Cross-section record. Not known to any social agency.)

Young Mrs. Limburg, though reported by a hospital where she had formerly been cared for to be alcoholic, gave little evidence of drinking habits while under care. Nothing seems to have been done beyond telling her that her reputation in this regard was known—nor does there seem to have been need of other action. (Selected record. Not known to any social agency.)

In the case of Mrs. Auerbach intemperance was the least of several pressing character and health problems, some of which have been and others of which will be discussed. (See Index, page 229, for page references.) Indeed the fact that she and her husband drank did not come to light until nearly the end of the record, when everything that this thoroughly disreputable young couple would submit to having done for them had been done. (Selected record. Not known to any social agency.)

The case of Mrs. Hughes presents the problem of intemperance only. Her husband, a recently discharged man, intelligent and with a good position in the business world, came to the Section in desperation, seeking help in a situation which had got beyond his control. He was supporting his wife, but refused to live with her until she should have changed her ways. She had an unfavorable heredity, both her father and an aunt having died of drink. The trouble had been growing upon her for the last five years; she had already been under care at a private sanatorium, and was at a city hospital when her husband appealed for help. Here she was said to be suffering from mental deterioration and loss of modesty, as well as the drink habit.

This truly desperate case was taken up by the visitor with the utmost intelligence and devotion. Following interviews with husband and wife the representative of a farm for inebriates and other special types was consulted, and Mrs. Hughes was taken to see a specialist. He did not win her confidence, advised against the farm idea, and in favor of employment and home life with her husband. This last point the husband was unwilling to consent to, but the wife was established in a very comfortable room and the doctor's recommendations tried out until another collapse landed her again in the city hospital. From there she was taken by the visitor to a deaconess's home, and when she had been put in order for the trip was sent to the farm considered before. There ensued several months of active correspondence between the visitor on the one hand and Mrs. Hughes and the mistress of the farm on the other, the woman's letters bearing witness to her utter reliance upon the visitor for encouragement and help of every sort, also to her increasing and quite desperate eagerness to be taken back by her husband. In the end, before the fourth month was up, the managers of the farm became convinced that the husband should give his wife a trial and persuaded him it was his duty to receive her, and against the visitor's advice she returned to him and to the temptations of the city. In hardly more than a fortnight she had relapsed again. The special point which the visitor had tried to make was that Mrs. Hughes should be kept in the country until prohibition had gone into effect. At the date of reading, contact seemed to have been lost with the couple. (Selected record. Not known to any social agency.)

The two discharged men present problems of intemperance which were somewhat alike in that the drinking seems to have been occasional only.

The Noonans had been helped a good deal during the husband's absence and after his return until he was established in work. There had been family quarrels before he went away, so it could not have been altogether a surprise to the visitor when, after an interval of several months, she found the couple again at loggerheads. The wife's complaints were of drink and abuse. The visitor made a point of arranging an interview with the man and hearing his story, a complaint that his wife was neglecting his children, and records her opinion that there was much on both sides. Doubtless in this interview she made an effort to influence the man to avoid drink, although there is no record of such action. Various proposed plans for readjustment of work and a country outing fell through, and at the date of reading the record seemed to have ended inconclusively. (Selected record. Not known to any social agency.)

Somewhat similar in handling is the case of Elof Landgren. His disability—an injured back—and the illness of his wife and children involved an immense amount of work, accompanied by very liberal relief and many interviews held with him. In the reports of these there is no mention of efforts to influence him regarding the use of liquor, although one feels sure that such efforts must have been made. (Selected record. Not known to any social agency.)

It may be noted that the period during which these two men were occasionally indulging their taste for strong drink was the fall of 1919, when prohibition was being gradually put into effect. It is probable that, had time permitted the further following up of these cases, later developments in them would have proved interesting; Landgren's case was under active care at the date of reading and Noonan's may have later entries.

Five cases that have come to our attention involve a combination of drink and non-support. Four are cross-section records, one a selected record.

Phelan was discharged in the fall of 1919 and soon after was reported to be working irregularly and drinking. Apparently no effort to see or influence him was made. (Cross-section record. Known to a family agency.)

The stepfather of three men in service was drinking and not supporting their mother. She wanted the "anti-loafing law" applied to make him work. One effort was made to find the man at a saloon he was supposed to frequent, and a few days later the mother was advised to go to the Domestic Relations Court. This is the last word on the subject. The woman was self-supporting and without dependents. (Cross-section record. Not known to any social agency.)

Tim Shanahan, a stone-cutter, with a son of seventeen in service and seven children at home, was drinking and giving so little support that his wife was forced to work outside the home. The visitor saw a priest who agreed to visit the man and try to get him to sign the pledge; whether this was done does not appear. She also had a "quiet talk" with Shanahan in which she asked his help and co-operation. He promised them and seemed ashamed that his wife was working. A month later he was said to be doing better and the wife was hoping to stop work soon; but when next heard from, after an interval of two or three months, things were worse than ever and Mrs. Shanahan was urged to have him drafted. This at last accounts she was planning to do, though so far the influenza epidemic had prevented the carrying out of the plan. Then, without explanation, the record comes to an end; apparently the volunteer visitor dropped off and no appeal coming from the family they were never visited again. (Cross-section record. Known to a family agency, the Bureau of Domestic Relations, and four other social agencies.)

Dick Norton three months after his discharge was working as a chauffeur but supporting his wife irregularly because of drink. He was visited at his place of business and an effort made to influence him to let liquor alone. At last accounts, a month later, he was doing well. (Cross-section record. Known to the Bureau of Domestic Relations and a diet kitchen.)

O'Neil was an habitual drunkard whose habits had been the ruin of his family. No direct work seems to have been done with him by the visitor, whose chief efforts were devoted to the solving of other problems and who called in the St. Vincent de Paul to find him work. While for months he showed no improvement, at last accounts he was working regularly and was said by his daughter to have entirely given up drink, also to be going to church. Whether this change was attributable to prohibition, to the influence of the St. Vincent de Paul, or to other causes, does not appear. (Selected record. Known to a family agency.)

Non-support without drink is of less frequent occurrence in the cases read than the combined problems. Indeed, it may be that the husbands in the only two cases that seem to fall under this head were actually drinking men.

In one the man was discharged and came home in March. He was said to work "off and on." In July his wife reported that he was abusing her and she feared for the children and was going to the Magistrate's Court to get a warrant for his arrest. No further entries had occurred up to the date of reading except a call in September in regard to a proposed outing; and we are thus left to our own conjectures as to why no backing was given the wife in a situation which certainly seemed to call for action. (Selected record. Not known to any social agency.)

Tommaso Sonnino, whose son was in the Army, failed to give proper support to his family and was abusive. Court action was urged upon his wife and she did make a complaint; but after the visitor had served the summons the couple made up. Interest was continued in the young daughter who had been driven from home by the father's behavior, but the parents and their younger children were thereafter, up to the date of reading, left strictly alone. (Selected record. Not known to any social agency.)

Desertion

Cases of desertion, of course involving non-support, are somewhat more numerous than those of home-staying non-supporters. We have however noted only twelve such—five cross-section, seven selected cases.

Mrs. O'Donnell, whose son was in service and her husband a deserter, was urged to go again to the Domestic Relations Court; there is no statement as to whether she took this advice and no evidence of other action. (Cross-section record. Known to a family agency, a hospital, the court, and the Salvation Army.)

The mother of young Mrs. Guffey appealed for help in compelling her son-in-law, who had recently been discharged from the service, to support his child. This had been a case of forced marriage following pregnancy. Investigation was made but no action of any sort is recorded. (Cross-section record. Known to the Bureau of Domestic Relations only.)

Stephen Wolff, said by his wife to have deserted her, was still in the service. He had claimed exemption from allotment, and when seen made various charges against his wife. Investigation brought out sharply contrasting opinions from friends and neighbors of theirs in the country town where they had lived, so that the reader of the record is left quite at sea as to which was more in the wrong. As no children were involved and the wife, a stenographer, was supporting herself, the Section did not concern itself further with the young people's differences. (Cross-section record. Not known to any social agency.)

The story of Mrs. Vizet, whose husband deserted her several years before the war, has been told somewhat fully in another chapter. (See page 54.) The man was believed to be in France, recently discharged from the service of that country, when his wife became known to the Section. She was already in touch with the district attorney's office and the French consul, with both of whom her visitor consulted: The latter had apparently made no effort to trace the husband and we are not told what action (if any) the former had taken. Home Service made three distinct moves to locate the man: through the Red Cross in France, through Ellis Island, and through the Canadian immigration authorities. The visitor also labored with the French consul to make him understand the importance of reaching Vizet and inducing him to send an allowance to his children, even though he was (quite understandably, in view of his wife's temper) unwilling to live at home again. (Selected record. Known to a family society.)

Isaac Bauman had been a deserter before he entered the service. His wife gave birth to an illegitimate child in his absence, and there was never any effort to secure support from him. (Cross-section record. Known to a family society, the Bureau of Domestic Relations, and another agency.)

Gus Hartmann laid his desertion to the fact of his having been compelled, after his discharge from the Army, to stay at his mother-in-law's, and this was due to his wife's having given up her home and attempted to follow him to camp, a proceeding which had irritated him exceedingly. The desertion was however temporary, and when he later went off to the country it is not clear whether he was deserting again or was planning, as his wife said, to send for her and the baby. The wife meanwhile wanted a place at service, and was sent with her child to the seashore cottage conducted under the wing of the Section, where she was kept on after her two weeks' holiday to help with the work. At the date of reading she was still there and plans for the future still waiting on the next move of the husband. (Cross-section record. Known to a family society and five other social agencies.)

Maurice Meadows' desertion was complicated by his mental condition; as has been already stated in another chapter (see page 129), he was on the verge of insanity, but said by the specialist who examined him not to be commitable. His wife had been under care before his discharge, and after it was helped to bring him into court where he was put on probation and ordered to pay $5.00 a week. This he did only once, then re-enlisted as a single man. Later, when his baby came, the visitor succeeded in reviving his interest by her letters and he was actually brought to a point where he made four successive monthly payments to his wife. He even wished to obtain his discharge so that he might support his family; but this the visitor discouraged, feeling it was much better for all concerned that he should remain under discipline. (Selected record. Known to a family agency, the Bureau and Court of Domestic Relations, the Department of Public Charities, and a church.)

Mrs. Downer had been aided financially and otherwise during many months, when she received word that her husband, who had been demobilized and had deserted her without returning home, was in

Washington. Inquiries were made for her through the Home Service Section there and a promise to help her proceed against her husband secured; and with a card of introduction to the Section, she started off. (Selected record. Not known to any social agency.)

A woman with several brothers in the service had been deserted by her husband and, with her five children, was in quite desperate straits when referred to Home Service. The husband was living in New York and had already been brought into court and ordered to pay $10 a week, which he did more or less regularly. The visitor consulted a lawyer and had the man brought into court again, where he was ordered to pay $15. He thereupon stated that he was willing to go home at once, and the probation officer, lawyer, and judge all urged immediate reconciliation. The visitor, however, knowing the man's record for neglect and abuse, "insisted it would be very unwise, so he was put on three months' probation, to be extended if necessary;" and the visitor was asked to assist the probation officer. At the end of three months the visitor again took up the matter with the court, and in spite of the fact that the man had fulfilled all the conditions of his probation the term was extended for another equal period. (Selected record. Reported not known to any social agency in spite of having been in court.)

Mrs. Emmet had been helped through her pregnancy in the summer of 1918, and later in the year had been aided again when her government checks were delayed. Upon Emmet's return in December he seems to have stripped her of her last cent, so that, according to her story, "she turned him out" in January. At the visitor's advice the woman went to the Domestic Relations Court and obtained a warrant for his arrest, but it was not until the following July that his whereabouts was learned—a hospital in another state where he was recovering from a severe industrial accident. In the preceding month a full investigation had disclosed that the woman was not Emmet's legal wife, that she had passed three years in an institution for wayward girls, and that the oldest child was another man's. The visitor took a day to visit Emmet in the hospital; he insisted that the children were none of them his, though the fact of his having acknowledged their mother as his wife, even taking her to his parents' home to stay, was established. Consultations were held with the chief probation officer of the court and the district attorney on the question of extraditing the man, and as to whether the case should be treated as one of bastardy or common-law marriage; it was decided to continue it as started, and a new warrant was issued, the old one having been destroyed. After this the visitor seems to have spent a great deal of time in rather futile interviewing of policemen with a view to being informed when the man returned, as it was expected he would. At the date of reading he had just been located (not apparently through the policemen) at a certain hotel, and his wife sent home to get the warrant. (Selected record. Reported not known to any social agency in spite of wife's earlier record.)

One man of education, a captain in the Army, was among the deserters. The case of Lawrence Buchanan was never clear: his wife, who was supporting herself and her two children by clerical work, professed not to understand his reason for leaving her, and none of the efforts to reach him by letter or through the Home Service Section in the western town where he was staying brought an explanation. Investigation of his business record produced only favorable evidence, and the wife was apparently of good character and devoted to her children. Differences between the parents as to the proper handling of the children are the only ones clearly brought to light. The wife seems still to have hoped for a reconciliation and reported having written her husband begging to be allowed to join him, and to have received in reply a letter urging her to make up her mind to the separation, get a divorce, and "marry some good man." One has a sense in reading the record that the wife's full confidence was never gained, and that perhaps a serious mistake had been made in the double approach made to the husband—writing him and at the same time asking the other Section to call on him—for soon after he wrote his wife reproaching her for having told the Red Cross so much and saying that he would not discuss his affairs with that organization. The only step toward legal action taken, up to the date of reading, was consultation with a lawyer about extradition. The appointment with the district attorney suggested by him seems not to have been made, the wife saying that she "did not think there was much use in pushing the case against Mr. Buchanan." (Selected record. Not known to any social agency.)

The one remaining desertion case is that of a mother who ran away from her children and was promptly followed by the visitor and induced to come back. The full story has already been told. (See page 48. Selected record. Not known to any social agency.)

Sex Irregularities

To one who is far from being a specialist in the subject it would seem that nearly every possible type of sex problem is represented in the Home Service records read. A majority of the serious current problems encountered are in the selected records; supervisors of certain divisions and their visitors were greatly impressed with the large number of irregular family situations met and found them extraordinarily difficult to deal with, which facts sufficiently account for the inclusion of a large number of such cases among those selected by them. On the other hand, among the cross-section records read there are a number of instances of a type of situation hardly represented among the selected records—that of belated marriage, in which sex relations, conception, and in a few cases the birth of a child, preceded the legal ceremony, which had taken place before the family became known to Home Service.

The history of these marriages is not usually given. We know that one was definitely forced by the girl's father, and that in another the couple had lived together several years, the woman, at least, "disbelieving in the ceremony" and agreeing to it only after she became pregnant and the man had been called into service. The attitude of the wife varied from that of the high-grade colored woman who was so ashamed that she was unwilling to go to her family in the South until her baby should be old enough to have its birth safely redated, and that of the gay young actress, who knew her family didn't believe she was married and decided she would fool them by producing a certificate after all. While knowledge of the previous irregularity may have modified the visitor's attitude in a number of cases, there is no one of them in which we find a distinct problem resulting. Even in the case of young Mrs. Carns, a pretty blondined little creature, the visitor would probably have made the same effort to back the departing husband's plan of getting her home to her mother if she had not known the history of their early relations. (This plan, we may add in passing, was successfully put through.)

The belated marriage as a type of sex irregularity bears interesting relation to certain other types, notably that of the unmarried mother deserted by the father of her child. While any statistical approach to the subject on the basis of the few cases read should be avoided, we cannot help being struck by the fact that the cross-section records yielded seven—probably eight—examples of marriages following conception or birth of children, and not one of a deserted unmarried mother; our only examples of the latter type were four included among the selected cases.

The cases of three of these three unmarried mothers have been touched upon under the section on care in Pregnancy and Confinement, and will here be reviewed with an eye to service bearing upon the moral and allied social problems involved.

Annie Sheehan was working in a hospital during the whole period covered by the record; she was never at all intimately known and up to the date of reading the only feature of her case that seems to have received attention was the question of support for the coming child from its father, Tom Glynn. About this the Bureau of Domestic Relations was consulted. She seems to have been a capable girl of good reputation. Her confinement was still some distance ahead at the date of reading the record and there is no evidence of her need of other help. (Selected record. Not known to any social agency.)

Amy Tulliver, the second of the unmarried mothers, was likewise of good reputation apart from the episode of her relation with the one man. Her baby died in a hospital when very small, and while she seems to have felt its death keenly, the problem of refitting her into society was of course simplified. Much good work was done by her visitor in finding a suitable home for her, helping her to work, and arranging for her gradual payment of a debt to her former landlady. The friendliest relations had been maintained with her by her visitor down to the date of our second reading of the record (some months after our first reading) and many good offices performed, such as the recovery of a coat that had been appropriated by the daughter of the former landlady, help in shopping, at the special request of the girl, etc. (Selected record. Known only to a hospital social service department.)

One criticism of the early handling of this case we do feel we must make. The manager of the home for working girls where it had been arranged to place Amy and her baby asked the visitor to explain to the girl in advance that she was to be Mrs. Tulliver there, with a husband overseas, and apparently this deception was agreed to. The situation put up to the visitor was indeed a difficult one, the plan having been already definitely set in motion; but we do feel that such plans rest upon an unsound basis and doubt whether they can ever aid in building up character or establishing a girl in the right relation to the world she lives in. Into what morasses of falsehood would such a tale as the one in question naturally lead a girl if, for instance, she was compelled to answer questions of housemates regarding the ship her husband was serving on, her experiences with allotments and allowances, etc.! Again, if unmarried mothers and their children are ever to obtain justice, will it not be in a world where such subterfuges are disdained?

Linda Antokolsky, the third unmarried mother, was only sixteen when she went through her critical experience. She had been for some time a decidedly difficult problem for her mother and the visitor, throwing up jobs or losing them almost as fast as they were obtained for her, taking no interest in the household, staying out late nights, and so on; indeed, her mother had once taken her to court, where she had been put on probation. Early in her pregnancy, and before her condition was known, all this suddenly changed. She worked steadily, assumed responsibilities for the younger children and for keeping the family accounts, stayed at home evenings. The visitor to the family had interested herself especially in Linda, trying hard in the earlier days to influence her to settle down, and had made a special effort while the mother was in a hospital to keep in close touch with the girl; but we are bound to admit that her zeal sometimes outran her discretion, as in her dealings with the young man in the case. Some months before their actual relation had become known to her, she had encouraged Linda to bring him to call, and on this occasion asked him point-blank if he meant to marry the girl, a question he answered by saying he didn't know. She then talked to him about taking Linda out more regularly—the point she had in mind being, as she explains in the record, that she hoped if the girl saw more of him she would get over wanting to marry him. With all her friendly efforts she did not win Linda's confidence—it was the mother who first received her confession. Later it was decided to bring the case against the young man into court, but this event had not been reached at the date of our reading. (Selected record. Known to seven social agencies but not to a family society.)

The fourth unmarried mother, Annette Privet, became known to the Section when her child was over three years old. Old Mrs. Privet had been a music hall artist and had educated her three children as cabaret dancers. She and her other daughter were scornful of Annette because the latter had never been as successful as her sister. Unhappy with her own people on this account, the girl was persuaded by a member of a traveling orchestra with whom she had become acquainted to go away with him. Six months later he abandoned her in England, just after she had been told by a physician that she was pregnant. In 1915 her baby was born. Placing the child with a foster mother she secured work, first in a factory, later as cook, and supported it until, in 1918, her health became so bad that Mrs. Privet, her mother, was persuaded to send money with which the girl came to the United States. Pressed by her family, Annette wrote to the father of her lover for information as to the latter's whereabouts, and received in reply an address, the information that the man had enlisted and had married an English girl, and an offer from his father of a home for the child. She then wrote to the child's father, and presently received an answer from his wife in England, to whom he had forwarded the letter, begging to be allowed to take the little girl and bring her up as her own, but offering no other help.

Annette's first application to Home Service was with regard to the possibility of forcing the child's father to contribute to her support. Other services rendered by the Section are elsewhere recounted (see page 66), but apparently the idea of attempting to force support was not encouraged, and three months later we read that Annette had abandoned all idea of such action and had concluded that her little girl was worth working for even if the father never helped. So far as her health permitted she did work, and at last accounts was doing well for herself and her child.

Four examples of pre-marital irregularity on the part of wives with men other than their husbands came to light in our reading. In two of these the women had been married several years.

The visitor's anxiety about Mrs. Neary, based on her earlier record as a delinquent girl, led to insistence upon her moving to the neighborhood where her mother lived. This was probably a wise precaution; though there was never the slightest reason, so far as the record shows, to suspect her of any impropriety of behavior during the period under care. (Selected record. Not known to any social agency.)

Mrs. Auerbach's story has already been touched upon in other connections. (See Index, page 229, for page references.) Her earlier record, as revealed by the investigation, is one of utter profligacy. As she was suffering from a venereal disease, the workers who were struggling with her felt it their duty to communicate the facts to the young soldier who had recently married her. Their pains proved to have been wasted, however, since he deliberately chose to continue his life with her. (Selected record. Not known to any social agency.)

In the case of Mrs. Inwood a serious need was neglected. She had been a wayward girl, and the young man who married her was said to be of good character and devoted to her. When first known she was living with a married sister in what seemed to the visitor very undesirable quarters in a basement. As, however, these living arrangements had been approved by the agency which previously had her under care, no effort was made to change them—a policy which on its face seems a mistaken one. Later the Section was notified by the Health Department that on account of tuberculosis in the sister's family Mrs. Inwood and her baby must leave, and that they had nowhere to go. Unfortunately this notification seems to have been lost sight of and no action taken; and it was several months later that the young husband came to the office greatly disturbed because his wife was living in another basement, among people not relatives and apparently of doubtful reputation. When a call was finally made the family had moved to Brooklyn. It will probably never be known just how serious the results following upon this lapse on the part of the Section may have been. (Cross-section record. Reported not known to any social agency, though record showed known to at least one.)

Mrs. Meadows, whose case has been mentioned several times (see pages 129 and 151), was known to have had an illegitimate child several years before her marriage; but though spasmodically accused of various crimes by a half-insane husband, she seems while under observation to have been keeping straight. No action directly bearing upon this point of character appears to have been taken by Home Service, or called for, though an immense amount of work was done with a variety of other family problems. (Selected record. Known to a family agency and four other agencies.)

Instances of a wife's infidelity during her husband's absence in service were to be expected, and four actually came to our attention—two among the cross-section, two among the selected cases.

One of the women told a story of having been betrayed by the use of a drug. Home Service contact with her was brief—a reference to an agency placing women with children in service, which undertook the responsibility of sending her to a convalescent home—and the fact of the baby's illegitimacy was not learned until after she had gone to work in Brooklyn. (Cross-section record. Not known to any social agency.)

Similarly Mrs. Bauman claimed that force had been used by an employer to make her submit to his attentions. Although she had previously been somewhat quarrelsome and complaining she worked on for months in the hospital where she had been confined and won the respect of those in charge. The visitor's service was largely in looking up the records of the husband and wife, which she did in great detail, and in trying to arrange a settlement between them. It was decided, on advice of a lawyer, that the man was not entitled to the divorce he wanted or to the custody of his child, the wife's first baby, as he had deserted and was giving no support, and there were stories of an earlier marriage of his followed by no divorce. (Cross-section record. Known to a family agency, the Bureau of Domestic Relations, and one other social agency.)

The case of Mrs. Young, which came to the attention of Home Service just as she was about to give birth to a baby not her husband's, remains somewhat obscure to us; for though a very full investigation was made and the family were known and helped through many months, we are still not altogether sure of the kind of woman she was. She lived in two furnished rooms usually dirty and disorderly, and most of the evidence would seem to indicate a pretty low grade of care for the children, although teachers testified that they came to school poorly clothed but clean and well patched. The Home Service visitor tried hard to persuade the woman to commit her children and take a position with the baby, but she refused. The Society for the Prevention of Cruelty to Children was called in but found no evidence sufficient to cause it to act while the husband was in France. A Big Sister, introduced by this Society, reported that she had won the woman's confidence, did not believe her bad, and thought she ought to be set up in a home of her own. It may be that if we had met this Big Sister we should discount her evidence even more than we ordinarily discount that of a new and probably amateur visitor to a family; but we cannot help noticing that the record contains little evidence that the Home Service visitor ever gained the confidence of Mrs. Young. However, the husband was notified by friends of his wife's infidelity, and when the father of her baby was discharged and came to live with her, any doubt that had existed as to the mother's unfitness to keep her children vanished, and the Society for the Prevention of Cruelty to Children, upon application by the returned husband, quickly took action and removed the children. (Selected record. Not known to any New York agency, but known to an out-of-town family society.)

The last of these infidelity cases is that of Mrs. Wood, an attractive young woman with three small children, parts of whose story have been told in other connections. (See Index, page 232.) She appeared exceptionally dependent upon her husband, whose discharge she insisted upon on several occasions, declaring that she could not get on without him. No help was given her in this direction as it was against the established policy of the Red Cross; but in other ways she was generously aided. When she had been under care for some fifteen months the talk of her little eight-year-old daughter and the almost simultaneous discovery that both little girls were infected with gonorrhea led to the discovery of the woman's relations with several men, which had been going on for some time. The visitor was overcome with distress at having as she felt failed, particularly in appreciating a need of recreation and supplying it. This comes out in a conversation with Mrs. Wood in which the latter finally makes it quite clear that nothing short of the society of men would have satisfied her. Her evidence then, and many earlier sayings and doings not understood at the time, together with her husband's statements later and the findings of a psychiatrist who examined her, combine to build up an explanation of her as an over-sexed and slightly deficient woman who had been devoted to her husband but who was unable to maintain her fidelity to him in his absence. A great effort was made to straighten her out by talking both with her and with the two men involved who could be got hold of, both of whom were brought to the point of promising to stay away from her in future; but the demoralization which the experience had wrought seemed to have been destructive of the very fibre of the woman's character, and though her husband on his return went back to her the family at last accounts was drifting rapidly on the rocks. Our own feeling is that Home Service had little if anything to reproach itself with in this case. The treatment was liberal and sympathetic; one lead only seems to have been disregarded, the woman's expression of a desire for work outside her home; and even if this desire had been gratified we see no reason to believe that the catastrophe would have been averted. (Selected record. Known to health agencies only.)

In addition to these known cases of a wife's infidelity there were several in which there was some reason for suspecting such a state of affairs but no definite proof; these we shall not attempt to comment on. Similarly, more or less well-grounded suspicions of the husband's infidelity came to light in a number of cases, but in only two was there a basis for action, and we shall therefore restrict comment to these.[1]

Mrs. Tully said her husband practised perversions which made it impossible for her to live with him. She suspected him of infidelity, also, and wrote him a letter in which she assumed knowledge which led to his admitting her suspicions justified. As she was anxious to obtain a divorce the Home Service visitor took her to see a lawyer and, when he could not take up the case, to the Legal Aid Society. Her evidence was found insufficient. (Cross-section record. Not known to any social agency.)

The wife of Eric Bjornsen was "a very pretty little Swedish woman with a charming use of English." Her husband, a naturalized citizen who had very recently enlisted, wrote asking the Section's interest in her as she was in need of "advice and cheer." She was working as an accountant and making a brave struggle to support her three small children, and in this she was generously aided; but it was not until four months later that a telegram from her husband demanding $300 to help him out of "difficulties" brought from her the first confidence as to his past irregularities, which had included both infidelity and dis-

[1] Several cases of bigamy will be later separately considered.

honesty. He appears to have been a very attractive young man, who always had been given another chance both by defrauded employers and by a forgiving wife; but the wife was now fairly driven to bay and asked help in finding out what the present unnamed difficulties might be.

There follows one of the most thorough pieces of investigation we have ever encountered. Letters and telegrams to army officials, to former employers and friends and, as the plot thickened, to many other sources of information finally revealed the true situation. In brief, Bjornsen had misappropriated funds and had violated the White Slave Act. Yet somehow he again evaded punishment, was honorably discharged, and retained his liberty. He was traced to another city and the facts gathered passed on to interested officials there. His wife desiring a divorce, the War Committee of the Bar was consulted and referred her to a firm of lawyers who undertook to handle the matter for her free of charge. At last accounts a huge correspondence was being carried on to obtain the necessary evidence. (Selected record. Not known to any social agency.)

A number of family situations may be grouped together by the one common characteristic that the woman passed as the wife of a man not legally her husband. The eight households making up this group represent every grade of morality, from those in which only the regularity of legal ceremony was lacking to others in which the assumption of the status of marriage was indeed a hollow sham.

Young Godonov was only twenty-one when he was referred, a discharged soldier suffering from deafness, to the Section. He and his wife had been married, they said, over three years before; but later when a marriage certificate was needed the true story came out. When the couple were only seventeen they had applied for a license, had been refused on account of their youth and had straightway set up housekeeping. They had always intended to legalize their relation and this the visitor helped them to do, arranging for the marriage at the bedside of the wife, then in a hospital. They were a very sound, wholesome young pair, quite evidently devoted to each other and to their two-year-old baby girl. (Selected record. Not known to any social agency.)

The Kendalls had been living together fifteen years, and were expecting their sixth child when they became known to Home Service. They were very poor and lived in an undesirable house and neighborhood, but the rooms are said to have been light, well kept, and clean. The man had a fair work record, though at the time he had lost his job as brakeman on account of failing eyesight and was having difficulty in finding work. The investigation seems to have been rather perfunctory, for though a church worker who knew their history was seen, none of the significant facts came out. It was not until six months later that the agent of the Society for the Prevention of Cruelty to Children (which had been called in for reasons that are not at all clear) reported that the mother had admitted to him having been married to a man who had left her and regarding whose whereabouts or present existence she had no information. Kendall had been a boarder in the home and had stayed on, and they had lived together ever since. The priest and church worker knew the couple and would like to see them married, but ignorance as to the husband's fate was a bar; help was being given them by the church and there is no evidence of any attempt to force a separation. In this case no action was taken; probably none was possible after the lapse of so many years since the husband's disappearance. (Cross-section record. Known to a family agency and seven other social agencies. Previously mentioned on page 52.)

Mrs. Walters, a very nice-appearing colored woman, came to the Section to see about her government pay. When questioned she admitted that she and Walters, though they had lived happily together for twelve years, had never been married. Their families and friends supposed them to be man and wife and she would rather, she concluded, go without government aid than undeceive them. Many letters addressed to "My dear wife" were shown the visitor, and after the latter had written the man regarding the desirability of a legal ceremony Mrs. Walters announced that he, as well as she, wished to get married. She was "very happy over it all, thought it all due to the Red Cross." Two months later the couple "called, proudly producing a marriage certificate. He was more jubilant than she, and they said they felt they wanted the Red Cross to rejoice with them as no one else knows or can understand how happy they are." (Selected record. Not known to any social agency.)

At the opposite extreme from these essentially normal households are two where the union seems to have been but one of an indefinite series.

Mrs. Tierney, though the man whose name she bore wrote the visitor that he was allotting to her, turned out to have a long history under another name. She also not only neglected her children but presently took to entertaining soldiers, serving them liquor illegally. Home Service called in the Society for the Prevention of Cruelty to Children and the children were taken away. (Cross-section record. Known to a family agency.)

Mrs. Treimer was known by her visitor from the beginning to be legally the wife of another man. She was living with her mother during Treimer's absence in service and was cared for as though she had a right to the name she bore. Later she ran away with a third man. (Cross-section record. Known to a family agency.)

The remaining three records are less clearly classifiable.

The Emmet family—mother and three children—have been mentioned elsewhere in this chapter. (See page 152.) They had been under care more than a year, and various relatives had been seen before it was discovered that the deserting father was not the legal head. Though Mrs. Emmet's first child was by another man, and Emmet when seen made other accusations against her, the fact that he had introduced her as his wife, even to his own family, seems to give color to her statement that he had wished to marry her but she had refused. The visitor labored long and faithfully to establish her on a self-supporting basis, as well as to get support from the man; but every plan, whether that of work at home (which seemed to succeed for awhile) or of work outside (though infinite pains had been taken to arrange for care of the children so as to free the mother) broke down. At the date of reading one could not help suspecting that sex delinquency might prove to be the explanation for the failure. The woman had been examined mentally and declared to be practically normal. (Selected record. Not known to any social agency.)

The history of the Sheas is a curious one. Shea, who came of an apparently respectable family but had a reputation for drink and general toughness, had been devoted to Mollie Shannon when she was a young girl, had betrayed her, had offered to marry her, but had been prevented from doing so by her parents. He had then, apparently angered by her refusal, disappeared for a time from her horizon. No child was born of this early union. After a few years he reappeared and persuaded her to set up housekeeping with him. It was not until some time later that she learned that he had been married during the interval when she was not seeing him. The legal wife was of dubious reputation; a priest interviewed in the course of the investigation said he believed she was living immorally. Shea accounted for his marrying her by the pique felt over Mollie's refusal; and for his leaving her by her unwillingness to bear children. His life with Mollie was far from admirable, as he drank and supported irregularly; but he seems to have regarded her as his wife, and at the time the Red Cross came to know her had allotted to her and was writing affectionate letters home. Many phases were gone through in the treatment of this family, but it was not until early in 1919, when the return of the man was recognized as possibly not distant, that the moral issues involved were squarely met. The whole situation was then brought before a seminar at the New York School of Social Work and the following plan agreed upon: (1) To keep Mollie apart from Shea, the Red Cross financing the plan and not asking him to care for the children; (2) To assure her of Red Cross support so long as she keeps away from him; (3) To place her at service with the new baby, and board the two older children either with her parents or with another family; (4) To make an effort to strengthen her church connections.

Up to the date of our reading the record ill health had interfered with the proposed placement at service, and as the man had not yet come home the plan had not been put to very severe test. In May Shea wrote home that he was going to have his marriage annulled, evidently so as to marry Mollie. The fact that the three persons concerned were Roman Catholics decided Home Service against seconding any effort in the direction of divorce. (Selected record. Known to a family agency, to another private agency, and to the Department of Public Charities.)

The last of our eight irregularly united couples—the Buicks—were of Protestant affiliation, a fact which doubtless has something to do with the very different treatment accorded them—though their characteristics and history probably had more, and we suspect that the personalities of visitor and supervisor also largely entered in. The story of Home Service dealings with them has already been told at some length and need not be repeated here. (See page 48. Selected record. Not known to any social agency.)

Four cases of bigamy came to light in the course of our record reading; one among the cross-section, three among the selected cases.

Mrs. Greer, a colored woman, lived with her mother and two sisters in a six-room apartment described as light, clean, and well furnished—"a very livable home and they seemed nice quiet people." She came to Home Service for help in getting the allotment and allowance due her, and also apparently with some hope that a second marriage contracted illegally by her husband might be annulled. Apparently, however, she did not wish to prosecute him though she is said to have been "discouraged" when told that the "second marriage cannot be annulled." The man's mother, seen later, stated that both wives "thought too much of her to have the man arrested." There was thus no basis for action in the matter of bigamy. (Cross-section record. Not known to any social agency.)

The case of Fred Carpenter, who bullied his wife into signing a paper saying that she was his sister, was mentioned under allotment and allowance problems (page 92). Mrs. Carpenter had been receiving

$20 allotment and allowance. The legal committee attempted to straighten out the matter, and after much correspondence received word from Washington that the man had married another woman and allotted to her as his wife. Correspondence with the Home Service Section in the town where the second wife lived, and with the man's attorney followed, and a vigorous effort was made to have Carpenter retained in the service and punished, but without result. At last accounts he had been discharged and had disappeared (the second wife disappearing from her home about the same time), and efforts were being made to locate him. Most of this work, as well as that of securing the allowance and allotment checks due the wife, was done by the legal committee. (Selected record. Known to a family agency.)

In the third bigamy case it was the hastily married wife of an ex-soldier, Louis Leonardis, who turned out to have a living husband. It was not until after she had run away with still another man that an investigation into her previous history in other cities was made which brought to light this earlier marriage. As the soldier-husband seemed to have a very genuine respect for the marriage bond, a great effort was made to follow up the woman and her lover, and (when at last they were found in another state) to induce her to return and permit service of papers. This she did not do. Efforts to secure court action freeing the man were, however, continued, though without result to the date of reading. (Selected record. Not known to any social agency.)

The fourth case of bigamy, brought to the attention of the Section by the Home Service Section in another city which was interested in the first and legal wife, has already been gone into in some detail and commented upon as an illustration of the freedom from conventionality of method believed to be characteristic of Home Service. (See p. 50. Selected record. Not known to any social agency in New York; wife known to Home Service Section in another city.)

The account of sex irregularities in the cases read would not be complete without mention of three other records, entirely different from one another.

The case of William Yeager, who lived alone with his stepmother, has already been referred to in connection with the insanity of the woman. (See page 129.) It was not until almost the end of Home Service relations with the family that evidence of neighbors verified what had been a mere suspicion: that immoral relations existed between these two. There followed almost immediately the forcible removal of the woman to a hospital for the insane. A physician interested in the case had indeed implied, a month or so earlier, that he could tell something if he would; but either he had been unwilling to speak plainly or the visitor had not made an effort to obtain his evidence. It is rather horrible to think that Home Service had been helping for months to maintain a home for these two, while striving to get the ex-soldier son established in work. After the removal of the woman arrangements were made for him at a Young Men's Christian Association, and there he was living at last accounts. (Selected record. Not known to any social agency.)

Maria Sonnino, eighteen-year-old sister of a man in service, confided to her visitor that her father had for many years, ever since she was little, been making improper advances to her. The mother knew the state of affairs and the case had been taken to court, but dismissed because of insufficient evidence. Apparently actual force had not been brought to bear, and the girl had always succeeded in escaping. She later left home and the visitor found a place for her to live in a working girl's home where she was very happy. This is one of several fine examples of relations between a visitor and a young girl in especial need which our reading brought to light. (Selected record. Not known to any social agency.)

Paul Darpegio was an ex-soldier who was suffering from bulbar paralysis. He had been in a military hospital for mental cases but expert examination proved his mind not affected. He expressed a strong desire to go home to Italy to visit his family, and arrangements had been made for his passage when the uncle with whom he was staying came to report that he had been guilty of malpractice with his two little girl cousins, aged five and seven, and the uncle was not willing to let him stay in the house another night. There followed a week of feverish activity in the course of which reports were secured from physicians of the War Risk Bureau and Federal Board; one of the psychiatrists attached to the Section, and two other specialists, examined the man, and still another was consulted about him; while the little girls were examined by a physician at the Health Center. From the beginning the issue was open between the view that the man was a criminal and should be dealt with as such, and the view that his immoral action was traceable to his physical or his mental condition. This latter view the visitor took and she vigorously opposed having him arrested. It became clear that, having his ticket and passport in his possession, Darpegio meant to sail in spite of the decision that he must not be allowed to go, so he was lain in wait for and with the aid of a detective sent to Bellevue in an ambulance but without formal arrest. All examinations failed to find anything wrong with the man's mentality, though one physician did say that there might be some "possible mental condition with latent symptoms." (This physician was merely consulted, had not examined him.) The visitor succeeded in getting the man out of Bellevue and into another hospital where his case was studied for a week by a specialist said to be the best equipped in the city to deal with his type of paralysis. This physician's recommendations were to avoid institutional care and send the man home where time and pleasant surroundings should ultimately restore him to practically a normal condition. His action toward the children the physician considered (so the visitor reported) not criminal under all the circumstances.

Thus far attention had been given chiefly to the man's health. The Society for the Prevention of Cruelty to Children was now asked to take the case over and arranged for a consultation with the district attorney, who agreed with the society's agent that court action would be useless as the children were too young for their evidence to have weight and that it was best to send the man back to Italy. This the visitor arranged for and he went.

Whether or not the decision to give first importance to Darpegio's physical condition rather than his criminal act (assuming it to have been such) was wise, in the end every medical and legal possibility seems to have been tried out and the man was certainly given the benefit of every doubt. Personally we feel that immediate reference to the Society for the Prevention of Cruelty to Children would have been the right action to take, though we cannot see that any better results would have followed. We are impressed by some features that do not seem to have impressed the visitor: one of the little girls reported that she had been misused more than once and that Darpegio had threatened to kill the children if they told what he had done. The physician who examined the children found them little injured mentally or physically, and believed that they would probably grow up to be normal women. We must hope that he was right in this; though the mother at last accounts was troubled by the way the older child continued to talk about her experiences. (Cross-section record. Not known to any social agency.)

Dishonesty in Adults

Our study of problems arising from defects of character has included a number of situations in which there was conflict with the law—cases of desertion and non-support and of bigamy. There is another group in which some form of dishonesty was involved. Only a very few of these problems were brought to Home Service in a way which necessitated definite action. All in which any adult was involved will however be referred to briefly.

Walker, a tuberculous Canadian ex-soldier who had left a hospital to come to New York and was trying to persuade his wife to live with him again, has been mentioned before. (See page 112.) The discovery of his criminal record did not affect the treatment of the case (though it helped to explain his wife's refusal to accede to his plan) since the one obvious duty of Home Service was to get him back to Canada where he had a right to hospital care. (Cross-section record. Known only to a settlement.)

Mrs. Cole, whose marriage had been a belated one and who was living apart from her husband, had a record in at least one of the stores where she had worked of minor theft. No action directly bearing upon her tendency to dishonesty seems to have been taken. As having an indirect bearing we may note the liberal relief, the plans carried out to establish Mrs. Cole on a firmer economic basis by training her for better paying work, and the friendly, stabilizing interest manifested in many ways. (Selected record. Not known to any social agency.)

The Russells were strangers in the city. Positive assurance was received from the Home Service Section in the western city where they had lived that the man had misappropriated funds and was considered an undesirable citizen. This information was accompanied by refusal of transportation but did not affect the treatment given, an account of which appears on page 205. (Cross-section record. Not known to any agency in New York.)

Gus Hartmann was discharged from the express company for which he worked because implicated in a theft of eggs. The visitor had apparently, before the discovery of this fact, held out some hopes of a loan to enable the family to go to housekeeping, and when she refused it the husband was exceedingly bitter against her for breaking her "promise," and there ensued something of a scene in which the visitor brought up the story of the alleged theft and the man defended himself, insisting that he hadn't stolen or he would have been locked up, had merely aided a man whose family was starving. It would seem that there might be something in this distinction but no further investigation was made. A more important point is perhaps the obvious defect in the visitor's method which made possible such an altercation; with a worker completely gentle, patient, and ready to hear and consider every point of view of even the most difficult client, a scene of this sort could hardly have occurred. (Cross-section record. Known to six agencies, including a family society.)

Two instances came to our attention—in addition to that of Bjornsen, mentioned on page 160 of this chapter—in which the person guilty of a dishonest act was in another city.

One, a wife to whom a ticket from a city in the Far West to New York had been delivered rashly by the Home Service Section there, sold it and made off with the proceeds. She had already proved herself so elusive a creature that efforts to punish her for the theft or to recover the money lost would have almost certainly proved wasted—even had such action been in line with the policy of the Section. (Cross-section record. Not known to any social agency.)

In the other case an old Italian mother, Mrs. Battista, who had been living in a middle western city with one son and was now in New York with another, was being defrauded of her government checks from a third son, which, continuing to come to her former address were indorsed and deposited by the wife of the son there, who chanced to have the same name as the mother. The Home Service Section in the western city, which had discovered the situation, was asked to force the son to deliver the checks, but this had not been accomplished at the date of reading. The legal committee had also written to Washington changing the mother's address, but we have no record of the arrival of any checks at her New York home. (Cross-section record. Not known to any social agency.)

Another somewhat similar case of forgery was involved with the bigamy case of Mrs. Greer, mentioned on page 164. Her husband who, as she knew, was living with another woman, had given his mother's address as his wife's in making out his allotment papers. For a time the checks came regularly and the mother handed them over; then the second illegal wife appeared on the scene, and (so the first wife believed) persuaded the mother to forge the wife's name and cash the checks. The wife's desire to take action was short-lived, for when her mother-in-law gave her half of a check just cashed she reported that she no longer wished to prosecute. (Cross-section record. Not known to any social agency.)

The Section's visitor had labored long and earnestly to solve the employment problem of Sam Hoffman, as well as to help his family in other ways. When he was brought into court on a second charge of theft, having been acquitted the first time, it was the Jewish Big Brothers, brought into the case by Home Service, who bestirred themselves; the Section itself seems to have left the handling of this particular phase of the family problem to them and we are not told in detail of their activities, though we do know that Sam was placed on probation. (Cross-section record. Known to a family agency, another private agency, and the Department of Public Charities.)

Mrs. O'Toole had been known through a period of many months and had been helped to secure her allotments from her two sons in service and in various other ways, when her worst trouble came to light.

A third son, Larrie, who had almost completed a term in prison, was to be tried for previous theft. The visitor wrote to the prison and received a letter from the warden which bore witness to the man's good behavior; backed the mother in her efforts in his behalf, performing such friendly service as visiting him in the Criminal Courts Building and taking him gifts from his mother; consulted the War Committee of the Bar on his case, and went with the mother to see the district attorney to whom she gave the warden's letter; and finally she appeared with Mrs. O'Toole at the trial, when happily Larrie was released on probation. There is a suggestion that the warden's letter had a good deal to do with this outcome, but naturally we are not in a position to know how much.

It would seem that Mrs. O'Toole had her hands full with Larrie, but as a matter of fact he was but half her trouble; Joe, one of the soldier sons, who had been discharged and had gone to work, came into conflict with the law before his brother's trial. The mother confided to her visitor in February that she was worried about him as he had been getting into bad company and had left home. At her request the visitor called up his employer, who knew only that the boy had been absent from work two days. A few days later the mother reported that Joe had robbed a liquor store and was in jail. The visitor then called in the Catholic Big Brothers who took up the case and were present at the trial. Joe was sentenced to an indefinite term. A week later the visitor obtained for the mother a pass permitting her to visit him. When he was released three months later, the Home Service visitor again sought the co-operation of the Big Brothers who promised visits. (Cross-section record. Known to a family society.)

Difficult and Neglected Children

All the delinquents thus far discussed have been adults. A few problems of conduct in children have also come to our attention.

Michael Dimattio, thirteen years old or thereabouts, was taken into the children's court for the theft of three eggs. The visitor met the parents at the court and talked with the probation officer. It was the boy's first offense and the judge put him on probation, telling him to thank the Red Cross visitor "for showing such deep interest in him." He promised good behavior and seems to have kept his word up to the date of our reading, over six months later. (Cross-section record. Known to a family society.)

Two children in families whose records were read may perhaps be classed as incorrigible.

The mother of Katie O'Donnell, fifteen years old, said she was uncontrollable and should be in an institution. No details are given, nor does any action seem to have been taken further than to advise taking the girl to the Medical Station, which does not appear to have been done, and this reference may very likely have been for some purely physical ailment. (Cross-section record. Known to a family society, the Domestic Relations Court, a hospital, and the Salvation Army.)

Very differently treated was the case of Ted Buchanan. His mother, an intelligent, educated woman, appealed personally to Home Service for help in deciding what to do with this wild boy of eleven who was altogether beyond her control. The visitor consulted with her supervisor and with the Children's Aid Society, which advised Brace Farm, and there his mother took him; but within a few days he ran away and returned to the home of his grandmother (the mother having taken a position out of town). The grandmother called in a truant officer and then was appalled that in consequence the boy landed at the Society for the Prevention of Cruelty to Children. The visitor now took an active hand in the case, endeavoring in many interviews to prevent his being committed to the Berkshire School. Finally he was paroled in the mother's custody on the understanding that the Boy Conservation Bureau and Home Service should see that he was placed in a good school. The visitor conducted the boy to a temporary home where he stayed ten days and did well. During this time he was examined at the Health Center, where the doctor declared him a fine specimen, mentally and physically. Then, after another visit to report at the Children's Court, he was taken by the visitor out to a school in the country. Here he stayed for a little over a month, when the master of the school asked to have him removed on account of "nasty habits and bad language." Back again to town the visitor brought the boy and to a mental clinic, where he was found to be retarded two years but normal. The visitor who had been working hard for some time to get the co-operation of certain relatives of the mother did finally induce the brother to appear in court; but no financial assistance being forthcoming, it was arranged for the mother to sign the boy over for three years to the Boys' Conservation Bureau, and he was fitted out and sent away to a carefully selected school in New England. This result had been achieved only a short time before our reading of the record. (Selected record. Not known to any social agency.)

Boys in three families were truants.

It was part of the plan worked out for the Oliver family that Harry, aged fourteen, should be placed in the truant school, but no record of any effort to accomplish this appears. This is one of the few records read which comes abruptly to an end because of the family's desire that relations cease. (Cross-section record. Not known to any social agency.)

In the Esposito family one boy was a truant. It is recorded that the visitor talked the matter over with the mother, whether with any result we do not know. (Selected record. Known to a family society.)

Billy O'Neil was a truant and his older sister felt he should be taken from the parents—a drunken father and a slatternly mother. The Society for the Prevention of Cruelty to Children was called in, but always at the time they paid a visit the father happened to be working and no action was taken. (Selected record. Known to a family society.)

The case just mentioned is to be classed, probably, as one of improper guardianship. Five others were read in which there was neglect of younger children. Three of these, in which children were taken by court action from a deserting, drunken, or immoral mother, have already been gone into in other connections.[1]

In a fourth case the father accused the mother of neglect—a charge that the visitor evidently felt had some basis, but which it is difficult to believe, as she had seemingly given good care to the children during the months of his absence. At all events the situation did not yet call for outside interference, the visitor acting merely as a friendly arbitrator of the differences of the parents—and like some other arbitrators not always having her suggestions accepted. (Selected record. Not known to any social agency. Case of Noonans, more fully discussed on page 147.)

The fifth case is that of the Woods, already dwelt upon in this chapter and elsewhere, in which the mother went to pieces morally in her husband's absence. As things continued to go badly after the man's return the couple were urged to give up the children to the Society for the Prevention of Cruelty to Children and let them be placed in an institution, but they resisted the pressure in this direction and finally solved their own problem (temporarily, at least) by separating, the father bringing in a housekeeper to care for his home and his children. (Selected record. Known only to two health agencies.)

[1] See stories of Mrs. Buick, page 48; Mrs. Gibson, page 146; and Mrs. Tierney, page 203.

CHAPTER VIII

EDUCATIONAL, EMPLOYMENT, AND HOUSING PROBLEMS

Educational Problems

Several different types of problem are grouped together under this general heading: problems of boys and girls in need of a prolonged schooling to permit them to finish the elementary grades or to pursue special courses; problems of especially gifted young people needing specialized training, and of adults needing to be fitted for better paying or higher type work; problems of housewives in need of guidance in buying and planning meals and instruction in cooking; and the problem of the unassimilated immigrant.

Scholarship Cases.—Regarding the co-operative arrangement between the Home Service Section and the Henry Street Settlement Scholarship Committee something has already been said (see p. 23). The scholarships given under this arrangement were of course a special sort of allowance; the amount ($3.00 in the earlier days, sometimes as high as $6.00 in the last year) was scarcely ever the equivalent of what the child might be earning—for all or nearly all these scholarship children were of working age and able to get their working papers. The family was therefore obliged to make some sacrifice to obtain this opportunity for the child except where other relief was given to supplement the scholarship. Children, to be eligible, did not have to show especially good records in school; some fairly stupid children were felt to be as much in need of an additional year or two of training as exceptionally talented ones.

The girl in one case, Sarah Farderber, was of quite an ordinary type, but her teachers said she would graduate if kept in school to the end of the year, and, with the aid of a scholarship, this was done. Discussion of a later effort to place her industrially belongs to the Employment Section. Cross-section record. Known to a family society.)

Another girl, Hilda Lund, had already left school when she became known to the Home Service visitor, and at first declared that she would not return. She seems to have been an unusually bright and decidedly conceited young person, who believed she could succeed (she aspired to be a writer) without more education. Whether through the visitor's influence or not she later became anxious to continue her schooling, and as it was difficult for her family to manage without her wages an exceptionally generous arrangement was made, the $5.00 scholarship being supplemented by a $10 a week allowance. This arrangement had only just gone into effect when we read the case. The reasons for such unusual treatment were not altogether clear to us from the record, which did not enlarge upon the girl's mental equipment, but this was strongly felt by the supervisor and visitor in charge to be exceptional. (Cross-section record. Not known to any social agency.)

The other four families were among those whose records were selected for reading.

In one, a boy of fifteen was helped to finish out his year and graduate; he then appeared at the office of the scholarship committee to say that he felt he should no longer accept the scholarship, was anxious to "get along on his own." At last accounts he had a good position. His family, of rather high grade, were most appreciative of the help given. (Selected record. Not known to any social agency.)

The story of Linda Antokolsky—a long one—is told elsewhere. (See page 155.) The only part of it which concerns us here is the early episode of her being given a scholarship and spending a few months in a trade school. She soon insisted on getting her working papers and going to work. Just the ground for this action we do not know; it was probably due to the same restlessness which kept her for a year following roving from job to job. (Selected record. Known to seven social agencies, though not to a family society.)

In the Marx family first one, then two, and finally three children were given scholarships. These were very self-respecting people with a little business of their own and unwilling to accept relief in the usual obvious forms. The budget made up by the dietitian, however, showed a weekly deficit of nearly $6.00, and the scholarships were evidently offered to supply the lack. The last one, given to a little girl of twelve or thirteen, is an exception to the rule that only children of working age are to be aided under this plan. (Selected record. Known only to a health agency. For previous references to this family see Index, page 230.)

Special Educational Experiments.—The Dorandos furnish examples both of an ordinary scholarship, given to a boy of fifteen to enable him to take trade training, and of help in developing special talent in an older brother. Michael, at eighteen, had impressed various judges of art with his ability. As he suffered from osteomyelitis and was far from strong he was sent to an art school at the seashore where his board, $12 a week, was paid for two months and all incidental expenses met. On his return he was entered at a school of fine and applied arts for an experimental term of three months, which had not yet been completed when we read the record. The planning of these special courses was in the hands of the scholarship committee, Home Service not only footing the bills but sending in several quarts of milk a day and supplying the two boys receiving scholarships with winter outfits of clothing. (Selected record. Known to a family society and three other agencies.)

In another family the son who had been in service showed some small talent in drawing and professed enthusiasm for art; but when his visitor arranged an interview with an artist who told him that he lacked fundamentals and it would take him three or four years to get anywhere even in commercial art, he decided that he must go to work at once, and did so, finding a position for himself. (Selected record. Known to a family society.)

In one exceptionally high-class family the mother felt that her two older children, a boy of ten and a girl of twelve, had musical talent and was anxious to have it cultivated. Lessons were arranged for them at the Music Settlement and excellent reports of progress have been coming from there; while opportunities for hearing good music which have come to mother and children through the settlement have been immensely appreciated. (Selected record. Not known to any social agency.)

The most exceptional case of talent known to the Section is that of a blind youth of twenty-one who possesses unusual musical gifts. He had recently graduated from an institute for the blind when he came to the attention of Home Service. As his tastes were along classical lines he found the idea of earning his living by producing cheap music intolerable, yet there seemed no prospect of further opportunity for study. Various efforts to find a way out had failed when a volunteer was introduced who possessed the private means as well as the interest and energy needed to bring results. She gave the boy a piano and engaged private tutors, one in French and English subjects, one in musical composition, who went to the home several times a week. Later, when a special fund from a benefit performance by a famous violinist became available for exceptional cases, the expenses of the young man's education were taken over and paid from it. Opportunities to attend concerts regularly were also given as a part of his training. At a recital arranged by the visitor the youth made an excellent impression and his teachers are enthusiastic over his progress. Their idea at last accounts was to equip him as a composer; he has already done some creditable original work. (Selected record. Known to one social agency.)

In addition to these instances of special educational opportunities supplied to young people of exceptional talent, three cases came to our attention in which training was given where no such talent existed.

A course in motor driving was given to one young fellow, Sam Hoffman, after many efforts to find him a job into which he would fit had been made without result. While a success as a course, it seems to have failed in its purpose of establishing him in regular work. The character problem was here the most serious issue. (Cross-section record. Known to a family society and two other agencies.)

Young Mrs. Cole, living with her dignified old mother and a small son, had drifted from one ill-paid job to another. She showed a decidedly flighty and unstable disposition. However, her visitor was not without faith in her possibilities, and in order to fit her for better paying work paid for a course in manicuring and hairdressing. At last accounts she had completed this course and secured a position much better than any previously held. (Selected record. Not known to any social agency.)

Mrs. Carpenter's desertion by her bigamist husband had left her in difficulties which have been elsewhere mentioned. (See page 164.) She was a woman of nearly thirty, with one little boy, and was evidently above the grade of work she was doing in a cigarette factory. A great deal of devoted care had been given her and the child in periods of acute illness, and several hundred dollars expended, when the plan was formed of getting her permanently on her feet by a course in nursing. She was accordingly fitted out and entered at a hospital, while a home was found for the little boy, the Section paying his board. At the date of reading she had been in the hospital about two months, was enjoying her work, and reported her boy "fat and well and perfectly happy." (Selected record. Known to a family society.)

Education of Housewives.—Under the head of educational problems also belong, as already indicated, those problems of ignorance on the part of housewives with which the visiting dietitians of the Section dealt. In all, 87 cases had been under their care for longer or shorter periods up to the date of writing. None of these happens to be among our cross-section cases, but a few are included among the selected records read. These cases naturally show a larger proportion of instances of successful work than would be found among the whole group. The visiting dietitian who has been longest with the Section assured the writer that she could "count on the fingers of her two hands" all the really successful cases, so difficult and discouraging is this type of work. Among the cases mentioned below the first is accounted by the dietitian a failure.

Mrs. Tannenbaum, a young Jewish wife accustomed to a high scale of living but quite shockingly ignorant as to the proper feeding of her two- and three-year-old girls, took kindly at first to the instructions offered, adopting the use of cereals and vegetables and profiting by other lessons; but after a time failed to keep appointments and finally declared she knew all she needed to know and saw no point in further lessons. (Selected record. Not known to any social agency.)

One fairly satisfactory case has been elsewhere referred to (page 69), and three examples of different types of families successfully dealt with will be cited here.

First there are the Lusks—young married people with a little boy of two and a baby, living in an apartment of four light rooms and bath. Mrs. Lusk kept her home clean but knew almost nothing about cooking or the choice of foods. Mr. Lusk was only recently out of service, had just taken a job, and would not be paid for a week when the dietitian first called, and there was nothing to eat in the house but a half loaf of bread. This gave a chance to start the family off with a stock of the right kinds of foods, including cereals, vegetables, bread, butter, eggs, meat, and fruit. Mrs. Lusk was most eager to learn and very soon had accustomed her small boy to the recommended milk, cereals, etc., while her husband, who had been suffering from indigestion, improved rapidly as his wife learned to cook. (Selected record. Known only to a health agency.)

This is the kind of intelligent young American family that might be expected to respond promptly to treatment. Another mother, with her tribe of seven and her heritage of Italian customs, was a different and more difficult type, but she proved equally co-operative.

When first visited by the dietitian, Mrs. Carillo's rooms were exceedingly dirty and disorderly, even to the beds which in any half-way well-regulated Italian household are usually in perfect order; and her household account for the first week showed a monotonous repetition of the same items—especially "bread, 50 cents" and "macaroni, 36 cents"—day after day. With gratifying speed, however, all this was changed as the instruction in buying and demonstrations in preparing meals went forward, and soon Mrs. Carillo was herself preparing excellent, well-balanced menus including cereals, vegetables, fruit, and meat, and was using all the various dishes taught her regularly. The children have improved so in appearance that the dietitian expects soon to have to give the prize she promised at the beginning for a pair of pink cheeks. Moreover, the appearance of the rooms has now changed so that, she says, the place is hardly recognizable, so neat and shining with cleanliness is it. (Selected record. Known to a family society.)

Our third successful case is that of a young woman of good standards and education, with a fair knowledge of cooking but little sense of the value of money. Chops and steak formed her staple articles of diet. The help given here consisted chiefly in showing Mrs. Newell how to organize her expenditures. At last accounts she was successfully keeping within the limits of a reasonable dietary budget, had paid most of her debts, and was saving money to meet clothing needs. It should also be noted, however, that she was working part-time, a fact which probably largely accounted for the improved condition of affairs. (Selected record. Not known to any social agency.)

Americanization.—The one instance coming to our attention in which a need of "Americanization" is noted—among many, doubtless, in which such a need existed—is that of two brothers of a man in service, Italians who had been in the United States two years.

Their cousin, when interviewed, called attention to this need. One of the boys, eighteen years old, was apprenticed to a butcher; the other, sixteen, was a hat cleaner; the mother had stated in the first interview that the family was in no need of relief. The general suggestion that they join some club or attend night school was followed up by inquiry as to the best Americanization center in the neighborhood, and the one found to be such, in a nearby settlement, was brought to the mother's attention. Advantage of this opportunity seems not to have been taken and a year later the visitor returned to the attack, suggesting the joining of an English class. The mother's reply was that the boys were not home until 7.30 or 8 o'clock in the evening and were then too tired to make the exertion required to attend a class. The visitor, however, persisted in looking up the Young Men's Christian Association English classes, and when the family added to their former objection that they could not afford the membership fees ($5.25 for each boy) she arranged for their admission without payment, giving the mother a letter of introduction to be presented by the boys. There is no record of the final outcome. (Cross-section record. Not known to any social agency.)

Employment Problems

With unemployment in the broad sense of the term our reading of Home Service cases hardly brought us in contact—a not-surprising fact, since during the war this problem virtually did not exist. Among the cases grouped here are some in which persons were seeking work for the first time, and others where for any one of a great variety of reasons a change of work or some readjustment in service was desired or seemed desirable. There have of course been included the problems of women and girls—wives, mothers, and sisters of men in service; and those of men and boys, both fathers and brothers left at home, and returned soldiers. The few instances encountered of illegal work by children are also noted. For the ends of the present brief survey the three headings suggested above may be used.

Employment of Women and Girls.—During the war period it was naturally the work problems of the womenfolk that chiefly came to Home Service; and it was to solve these, primarily, that the Section formed its own employment bureau and that the Red Cross workrooms were started, of both of which ventures some account has been given.[1] Naturally, therefore, women and girls encountered in the homes who were out of work or who expressed a desire for better jobs were referred quite usually to the Bureau. Of results in most of these cases we know little; sometimes the matter of employment is not referred to again, sometimes it appears later that a job was found but how is not stated. No general statement regarding results is therefore possible. All we can do is to gather together a few notes on certain types of problem and the more conspicuous failures and successes recorded.

A few instances of difficult adjustment may be noted first.

Lois Burian, sister of a man in service, had been an operator on caps. She wished a position as governess for which she was obviously unfitted, and did not care to take the job at Huyler's which, at the

[1] See pages 24 and 25.

moment, was the only one that could be offered her. A letter from her, written several months later, says she is still employed at the gas-mask factory "the place you referred me to," though no other record of this reference had been made. (Cross-section record. Not known to any social agency.)

The granting of a scholarship to Sarah Farderber, fifteen years old and one of several children at home, has already been mentioned (page 173). Soon after her graduation from school, she was given a letter of introduction to an employer who was a friend of the visitor. She called upon him but did not get the job, his explanation to the visitor being that "she did not seem the least bit intelligent or polite and did not look a bit tidy." The regrettable feature of the incident, from a case-work point of view, was that it was never apparently talked over with the girl, nor any effort made to correct her faults and help her to another opening. We simply do not know what the outcome was for her. (Cross-section record. Known to a family agency.)

In another case, that of a young wife obliged to break with an abusive and immoral husband, every conceivable care was given. She was placed at a suburban Young Women's Christian Association where her board was paid and many efforts to place her made; but job after job was taken by her only to be dropped after a day or two. Mental examination revealed that she was hardly responsible. (See Glynn, page 116. Selected record. Not known to any social agency.)

A young woman, Mrs. Emmet, first supposed to be the wife of a man in service but later found to have no legal claim on him, was given an opportunity to make babies' shoes at home, and did this work for a time declaring that she liked it and found it well paid. It is not clear why the work was dropped. Later, though the care of Mrs. Emmet's children was arranged so that she could be free to work, and though she seemed to have little difficulty in finding jobs, she lost them with equal facility, never staying in one more than a few days. Tested, she was found to be of practically normal mentality. At the date of reading, the record afforded no clear explanation of her employment problem. (Selected record. Not known to any social agency.)

Linda Antokolsky's story has been elsewhere told (see pages 155 and 174). After a scholarship had been given her for a few months she decided she preferred to go to work. For nearly a year thereafter her record was one of most irregular employment in jobs found sometimes by Home Service, sometimes by herself, with constant changes. Then, quite suddenly, she settled down in one of the positions obtained for her and worked steadily, achieving in due time an increase in wages. (Selected record. Known to seven agencies but not to a family society.)

Two elderly women of drinking habits were among those successfully placed.

One position may have been held only a short time—the report we have covers only the first three days. The other, in a hospital, seems to have been held for months, down to the date of reading. (First, a cross-section record and known to a family society. Second, selected and not known to any social agency.)

Three women with babies were sent to the State Charities Aid Association for placement.

One of them when next heard of was living with a former employer in Brooklyn; another was placed through the association, but because of illness the arrangement was soon broken up; the third secured a position but was prevented by illness from taking it. (First two, cross-section records and not known to any social agency. Third, selected record and known to a family society and two other agencies.)

Two wives worked for a time at the Red Cross workrooms.

With one it was for a very short time only, illness intervening; with the other, part-time work seems to have been done during twenty-one weeks running through a period of some six months, the average weekly earnings being about $4.50. (First, selected record, family unknown to any social agency. Second, cross-section, known to a family society.)

One young wife living with her mother was introduced to the Young Women's Christian Association needlework shop and did some work for it which was satisfactory. (Cross-section record. Not known to any social agency.)

In two families sisters of men in service were helped to better jobs; in one the wage advance was from $8.00 to $12 a week, and in both emphatic satisfaction was expressed by the girls. (One a cross-section, one a selected record. Neither known to any social agency.)

In two instances fine all-round work was done with exceptionally high-type women, including the finding of suitable employment for them.

Mrs. Drew had done some sewing at home and wanted more which she was helped to get. Later when it seemed desirable that she should have part-time work outside her home a position as waitress in a club was found for her which she filled satisfactorily for several months.

When this proved too great a strain a position as switchboard operator at a club—five hours in the afternoon and evening five days a week at $25 a month—was brought to her attention and filled by her for some time. Still later she was able to return to her original plan of skilled sewing at home. (Selected record. Not known to any social agency.)

Mrs. Marlton was a woman of cultivation who spoke French fluently. An arrangement was made for her to talk French with a little girl, work carried on for several months to the satisfaction of all concerned. Later a position as companion was offered and successfully filled. (Selected record. Not known to any social agency.)

Employment of Men and Boys.—Naturally the employment of the ex-soldier would be first thought of under this head. However, there is comparatively little to say about him since at the beginning of demobilization the Section decided to discontinue its own employment service and work through existing agencies, especially the United States Employment Bureau.[1] Accordingly, able-bodied discharged men seeking jobs were quite uniformly referred to this Bureau or to the Reemployment Committee of New York for Soldiers and Sailors. Where later references are made to jobs secured by such men there is scarcely ever any indication of how these were obtained. Quite exceptional, in our cross-section reading, is the case of a young Bohemian sent to the Reemployment Committee and who promptly reported having got a job through them. That there were many such cases we do not doubt, but evidence as to results has rarely come to our attention. Two discharged men among our selected families were indeed sent direct to jobs which they secured and held; but more frequently there is record of a man's being referred to an agency, and then the statement that he is working at such or such a job but without any intimation as to how it was obtained.

Sometimes, as strikingly in the case of young Yeager, there is a long record of struggles, extending in this case over several months, to induce the man to take work offered, at the end of which he sud-

[1] To enable this Bureau to carry on its work, for which appropriations from the government were lacking, the Executive Committee of the New York County Chapter of the American Red Cross appropriated for its use, between March, 1919, and November of the same year, the sum of $11,900. Appropriations totalling $3,000 were likewise made, during November and December of that year, to the Reemployment Committee of New York for Soldiers and Sailors, which later returned $594.20.

denly finds a job for himself and keeps it. (Selected record. Not known to any social agency.)

Occasionally there is record of a readjustment in work, as in the case of Conrad Limburg, who was being employed only half-time as a driver; his employer was interviewed and the following week the man reported that he had been given full-time work. (Selected record. Not known to any social agency.)

Occasionally, also, an apparent need of readjustment seems to have been disregarded; as in the case of Helmer Knut, who is said to have formerly earned $40 a week and to be earning, when visited, only $15. Needed nursing care for the man and his wife was provided over a period of several weeks, but there is no evidence that the employment situation was ever discussed with the family. (Cross-section record. Not known to any social agency.)

In the case of disabled men the main point was usually to induce them to go for examination to the War Risk Insurance Bureau and make application for compensation there and for training with the Federal Board for Vocational Education; and when these steps had been taken, to co-operate with the Board in any plans made for the man's care or advancement. However, independent attempts at adjustment were sometimes made.

Thus, a former employer of Peter Bellaro (who had lost a leg in service) was seen, and agreed to give the man part-time work at his trade of tailoring; but it turned out that Peter was really in need of hospital care, though he refused for a long time to submit to it. (Cross-section record. Not known to any social agency.)

Again, there was John Rittario, formerly a chauffeur, who had put in a claim for compensation on account of injured feet; he was referred to the Red Cross Institute for Cripples, but evidently did not make use of the opportunity as he reported, when last at the Home Service office, that he had been told if he worked he would not be compensable. (Cross-section record. Not known to any social agency.)

Another man, suffering from a form of paralysis, was given beadwork by his visitor while waiting for the question of his compensation to be settled, and made no less than eight chains at $10 each. Such a temporary measure, while very appropriate under the circumstances, can naturally not be regarded as the solving of an employment problem. (Cross-section record. Not known to any social agency.)

Fathers and brothers at home were sent to jobs sometimes by the visitors direct, sometimes through the Home Service Employment Bureau and, as with the other groups, results are recorded so seldom as to have little significance. There are a few records of proffered help being refused: one father, a peddler who said he was making about $6.00 a week, had no explanation to give for his refusal; another, a letter-stamper, gave the seemingly excellent reason that he was well known in his trade and would obtain work if there were any. Sometimes employers or former employers were seen in the effort to make favorable adjustments for men.

A man on account of failing eyesight was disqualified for the job of brakeman on a railway which he had filled for years. His chief in the service was seen and said he had already promised the man a job for which the passing of an eye test was not required. (Cross-section record. Known to a family society and seven other agencies.)

The employer of a man for whom a needed operation had been arranged was seen both before the operation and afterward, and his place assured to him upon his return. (Selected record. Not known to any social agency.)

An elderly tailor asked for help in obtaining better paid work and was referred to the United States Employment Bureau; whether anything in the way of a new job resulted we are not told. Later he appealed for help in persuading his employers—a large department store—to give him full-time instead of part-time work. A letter was written, but no result is recorded. (Cross-section record. Not known to any social agency.)

A position left vacant by a tuberculous man who had been sent to a sanatorium was obtained by his younger brother on the recommendation of the visitor. (Selected record. Not known to any social agency.)

The most difficult employment problems were naturally those in which some infirmity, moral or physical, complicated the case.

In one, where the efforts of the visitor were chiefly concentrated upon helping a neurotic sister, one serious talk was also had "about his responsibilities" with a young brother who was said to work occasionally and to spend what he made, and to be the "black sheep of the family." He assured the visitor that he was anxious for work. She then saw the Young Men's Christian Association regarding a job for him, but upon next inquiry of the mother was informed that he had gone to work. Whether anything had been accomplished in the way of influencing him we cannot tell. (Selected record. Not known to any social agency.)

In a few cases the help of the Big Brothers was asked and generously given; in one the St. Vincent de Paul Society gave splendid co-operation.

Harry Cohen, sixteen years old, was continually out of work and growing steadily more unruly, his last escapade having been the pawning of a suit of his mother's. As the home had to be broken up on account of the mother's health, the Jewish Big Brothers were called in. They found the boy a home and a job. This job he did not keep, and in first one home and then another he failed to fit, his smoking being apparently the thing especially objected to. A little later he went off to his grandfather in another city, where he did not work and after about a month's trial was put out. There follows a note of an effort to get an uncle to take him to the country where he was soon to open a summer boarding house; whether this was accomplished does not appear and there is no later mention of the boy. (Selected record. Known only to a settlement.)

Sam Hoffman's story has been already told in fragments (see pages 169 and 176). He was the subject of endless efforts at placement both by the Home Service visitor and by the Jewish Big Brothers, but seldom took and never held a job. How the visitor finally discovered a special interest on the part of the youth, and arranged for him to take lessons in motor driving at the Young Men's Christian Association; how, marvelous to relate, Sam took a vivid interest in the course and actually obtained his license at the end; and how he just then committed a theft, thus bringing all constructive efforts in his behalf to naught, has been elsewhere related. (Cross-section record. Known to a family society and two other agencies.)

Another brother of a man in service, Larrie O'Toole, was (as related on page 170) a prisoner when Home Service first became acquainted with his mother. After he was released an organization which interested itself in ex-prisoners was consulted regarding possible work for him; a letter was written on his case at the request of this organization, and he called at their office but seems to have received no help and ultimately found work for himself. Later he was working at a second and somewhat better (though still ill-paid) job and his mother reported he was doing well. Another brother had meantime been arrested, imprisoned, and released. His former employer was seen and held out hopes of re-employment, but he did not get his job back. At last accounts the Catholic Big Brothers had been asked to interest themselves in the two boys and had promised visits. (Cross-section record. Known to a family agency.)

In a Bronx division the St. Vincent de Paul Society was asked to find work for the drunken father of a family and did so repeatedly. O'Neil was a steamfitter and a capable workman when sober. Up to the date of first reading of the record no change in his habits had occurred; but on taking up the record several months later we found to our amazement that he had become in the interval a sober and industrious citizen. The causes which led to this result are obscure; some possible ones are suggested in an earlier paragraph on this case. (See page 149. Selected record. Known to a family society.)

Physical infirmity created work problems that sometimes proved insoluble.

Poor old Mr. Rolf, an educated gentleman who had formerly worked as a book agent and a librarian, was incapacitated by deafness. An effort to place him in the New York Library was made, but the visitor was told that he was already known and that his case was hopeless. (Cross-section record. Social Service Exchange was unable to identify as information was insufficient.)

A painter who suffered from painter's colic desired a change of work. A job was found for him, but it proved too hard and he gave it up, going back to his painting. (Cross-section record. Not known to any social agency.)

An old Jewish peddler was just recovering, when first known, from an operation for gallstones. After he had been to a convalescent home he asked help in finding work and was advised to come to the Home Service Employment Bureau. The Bureau, after talking with him, expressed the opinion that he could not be placed, as he spoke little or no English, was partly blind, and apparently inefficient. Again, later, they reported that they would not give him a job "as they say he is an active tb. case." The man's physician, consulted, stated that he was not tuberculous but a sufferer from chronic bronchitis, and that there was no reason why he could not work. He was told that he could and should work, and replied that he was willing to do anything anyone would give him to do, but preferred outdoor work. This is the last word on the subject that the case contains, though later efforts were made to help the young daughter of the family find work. The record is an especially poor one. (Cross-section record. Known to a family society.)

Another elderly man, a sufferer from lung trouble, "probably not tuberculosis," was first sent to a bureau for the handicapped, where he registered but seems not to have obtained work. Later a job as watchman was found for him through the United States Employment Bureau, but he refused to take it as he had the prospect of a better one. This he later proved unable to hold. (Selected record. Known to a family society and a clinic.)

We have reserved for the last what was certainly as discouraging a case as any read, in the hope that the brilliant success it records may restore hope in bosoms which have found little to enkindle such a feeling in the foregoing recital.

Peter Trotsky, brother-in-law to a man in service, and father of six children, was found to be suffering from a growth on the right wrist which made it impossible for him to use that hand. He was working for wretched wages, as a rag picker in a dark basement. From the first he showed pathetic eagerness for better work which would enable him to support his family; and when, after he had received every possible help along surgical lines, he was sent to the Red Cross Institute for Cripples, he went eagerly. The outcome may be told in the visitor's own words:

"Visitor called at the Red Cross Institute for Cripples. She there learned that Trotsky had been placed in a job at $18 a week with the Blank Co., Grand St., as watchman. The woman in charge said that they were very impressed with the man's desire to support his family. He came to them every Monday morning before he went to his rag picking to find out if there was any chance for him to get a better job. She said they had never had a a case of more active co-operation between the man and the office than the Trotsky case.

"Visitor was greeted by the entire family, including the boarder, with much enthusiasm. Mr. T. was so happy that he talked Polish and English all in one breath. This is the first time, the boarder said, that he had ever been able to earn more than $10 a week, and he had to work so very hard for that. He explained to visitor that his present work consisted of carrying a timeclock around his neck and winding it every hour with his good hand. He said he could hardly believe that he really had a job and that he never let his eyelids close for a moment during the whole night for fear he might lose his job. Every time he thinks of the rags and the pain they used to give him in his stomach and arm, he doesn't see how he ever stood them as long as he did." (Selected record. Not known to any social agency.)

Illegal Work of Children.—Our reading brought us only three cases in which a question of illegal work for children was involved.

Esther Teitelbaum, a delicate girl of fourteen, was the daughter of a most self-respecting family who were making every effort to get on without financial aid. She was working, earning only six or seven dollars a week. Her visitor brought her to the office to consult the employment bureau and there it was learned that she had no employment certificate. No effort was made to readjust the situation, and though there was talk of reporting her employers to the authorities later, when she should have left them, this does not seem to have been done. Three or four months after discovery of the lack of working papers it was learned that the girl had been obliged to give up her work for health reasons and had gone to the country to stay with an aunt. It would seem that an effort to get her back into school on a scholarship basis, or to the country if her health demanded it, should have been made. (Cross-section record. Not known to any social agency.)

Mrs. Niles, whose income from several lodgers more than paid her rent, felt quite desperate when she was told, early in December, that the allowance she had been receiving from Home Service would be discontinued as she was receiving her government checks and it was felt her stepdaughter, living with her, should be contributing. Later in the month the visitor discovered that the little daughter ten years old had been placed by her mother in the toy department of one of the large department stores where she was earning $8.00 a week. Greatly distressed, the visitor expostulated, then arranged to pay an allowance of $2.50 if the child was returned to school. The mother "seemed most grateful" saying she "could manage beautifully on that," and after the holidays the arrangement went into effect. In the following July, when the husband had returned and gone to work and the allowance had been discontinued, the little girl was found to be working again; but after a serious talk the mother promised that the work would end that week and seems to have kept her word. (Cross-section record. Known only to a diet kitchen.)

Mrs. Dorando worked at home, making cork sponges for bottles. She had six children of school age or under. It is related that "all the children work steadily on the corks for the shoe-blacking bottles," yet the case contains no evidence that the visitor recognized this state of affairs to be undesirable or illegal. (Selected record. Known to a family society and three other agencies.)

It would obviously be absurd to generalize from three instances. All we can do is to record the question raised in our mind as to whether Home Service visitors were quite sufficiently impressed, as part of their training, with the duty of doing their part toward seeing that laws for the protection of children were enforced.

Housing Problems

Housing problems were recognized and commented on in a mere handful of families; but few as they are they represent the commonest types of housing difficulty met with in New York tenements.

In two cases it was neglected repairs that gave ground for complaint.

Mrs. O'Toole's plumbing was out of order. The visitor spoke first to the janitor, and when no action followed wrote to the landlord, after which the work was done and the gratitude of the housewife earned. A later letter to the landlord brought similar results. (Cross-section record. Known to a family society.)

Mrs. Torquato's walls were badly broken and very dirty; the landlord was first approached on April 30th and promised painting and repairs; then, when no action was taken, the visitor complained to the Tenement House Department and in June the work was done, to the immense satisfaction of Mrs. Torquato. (Cross-section record. Known to a family society and another agency.)

Three cases of overcrowding are noted.

In one the condition was due to the addition of a second woman with her children to the original household consisting of mother and three young ones. As the rent was only $12, there can hardly have been more than three rooms. The visitor protested vigorously and often, also offered addresses to the visiting friend to help her in her own plans; and finally, after more than a month, she seems to have disappeared from the household, though the event of her departure is not recorded. (Selected record. Not known to any social agency.)

In the other two overcrowded households there were eight and nine persons in three rooms—at least two rooms, in each instance, being of the dark interior type. Nothing is recorded as having been done.

One of the families was never very intimately known and was always self-supporting; their income seems to have been sufficient to justify a larger expenditure for rent, but it is easy to understand that a visitor who had known the family only a month or two, and in that time had given only some slight attention to health and employment and sent the children to the country for a vacation, would not be in a position to exert much influence in persuading them to move. (Cross-section record. Known only to a health agency.)

The other family was intimately known and a great deal of help of many kinds had been given; at the end the total income had been greatly increased and seems to have been sufficient to justify a move; the visitor might also, it would seem, have been in a position to exert some influence in the matter. She may, of course, have attempted to do so, or may have been quite sure, for good reasons, that the attempt would be useless; or may merely have overlooked the question, though in a case where exceptionally thorough work was done this hardly seems probable. (Selected record. Not known to any social agency.)

In two other cases of undesirable housing no action was taken.

Perhaps if other events had not occurred to break up the Buick home a move from the "dark, damp" rooms occupied would have been made, as the young mother was fully alive to the need of better quarters. In the other case the visitor encouraged the family to seek an apartment with better light and air, but up to the date of reading none had been found. With the present extreme shortage in housing accommodations this is not surprising. (Selected records. First unknown to other social agencies; second known to a family society and three other agencies.)

Four families actually did move to better quarters. In two of these cases we have no evidence (except, in one instance, the increase of rent from $9.00 to $11) as to improved conditions in the new rooms; the visitor does not seem to have seen them in advance nor to have commented upon them in the record afterward. In the other two, rather odd situations arose.

A great deal of pressure had been brought to bear on Mr. Carnegie to get him to the point of moving his family from three poor rooms, two interior, in a "shabby, dirty, smelly" house in a bad neighborhood, which are said to have been rented at $5.00; but the visitor was quite overcome to find the family one day installed in "four bright, airy rooms" at $15, and straightway took up with them the question of a smaller apartment or a roomer—without result, to the date of reading. (Cross-section record. Known to a family society and another social agency.)

Mrs. Neary was moved twice; the first time it seems to have been not bad housing but a belief that the woman should be near her mother, which led the visitor to insist as she did on the change. She personally visited the new rooms and paid for them in advance, reporting: "Found that the rooms have been newly painted and papered and all three have windows that admit sunlight. The rooms are small and in the rear, but there is a private toilet and the neighborhood seems very quiet." After this it is a surprise when, some nine months later, another visitor backed the woman in her desire to move to a front apartment on an upper story, explaining to the landlord that "the Red Cross could not think of letting one of its families live in such a dark, damp place." As we have not seen the rooms we can only confess ourself puzzled. The season may possibly in part account for the difference in judgment, the first inspection reported having been in August, the second in May. (Selected record. Not known to any social agency.)

In one other instance the visitor exerted a decided influence in bringing about a move. Here it was not the house that was objectionable but the location—in a very bad neighborhood facing on railway tracks. The visitor encouraged the mother in her plan, at her request visited the new apartment she had found, and having approved it gave her the money for the first deposit. (Cross-section record. Known to a family society.)

To one familiar with housing conditions in Manhattan it seems certain that among the five-hundred-odd families whose records were read there were a number of others who were living in unfit quarters. If such situations were overlooked the oversight was probably due in part to a lack of training in housing standards, in part to the extreme pressure of work which accounts for so many sins of omission on the part of the Home Service visitors. The growing scarcity of available apartments during the period covered should also be borne in mind.

CHAPTER IX

RELIEF PROBLEMS

In considering the vital problems involved in the administration of relief by Home Service, statistics can give us little or no aid. The wisdom of decisions as to whether relief shall be given at all, and if so how, in what amounts, and under what conditions, can only be judged case by case, taking into account all the complex factors which render each family situation different from any other. There are, however, certain considerations having a general bearing on the case-work problems involved which may be statistically expressed and which it is proposed to set forth in a brief preliminary statement, even though the value of the data presented is recognized as very slight.

General Considerations

First, then, it is of some little interest to inquire in what proportion of the cases read in the two periods the question of giving financial aid seems to have been considered, and in what proportion of cases such aid was actually given.

Taking the 217 case records dating from May, 1918, we find that in 127, or 59 per cent, the possible need of a grant or loan was apparently considered, while in 84, or 39 per cent, financial aid was actually given in larger or smaller amounts. Of the 237 records dating from May, 1919, on the other hand, only 35, or 15 per cent, contained evidence that the giving of relief had been considered, and in only 24, or 10 per cent, was a grant or loan actually made.

The great difference between the proportions in the two periods is, as has been already pointed out, to be explained chiefly by the fact that in 1919 many of the cases coming to Home Service was purely inquiry cases, while such cases were comparatively rare in 1918.

However, that the above fact does not fully explain the difference between the incidence of relief problems in the two periods appears when we restrict our consideration to the groups of cases involving peace-time case work problems—168 in the 1918, and 77 in the 1919 period.[1] For on this basis the records in which the question of giving financial aid was considered formed 76 per cent of the 1918 group and 45 per cent of the 1919 group, while those in which relief was actually given formed 50 per cent and 31 per cent in the two periods respectively.

It is evident, then, that an additional explanation of the difference in proportion of families possibly needing financial aid and families actually aided in the two periods must be sought. Probably such an explanation is to be found in the supposition that families which had succeeded in getting through the war period without resort to the Red Cross were likely to be possessed of more ample resources, and so naturally more frequently came to the Home Service Section, when they came, for forms of service not involving financial aid.

However this may be, the point of chief interest is that, of a group of impartially chosen cases originating in the midst of the war period, less than 60 per cent involved any question of relief and less than 40 per cent received financial aid; while even in a more restricted group of records which presented case work problems, only 76 per cent, or just over three-fourths, involved such questions and only 50 per cent, or exactly one-half, received such aid.

An attempt was also made to determine whether any difference in status between families receiving and families not receiving relief could be determined by the test of their previous acquaintance with relief-giving agencies. We have record of such acquaintance, or its lack, for 351 families. One hundred of these received relief from Home Service, and of these just 25 had previously been known to relief-giving agencies; 251 never received relief, and of these 12 per cent (31) had been known to such agencies. As this second group includes many of the mere inquiry cases, it is interesting to find that even so many as 31, or 12 per cent, had been in contact with agencies giving relief;[2]

[1] In these restricted groups are of course included all cases in which the giving of relief seems to have been considered.

[2] This includes the three family societies and two other agencies that give relief.

while it is certainly enlightening to learn that approximately three-fourths[1] of the group of families given financial aid by Home Service were receiving such help for the first time.

Returning to the cases in which relief in some form and amount was given—84 in the 1918 and 24 in the 1919 group—it will be interesting, as we consider the policies governing decisions and detailed methods of administration involved, to divide them into three groups: (1) cases in which the only relief given was in the form of grants or loans for special purposes—as transportation, vacations, hospital expenses, or clothing—a small and fairly clear-cut group; (2) cases in which single or occasional grants or loans were given, largely of an emergency character, to cover general living expenses—often in addition to grants or loans for special purposes; and (3) cases in which an allowance, or planned regular help over a period of time, was given—often in addition to relief of the two types already described. This classification is based not at all on *amount* of relief given. For example, the second class included cases in which a single dollar or $5.00 was granted in an emergency, and—at the other extreme—one in which successive loans or grants totalling over eighty dollars were made; and the third class, cases where a quart of milk a day, sent regularly for a month or more, was the only relief given, a few in which an allowance was started and immediately discontinued, and still others in which the total expenses of a family, amounting to hundreds of dollars, were borne for a year or more.

While there is no particular significance in the figures, it may be noted in passing that of the 108 cases, 41 received an allowance (in the meaning given above);[2] 54, single or occasional grants or loans to meet emergent or miscellaneous needs, but no allowance; and 13, grants or loans for special clearly defined purposes only.

Among the selected cases it is not surprising to find the percentage of cases receiving relief much higher than among the cases chosen at

---

[1] A family's having been known to an agency which gives relief is of course far from being proof that it received relief.

[2] It should be stated that we have not always followed the terminology of the cash cards kept in the treasurer's office in deciding which were allowance cases, but have determined our classification by what seemed to be the facts of the case. It is quite possible that another person might have classed some few cases differently, but we believe that the grouping given is approximately correct.

random, since naturally illustrations of the best case treatment in their divisions would be chosen by the supervisors from among the cases on which most intensive work had been done, which are usually those presenting the most numerous and difficult problems; and these seem ordinarily to occur, or at least are usually discovered, in families where the income is deficient. As a matter of fact, of the 77 selected cases read, 69, or nine out of every 10, did receive relief and in 55 cases, or in eight out of every 10 receiving relief, the relief was in the form of allowances.

A question which we should like to be able to answer is: In what proportion of cases was the need of relief wholly the result of war-time conditions, and in particular of failures in the working of the government plan of allotments and allowances; and in what proportion would that need have existed even had the man not been in the service? A very brief experiment was, however, sufficient to convince us that in a large proportion of cases a clear-cut answer to this question was impossible. It is evident enough that financial need in a family where the son in service never made regular contributions to the family income, or contributed only enough to pay his own board, cannot be due to his absence in service; and that such need in the family where the husband and father had been the sole and adequate support is clearly due to war conditions. But what of the family where the son in service had formerly contributed $40 or $50 a month to the family pocketbook, in place of which a $25 allotment and allowance check now comes from the government in his absence; while a younger sister, also a contributor to the family income, suddenly breaks down and has to go to a sanatorium? What of the family of which the head was an irregular supporter, due to misfortune or bad habits, so that it is impossible to say whether the income from the government does or does not equal his former contributions? These are only examples; the combinations of causes operating in individual cases are almost infinitely varied.

The question of how far other possible sources of financial aid were tapped before relief other than emergency was given by Home Service is hard to answer, as there is a marked difference in this regard in different divisions. There are many instances where the relatives were pressed to contribute in the traditional manner; for example, the case of old Mrs. Ames, where it was decided that the children should support their mother and the allowance begun was stopped. At the other extreme are cases where, even when there were known to be well-to-do relatives, no attempt to get help from these was made—for example, the case of Mrs. Dutcher (page 44), and that of Mrs. Drew (page 42).

The mother of the latter had a prosperous rooming house in a good locality which her daughter said she had recently bought; but though she was visited, no effort seems to have been made to induce her to help her daughter. She was a German in sympathies as well as birth, and not on the best of terms with her daughter's family as she had never approved of her early marriage and had not been able to get on with the grandchildren when the attempt to combine the two households had been made; so that Mrs. Drew had thought it best to withdraw and take a little apartment of her own, the rent of which was just about the amount by which her income from the government fell short. These facts may furnish the explanation of why no approach to the mother on the financial side was made before the allowance of $15 a month was arranged for Mrs. Drew. (Selected record. Not known to any social agency.)

The Withholding of Relief

Among the cases in which the giving of relief seems to have been considered, but none was given, many different types of family and of situation are represented. Several families whom the Section was asked to visit because of supposed financial need were surprised at the call and stated that they were in no need. Several others admitted difficulties but wished to get on if possible without aid, or absolutely refused to consider it though obviously in sore straits. In the case of one woman who asked help the St. Vincent de Paul Society was consulted and reported that she had an income of about $80 a month. A boy for whom a scholarship had been arranged decided to take a job at $15 a week. A number of families in fair circumstances, though with depleted incomes owing to the absence of sons in service, were refused loans. Whenever it was evident that a family had resources which put it beyond the need of a grant, it was naturally a question whether a loan might not better be sought by it through the ordinary channels, as from friends or business associates, than from the Red Cross; and though we have sometimes questioned whether the refusal was wise, we have in none of these cases been prepared to maintain that it was surely a mistake.

One husband in service wrote—the letter of an educated gentleman—asking that his wife be aided. The wife, visited, said that a loan was not an absolute necessity, and spoke of relatives to whom she was going as able to help. The husband, in reply to a letter reporting on this call, wrote that his wife's statement had been dictated by pride. Another visit was paid but she had left town to go to the relatives previously mentioned. Was there a real need here, which the wife had been unwilling to confess—possibly because of something in the personality or manner of the visitor which made such confession difficult? Or had the husband, who wrote of having read a Red Cross booklet and of "feeling quite relieved," mis-read what was said therein and had false hopes raised? (Cross-section record.)

There are a few cases, however, in which all the evidence given points to the need of relief.

Young Mrs. Baronez lived with her baby in a well kept three-room apartment for which she owed two months' rent, and—no allotment having come through—was dependent for her food on a poor cobbler uncle with a family of his own. The uncle was not seen nor was any investigation made. A week after the first visit a letter written to the man's commanding officer who had referred the case stated that the "wife and baby have no visible means of support and are being fed by an old uncle." The next visit recorded is over a month later, when a check for $76 had, happily, arrived. (Cross-section record. Not known to any social agency.)

Such also was the case in the Schiff family—father, mother, and five children under working age, the one boy earning having left to go into the service about a month before. Their apartment was neat and well furnished, though in a dirty, run-down house, and all the evidence points to their being a good type of family. The father had been ill and out of work for four weeks. The little girls were reported by a clinic to be suffering from malnutrition. Perhaps the existence of a married son who was said to be earning well explains the lack of aid, but we confess to not being satisfied. (Cross-section record. Known only to a diet kitchen.)

It seems hardly worth while to take space for the three or four similar cases that might be mentioned. Facts known to the visitor though not appearing in the record might, of course, explain most of them.

Grants and Loans for Special Purposes

Among the cases, of which there were 13 among the cross-section records of the two periods, where the only relief given was in the form of grants or loans for special clearly defined purposes, transportation was the commonest special need met, appearing in seven.

In three instances comparatively small grants were made, ranging from $12 to $32. One was to enable an ex-soldier who had rashly left a Canadian tuberculosis hospital to return to Canada where he promised to place himself again under care; one was to enable a mother to go South to visit a tuberculous soldier son in a government sanatorium; the third was sent, through the Home Service Section of the town where he was sojourning, to a somewhat erratic young man recently out of service who was stranded at a distance and who stated that he wished to return to his family in New York. He used the money to go to Washington, a fact apparently indicating that the Section in question handed him the cash instead of buying his ticket and seeing him on the train.

In three other instances large loans of $73 to $150 were made. The smallest, covering back board in New York as well as a ticket home, was advanced on the request of a Southern Home Service Section to a young colored man stranded here and was promptly repaid by his father, a prosperous farmer. The other two were for the transportation of young wives of soldiers to points in the distant West. They were made after exchange of telegrams, in one case with the man's family, in the other with the Section which interviewed his mother, and in both instances were promptly repaid.

The seventh case was more complex. A young man in service came to the Home Service Section asking to have some one meet his wife at a Pacific port where she was soon to arrive and start her on her journey to New York. His family, who were visited, appeared to be prosperous and respectable and he advanced $50 toward expenses. A long correspondence, chiefly by telegraph, was entered into with the Home Service Section at the port, but the wife proved illusive, appearing and disappearing at irregular intervals much to the distress of the young husband. Finally the Western Section sent word that they had bought the ticket to New York and that the young woman was to arrive on a certain day. She did not appear, and some little time later the young man received a letter from her stating that she had sold the ticket and gone to another city. He was very naturally indignant at the failure of the Home Service Section to see his wife on the train, though clearly mistaken in attributing her failure to arrive to this cause as there are many points west of New York at which one not wishing to finish her journey could have dropped off. His demand for the return of the $50 he had advanced was not granted, but the New York Home Service Section lost a considerably larger sum advanced by the Section in the West. Review of the case does not, however, reveal any fault in the correspondence, the one mistake made having been that of entrusting her ticket to an obviously unreliable young woman. (Cross-section record. Not known to any social agency. See page 169 for previous mention of this case.)

In two cases the special grants made were to cover hospital expenses—one, confinement expenses of a soldier's wife at the Booth Memorial Hospital ($17); the other a bill of $146, which the British recruiting officer acknowledged responsibility for on account of promises made to a new recruit.

In two other cases trusses were provided, one for the father and one for the mother of a man in service. In four cases (one of which also received a transportation grant while another was one of the truss cases just mentioned) vacations were paid for. In one of these the children of a tuberculous mother were sent to a sanatorium for Hebrew children while she was in the country; in another a young girl's board in the country was paid for a week and her wages for the same period made up to her—she was badly run down following an attack of influenza. In the third the little sister of an ex-soldier was sent to the country, to return "much improved"; and in the fourth, $70 was spent in giving the two children of a soldier a vacation.

In all the above 13 cases expenditures were fully justified, and the only errors noted were those of the two co-operating Sections which failed to put their clients on the trains which they were supposed to take.

In most of these cases, also, it is clear, from the record, that the financial help given was adequate to the need. This is not true, however, in three instances.

In one we have to do with a young wife and mother of three small children, "a good looking young woman with a pleasant smile" of whom it is said that "notwithstanding a winter of anxiety she seems to have retained all her sweetness of disposition." This is about all we are told of her, except that she is a waitress earning $6.00 a week, and asks a loan of $25 to carry her along until her allotment and allowance check arrives. No facts to explain why this service was not rendered are given, and it is of course quite probable that the visitor, in discussing the young wife's situation with her, found that there were other resources—such as income from tips—which might tide her over. It was about six weeks later that the opportunity to send two of the children to the country was offered and accepted, and nothing is told us of the financial or health situation, then or later. (Cross-section record. Not known to any social agency.)

The second case where the adequacy of the relief given seems doubtful is that of the mother who was sent south to visit her tuberculous son. The family was a most respectable Bohemian one, living in five "extremely neat" rooms, and at the time when this was done another son had been discharged and was working. But eight months earlier all three of the sons had been in service and an allotment and allowance, amounting to $25, was being received for only one; the mother and little daughter, the latter earning $7.00 a week, were at home alone and were owing two months' rent.

Again it is probable that the visitor took up the situation carefully with the mother and found that for some reason financial aid was not needed; but the record fails to give the explanation which might have satisfied us. Fortunately the most difficult period for the family was brief, as one son was almost immediately discharged. (Cross-section record.)

The third doubtful case is that of the mother and daughter mentioned on page 105. From the report of the visit paid just after the girl's return to work following her attack of influenza we cannot be sure that financial relief was needed; but in view of her seriously rundown condition several months later, said to date from this illness, we are led to suspect that convalescent care or a special temporary allowance to build her up would have proved the stitch in time. (Cross-section record. Not known to any social agency.)

Emergency and Occasional Relief

There is probably no group of cases about which there is less of interest to say than about the cases in which emergency relief alone was given, or emergency relief combined with minor grants for what we have defined as special purposes. The families were in general little known, and the more serious problems calling for case work, whether or not they existed, were not discovered. In almost half the cases relief was given on only one occasion—once in the form of a grocery order, once in the form of a payment for medicine, 16 times in the form of cash payments of less than $10 (three times of $1 only, usually $5.00) and six times in the form of payments of $10 or more, the largest being a rent payment of $22 made direct to a landlord. There were also a few cases in which there were two small grants, one in cash and one in goods, a few in which there were two cash payments (the largest totaling $30), and one in which, in addition to $5.00 in cash, $7.75 was paid out for an abdominal bandage. There remain 17 cases in which relief was given three or more times, in a few of which there was an approach to the more thorough acquaintance and the sort of planning usually given a family which receives an allowance. The value of relief given in these 17 cases ranged from less than $10 (in the one instance where the client was given food and lodging but no cash beyond a few cents for fuel) to $89.

What shall we say of the manner of handling the relief problems in this most miscellaneous group of cases? To begin with, rather less than half of them can be classed as pure emergency cases which never became anything more. Such an one is presented by the soldier who appeared with an attractive young wife whom he had married three days before, asking care for her over night as he was entirely out of funds and must return to his post. She was placed at the Young Women's Christian Association Hostess House, and next day, when he came in to say that he had made arrangements to have her received on the island where he was stationed, he was given a dollar for luncheon—since when no word has ever been received from the couple. Such were the several cases in which embarrassment was due to nonreceipt or delay of checks, which arrived within a few days of the granting of relief and, as there was no later application, probably continued to come with sufficient regularity to meet needs. Such was the case of the wife whose check was delayed, who was moving and claimed to be not well and who, after the move, was never heard from again.

In a few of these cases the reviewer is in some doubt as to the wisdom of giving aid—which is not strange, as the visitor was probably in more doubt, and inevitably, in view of the need for quick decision on insufficient data. But in the main, so far as it is possible to judge from the records, action was right so far as it went and there was usually some fairly obvious reason why it did not go any farther. In only two instances did later investigation reveal that relief had been given on false pretenses; in one the entire story of a man seen only once at the office proved to be false, including (probably) his claim to be a discharged soldier; in the other, a particularly clever bit of investigation disclosed the fact that a man who had claimed to be out of work really had a large, successful-appearing business of his own. In another case two $5.00 grants had been made before it was discovered that the family was under the care of a family society and receiving an allowance from them.

In two instances there was an unexplained gap or total lapse in the treatment. In one of these the visitor, reporting on a call, states that no money had been given, as the regular visitor was due there on Friday and the client "seemed to have enough to tide her over till then"—after which a gap in the record of nearly a month occurs. However, as already elsewhere pointed out, there is little to be gained from a rehearsal of such sins of omission as one can never be sure as to causes—beyond the general, ever-present one of excessive pressure of work.

Some of these small grants were for fairly definite purposes. Thus, in one instance $5.00 was given to help a mother move from an especially undesirable neighborhood facing on railway tracks. In another, the $7.00 given was specified to be for clothing for a child, the relatives agreeing to meet other needs; in still another, $6.00 was given for shoes for the children. In five cases rent was paid. This was rather exceptional action for the Section, as soldiers' families came under the protection of the Civil Rights bill and were in no danger of being ousted until three months behind with their rent, and the cases contain no special explanation of it. Three of the families were decidedly above the average in standards of living and seem to have made an especially favorable impression. Insistence by the superintendent of the building that the May rent be paid before June first, taken with the delicacy and unusual sincerity and uncomplainingness of the mother and the high terms in which the superintendent spoke of her, may very likely account for the action in one case; serious illness of the father in one, and death of the father in another case may be responsible; in a fourth, the request was for a loan pending receipt of a government check, and rent for one of the two months advanced was actually repaid; in the fifth, a Canadian case, a check arrived soon after the single payment of a month's rent and the family was able to manage thereafter. In none of these cases is there any special ground for criticism; though in several, investigation was slight or almost lacking so that one cannot be sure as to the wisdom of action taken. We all know that in times of emergency pressure such risks have to be run.

Turning to the cases in which relief cannot be classified as emergency merely, what shall we say of its administration?

In general, as we might expect, these families are better known than those who received one or two emergency grants only, and reasons for action emerge more clearly. There are several in which ill-health clearly created the need for relief and in which that need seems to have been fully met.

Mrs. Winship, living alone now that her son is in the army, was thought by her physician to be in need of an operation for appendicitis. She is described as having "auburn hair and a very sweet personality," and had been a seamstress. In the hospital where Home Service had arranged to pay $14 a week for her, her blood count showed a poor condition and it was decided not to operate. At the end of a week she came home very much in need of building up, and during the next ten weeks seven small sums, aggregating $37, were given her at irregular intervals to supplement her income and enable her to get into better shape. Evidently she must have improved, as at the end of this time she took a position as housekeeper for a physician. When next seen, four months later, she was recovering from the postponed operation and was very well situated; her son had returned and gone to work. (Cross-section record. Not known to any social agency.)

A young vaudeville actress whose husband had enlisted in the Canadian forces was ill and out of work and had not yet received her pay. Aid was given her at first in meeting living expenses, then to help her get off to another city where better work awaited her. It amounted, during about eight weeks (part of which she worked at a job found her by the Red Cross Employment Bureau) to $50. We have no criticism to offer on this or any other phase of the work in this case. (Cross-section record. Not known to any social agency.)

Mrs. Tierney was reported by her first visitor as a "very nice and neat appearing woman," and her rooms were said to be "very neat" though "very scarcely furnished." She had made arrangements to be confined at home and relief amounting to some $37 was given during the period of her illness. It was not until she was up and about again that her history (under another name) was discovered, and a very different line of action found necessary. The relief given was clearly called for in the circumstances and seems to have been adequate. (Cross-section record. Known to a family society.)

"A most attractive-looking colored woman," living in a very neat and well-furnished apartment of five rooms, was aided in securing her allowance and allotment and loaned $10 pending its receipt. Several months later, after her confinement (for which she had made all arrangements herself) she appeared one day at the office with the baby, "a picture of neatness," and "very hesitatingly asked for a little help." Five dollars then and a similar sum a week later were given. Presumably a delayed check then arrived as there was no later record of action. (Cross-section record. Not known to any social agency.)

One of the most appealing cases in our collection (though not one of the most desperately needy from a purely financial standpoint) is that of an old father who, when his son enlisted, had held a small position in which he barely supported himself, but who had since been disabled by rheumatism and was very feeble. He was living with two unmarried daughters in the home of a married daughter and found dependence upon his son-in-law very painful. While efforts were being made to secure an allotment from the son a little help was given him from time to time to provide and repair glasses or supply some pressing need, and the old man's pathetic efforts to find work were seconded; but the request of the family for $10 a month toward his board was not granted, even after the son had written that he had made allotment and applied for an allowance. It is probable that the total income of the family was sufficient to meet absolute necessities—though as the dietitian was not called in we cannot be sure of this—and that Home Service was justified in refusing the allowance; but we confess that this is one of the cases in which we should have liked to see a little concession made to a psychological feature of the situation—the evident mental suffering of the old man. (Cross-section record. Known only to a church.)

A father incapacited for work, a mother, and one daughter, a milliner earning $12, were found living in what was described as a good class apartment in a good neighborhood, rent $37.50. The son in service was an accountant and had claimed that his parents were entirely dependent upon him, but had been drafted nevertheless, there being a record of his father's earning $40 during the preceding month and $750 during the preceding year. Ten dollars was given the mother on one occasion when she called at the office, but the visitor seems to have felt strongly that there was no very acute need; and after the mother's death, by accident, an apparently well-to-do relative appeared and took charge, who, at last accounts, was engaging a $35 apartment for the father and daughter. (Cross-section record. Not known to any social agency.)

The one case in all this group which to our mind was most evidently ill-handled should be cited, since its mistakes are not traceable to the pressure which makes it unprofitable to discuss the majority of shortcomings.

Mrs. Hartmann, pregnant and with a baby of ten months, came to the attention of the Section immediately after her husband's induction into service, as he had been a poor provider and she was left quite without resources. Her three rooms are described as "clean and comfortable though sparsely furnished." Her mother was a widow with three children at home, struggling along with the aid of a pension from the Child Welfare Board, and there appears to have been no other relative or friend able to help. During a period of six weeks, up to the date of arrival of her first check, Mrs. Hartmann was aided irregularly, usually to the extent of $2.00 or $3.00 at a time, the total given in this period being $24. Just how she was expected to live is not clear; one is loath to believe that it was intended that she should depend upon her mother. Perhaps the niggardliness of the relief given is explained in part by the fact that during this time, although the husband was still in this country, the wife was being urged to give up her home and go out to service with her baby. While she repeatedly agreed to this plan she never acted upon it. What she actually did—during a period of several months following this first period when she was unvisited by Home Service—was to give up her home and follow her husband to camp, an act which he bitterly resented.

It is hard to avoid the conclusion that responsibility for this action, with its train of unfortunate consequences, is to be laid in part at the door of an inadequate relief policy and unwise advice. (Cross-section record. Known to a family society and to five other agencies.)

An interesting contrast to the case just cited is presented by the family, of all this group, upon which the largest sum of money was expended. Little was learned from outside sources about this family and that little was not to their credit.

A husband and wife, accompanied by the man's mother, appeared in the office one day, recent arrivals from a city in the Middle West. Mrs. Russell, a cashier and bookkeeper, did most of the talking: she had married Russell recently, she said, upon his discharge, in fulfilment of a promise, although he was in very bad nervous shape. Soon afterward he had disappeared, and she and the mother had been so distracted with anxiety that when a letter was received from him in New York they used all the money they had to follow him there, and all three were now stranded and anxious to secure transportation home. Her marriage certificate, she said, was in a certain buffet drawer in her apartment.

The telegram of inquiry to the Home Service Section in the family's home city brought word that no certificate could be found and that transportation would not be given as the man had left the hospital in debt and had misappropriated subscription funds. Evidently the wife had made a decidedly favorable impression, and when the couple were thus left high and dry and she announced their intention of getting work and earning enough to pay their way home, the temporary arrangement which had been made for them at the Salvation Army Hotel was extended until they should get started. The mother meanwhile borrowed enough to pay her way home. Both the husband and wife did find themselves jobs, and she at least worked persistently; he met with an accident and had to lie by for a time. In all, $89 was expended as a loan, largely in hotel bills, upon the couple, who at last accounts were both working. What finally became of them does not appear. This is one of the cases, typical of Home Service, in which the benefit of every possible doubt seems to have been given in dubious circumstances; we confess a liking for the mental attitude shown, even though we cannot declare our certainty that this couple could not have managed with less than was given, and even though—as was certainly to be expected from their story—no dollar of their indebtedness to Home Service has ever been paid off. A full report of an adequate investigation in their home town might have thrown a clearer light upon their situation and needs. (Cross-section record. Not known to any social agency.)

The case of a young American wife of a Canadian soldier illustrates the more or less distinctive handling which we shall find characteristic of Canadian allowance cases.

Like many British and Canadian cases it was referred by the Recruiting Mission, so that the status of the wife was to a certain extent known. Her rent was due and she owed $87 on her furniture—debts from the forced collection of which she was not, as were the wives of our own soldiers, protected by the Civil Rights Bill. On the first visit $20 was given and a card of instructions left in case of future need; and two or three months later, when she was in poor health, the wife was aided with additional grants bringing the total to $40. She had been living alone in a "very clean little apartment of four rooms," rent $14, and had been working when able; but when, a month after the last grant, it was found that she had moved to a $21 apartment, was receiving $45 from Canada regularly and earning $40, it was decided that "she could manage," though she asked help again. (Cross-section record. Not known to any social agency.)

Naturally, in a group of cases receiving occasional unplanned relief, one would not expect to find a high percentage of returns on loans; contacts were too easily lost and the amounts involved did not make an effort to secure return seem especially worth while. There are, however, a few cases worth citing as instances of return or non-return of loans.

A professional dancer was temporarily embarrassed but expected to go to work in a few days. Little investigation was possible beyond verification of her engagement, as she was from out of town, a transient at a hotel. After she had been loaned $15 a report was received that she was earning $300 a week and that her husband was a professional gambler. A fortnight later she appeared at the office to repay her debt. (Cross-section record. Not known to any social agency.)

Another loan that was repaid was one of $10 made to a janitress to enable her to move to rooms where she would be free to go out to work. (Cross-section record. Known to a family society.)

A young wife, temporarily unable to work on account of pregnancy, was advanced $30 in all; meanwhile she had returned to work, and finally received two checks for $30 allotment and allowance, which she decided to spend on replenishing her wardrobe, waiting until the following month to repay her debt. Before this time arrived she had disappeared, leaving no address; but when she was located several months later and visited at her place of business, she promptly repaid all she owed. (Cross-section record. Not known to any social agency.)

This is the only one of the cases on which there was repayment where the method of handling, involving as it did a perfectly definite follow-up, was clearly responsible for the outcome.

A characteristic "after care" problem involving a loan not returned is presented by the discharged soldier who reported himself just taking a job and asked an advance. The only investigation made was in verification of his possession of the alleged job. Loans amounting to $25 were made in the course of a week and an effort made to persuade the landlord not to dispossess the young couple. When next called upon they were found to have moved to Brooklyn. Efforts to collect the loan were unavailing. (Cross-section record. Not known to any social agency.)

In another similar case—except that this young couple were childless—a much more careful investigation of work references was made, with results entirely favorable to both man and wife, and nearly $40 was advanced. It has never been repaid, though at last accounts both were working. No effort to secure return of this loan seems to have been made. (Cross-section record. Not known to any social agency.)

The instances are obviously too few to permit the drawing of deductions regarding the relative likelihood of return of loans by wives in the absence of husbands and by the returned husbands themselves. We are reminded by the last two cases cited, however, of a statement made to us by several of the supervisors of the Section to the effect that the returned men were more likely than their wives to repudiate debts contracted in their absence. The cases cited above do not, of course, fall into this class as the loans were made to the men themselves.

Among these cases there are naturally a number in which, after one or more small loans or grants, an additional request was made which was refused. The reasons for refusal are usually at least as obvious as the reasons for previous acquiescence; indeed, we have record of no refusal which seems to us clearly unjustified, unless it be in one case when it is not evident what had occurred between the payment of a first month's rent and the refusal of a second to account for the different answer.

The Olivers indeed presented many unprepossessing features: the mother had a record for drink, though she had not been seen intoxicated, the home was "dingy and ill kept" as well as dark, and the boys were truants. Still, all these facts had been known at the time of the first grant, and no facts as to larger resources appear to have come to light in the interval. It was probably a case in which much work and much money would have brought small results; still we are not quite satisfied that a very full investigation should have been followed by so little action, and are just a bit inclined to sympathize with the disappointment and irritation which the family too forcibly expressed; for after all, the father who had supported them had died and no substitute for his income was in sight. (Cross-section record. Not known to any social agency.)

Another case of refusal may be cited as one in which the grounds of action were wholly clear.

Bauman had thrown over his wife because of the birth, in his absence, of a child not his. A small amount of relief had been given to the wife before she had found a position in which she was supporting herself and her two children. But when the husband asked a loan of $20 to help establish himself in a news-stand he was very definitely told he could not have it as he was already earning enough to support himself. (Cross-section record. Known to a family society, the Bureau of Domestic Relations, and another agency.)

All the cases which have been discussed thus far, under both "special purpose" and "emergency or occasional" relief, have been from the cross-section groups. Among the selected cases there are but 14 which can be classed under either of the above heads. Thirteen of them received emergency or occasional relief, and there is nothing of special interest to be said of them with the exception of three, in which large grants or loans for special purposes were made as well.

One of these is the case of the psychoneurotic girl rescued after seven years' confinement, whose case is discussed on page 125. Over four hundred dollars had been expended up to the date when we read the record in the treatment which brought Hannah O'Neil up from the depths in which she was found to the threshold of a normal life. As already pointed out, one measure in her behalf, though taken under expert advice, turned out badly; but, in spite of this, and even if she should never become a fully independent and self-supporting human unit, we are convinced that the money was on the whole well expended. (Selected record. Known to a family society.)

The second case that seems to us worthy of special comment is that of Larkin, a deserter from the Army. When his young wife became known to the Section he was in a camp stockade and she was within two months of her confinement. Both proved to be of excellent character: the wife was an exceptionally fine, honest young woman; the husband, in sheer desperation at her situation, had run away to come home and take care of her. She was helped through a period of several months when ill health incapacitated her, and was always co-operative, intelligent, and appreciative of everything done for her. The husband, meanwhile, had been sent to a disciplinary barracks in the West, and when he was released the Section paid his transportation home, a loan which he returned only a little more than a month later. (Selected record. Not known to any social agency.)

The third and last instance to be cited under this head, and also the most striking—as representing probably the widest divergence in relief practice from that of established social agencies which Home Service has to offer—has already been mentioned. (See page 48.) Clement Evans, a young professional man, had thrown up a good position in the Far East on our entrance into the war and, with his wife, had come rushing home. After a year and a half in service as a captain his savings were exhausted. He was very anxious to return to the East where he was promised an excellent opening, and asked a loan of $1,500 to enable him to do so. Meanwhile he took temporary work and was loaned $50 to carry him along until the question of the larger loan could be considered. Investigation showed that he was of good standing in his profession and personally; the case was brought before the consultation committee and it voted to make the $1,500 loan. The original loan of $50 was returned before he left New York; in the year following only one letter has been received from him, written on his journey, and the $1,500 has not yet been returned. An insurance policy on his life had been taken out by the Section to cover the amount of the loan, and the second premium has been paid by him.

We have already confessed that we are disposed to differ from the decision of the consultation committee in this case. The man had work in New York which promised fairly well, and his wife expressed the opinion that it would be better for him to work and accumulate the money to take them back to the East or to wait for some other opening; she even says, in a late interview, that her husband is becoming resigned to the probable delay. We cannot see that there was sufficient reason for risking so large a sum of money—for however honest the man, it is evident that there was a risk. (Selected record. Not known to any social agency.)

Allowances

The cases grouped under this head are somewhat less numerous among the cross-section cases than were those receiving emergency and occasional relief, but among the selected records they form a large majority. In all, 96 cases—41 cross-section, 55 selected—contain record of an allowance given for a longer or shorter period. It is of course understood that many of these received also relief for special purposes and emergency or occasional relief before, during, or after the periods when allowances were given. We shall here concern ourselves, however, chiefly with the allowances.

These divide naturally into those planned by the dietitian of the Section on the basis of a scientific budget, and those not so planned. As the dietitian came to the Section in October, 1918, all allowances given prior to that month were without the benefit of her planning and it naturally took her several months to work through all the records needing her review. When once she had got abreast of the current work she was supposed to plan all new allowances given in any of the divisions, and to review each such case once in three months so as to make sure that changes in the family situation and changes in prices were duly considered and any needed modifications made. To this rule there seem to have been some exceptions, especially among allowances planned for relatively short periods.

Forty-four cases read by us—9 among the cross-section group, 35 among the selected—had benefited by the dietitian's planning. Many of these had of course been receiving allowances before her first review, and it is of especial interest to note the changes made under the new budget system. The great majority of the cross-section allowance cases, on the other hand, and a number of selected cases, never reached her hands. These it will be well to consider first, especially such of them as represent the earlier efforts of the Section to solve problems of continued relief. Canadian and British cases also form a special group which received somewhat different treatment from others.

Eight cases are grouped together because the only thing entitling them to be considered allowance cases was that milk (or milk and eggs) was regularly sent in for over a month. In six of them the presence of a small baby was probably the deciding factor in determining the giving of the milk; a small amount of emergency or occasional relief was also given.

In two of these cases relief was evidently closely restricted because the male head of the family was at home and should have been supporting. There were rumors of property in another which, though not verified in the very careful investigation made, probably influenced the visitor against the giving of larger relief. In this and a fourth case young mothers of babies about a year old were urged, at the time the milk allowance was discontinued, to go out to work. Both were living with their own families and were said to be in sufficiently good health; but whether the advice was wise or not we really do not feel able to say from the facts given. It was not taken in one case; in the other we do not know the outcome. The fifth mother was scarcely ever found at home and did not accept the invitation given to call at the office, so that the lapsing of the relief was inevitable. The sixth was living with her mother's family in a very comfortable old-fashioned ten-room house in the Bronx, but said she could not afford the milk her baby needed since it had been weaned.

The two remaining cases involved older children in delicate health.

The father of three small children in one was abusive and did not give proper support. The mother was urged to bring court action, and the milk was ordered at this time to supplement the earnings of the eldest daughter; but when the couple made up their differences this aid was withdrawn. (Selected record. Not known to any social agency.)

The last case was that of the little tuberculous girl, Emilia Vaccaro, whose treatment is described on page 54. As there was a father at home working, and as the son in service had married and so would not be coming back to help, those in charge decided to refuse the request for aid made when his allotment and allowance ceased to come; but when the mother asked milk for the child it was not refused. This concession was surely justified—indeed a larger one, to cover a complete building-up diet, would have been if a budget study had proved it necessary; as no such study was made we cannot judge whether the aid given was sufficient or not. The basis, stated above, on which the general refusal of aid was grounded, does, however, seem to us a wrong one, being in apparent conflict with the principle that Home Service help to families of soldiers was not to be limited to needs which those soldiers would have met if at home.[1] This case originated in 1919, so that it should have been possible to benefit by the dietitian's budget study. (Cross-section record. Not known to any social agency.)

Passing from this small special group of milk-allowance cases to the much larger one in which cash allowances were given, we shall find it best to split it up into smaller groups. Under some heads we shall discuss only a few examples, as many cases have already been covered under other topics,[2] while in others the relief problem *per se* is not of especial interest.

Such a group is that of expectant mothers, all of whom have been mentioned under Pregnancy and Confinement. (Pages 94 to 102.) Of the five who received unbudgeted allowances—all cross-section cases—three were adequately aided from the outset, while two were left to struggle along for some weeks with the seemingly insufficient aid of relatives, though neither was receiving government checks or in

[1] See page 39. Also decision of consultation committee, Feb. 15, 1918: "If the family of a bachelor requires assistance because he enters the service, and the man subsequently marries, assistance to his family shall be continued."

[2] See especially Educational Problems for scholarship cases, page 173.

condition to work. A large check came to one of these young women just after an allowance had been started, and the other seems also to have begun again to receive her allotment and allowance a few weeks after she became known to the Section.

A group that has not been so fully discussed is that of elderly parents without children at home or insufficiently cared for by such children.

Old Mr. Rolf was treated with the utmost kindness and received an allowance of $7.00 a week for eighteen weeks, while every possible effort was being made to induce his only son to allot to him. When the young man's commanding officer wrote that his "character was found to be such" that it was impossible to persuade him to provide for his father, it was decided that the old gentleman, who was of English birth, was really not a Home Service responsibility, and arrangements were made to have the care of him assumed by a British society which was already interested. (Cross-section record. Social Service Exchange reported information furnished insufficient for identification.)

Another pathetic figure was a blind old father. The one son at home was a ne'er-do-well, so that the giving of relief was a difficult problem. How the ingenious idea was finally hit upon (after various other arrangements had been tried) of asking a friendly housewife across the hall to give the old man his meals has already been related in another connection. (See page 46.)

Three old mothers are on our list:

Mrs. Intaglia was living alone with a daughter of twelve; she had a lodger who paid about half her small rent, but how she met her other expenses does not appear, her allotment having failed to come for two months and her relatives being, so she said, unable to assist. This is one of the poorest records we have read: there was no investigation, so that we cannot tell whether the failure to give any relief during the first eight weeks of acquaintance was the serious blunder that it appears to be or whether the giving of $5.00 a week for the second eight weeks was justified—and if justified, whether it was adequate or inadequate. We are pretty clear, however, that the last entry in the record represents a wrong point of view, quite out of harmony with the usual practice of Home Service. It reads: "Advised woman that Red Cross could not continue granting weekly financial assistance. That her son had been in service for a very long time and she had not received any money, which was probably an indication that her son had not made any allotment and therefore if she wished a weekly allowance she would have to go to the Red Cross workrooms and work from 10 a. m. to 3 p. m. Woman complained and pointed to her hand. Her knuckles are slightly swollen and she seems to have rheumatism. She does her own housework, which is certainly much harder than the work at the workrooms." In the rigidity of its interpretation of the terms on which relief could be given and its casual treatment of a perhaps minor but hardly negligible physical ailment, this smacks of what we should like to believe a bygone era in charitable work. We suspect that irritation with a "begging type," rather than a sense of justice, was in the ascendant at this point. (Cross-section record. Not known to any social agency.)

Mrs. Battista's case was much more carefully considered. We have already told the story of the theft by her son in the West of her government checks (see page 169). She was living with another son and had no proper place to sleep; so $3.00 a week was paid to a neighbor who gave her a bed until her son's family moved to a larger and very comfortable apartment where it was felt she could be taken care of. That the son who had steady work and a small family should be expected to feed and otherwise care for her, was very reasonably felt. (Cross-section record. Not known to any social agency.)

It is by no means so clear that the decision in the case of the third old mother, Mrs. Ames, was right. She was receiving only $10 from her son in service and was living with a married daughter whose husband was crippled and ill much of the time, but evidently no shirker. Other relatives were seen, and in a conference with mother, daughter, and daughter-in-law it was agreed to give a small loan allowance. Three dollars were actually given in two successive weeks. Under the date of the second payment we read that a conference was held with the supervisor and it was decided to discontinue the allowance as the son-in-law was working and the married children should help. There is no indication that this decision was explained to the client or her relatives; and as, on a call made in relation to another matter more than a month later, the son-in-law asked why the payments to the mother had ceased, we are inclined to believe the oversight real and not a matter of recording only. It is clear that an abrupt change in a definitely made plan should not have been made without notification and statement of reasons to those with whom the former agreement had been entered into. (Cross-section record. Known to a family society and to the Bureau of Domestic Relations.)

The Meixners, an old Jewish couple with two sons in the service, were receiving when first known only $10 a month from one son, and in spite of most persistent correspondence with the sons, their commanding officers, and government authorities, seem never to have received the full amounts due them. They were under almost constant care for a year, until after the return of one son, receiving over two hundred dollars, mostly in the form of a weekly allowance of $5.00. The care given, as indicated by this and treatment of other needs, was thorough and kindly; whether relief was adequate, and why the family was never referred to the dietitian for budget study, are questions we cannot answer. (Cross-section record. Not known to any social agency.)

One of the few sisters of men in service who were objects of Home Service care in the records read was Mrs. Connolly.

She had two little daughters of nine and five, kept a very neat home, and was well spoken of. She was receiving, as a widow, an allowance from the Child Welfare Board of only $17 and no allotment from the brother who had lived with and helped her; and she was in poor health when first known to the Section. An allowance of $8.00 a week was very promptly begun and kept up for seven weeks while the brother was written to and negotiations entered into with the Child Welfare Board. A letter from the Board saying that its allowance would probably be increased to $26 a month at its next meeting perhaps explains why the Red Cross allowance came to an end a month later, though there is no definite statement of this increase having gone into effect. Even if it did, obviously there would still have been need of supplementary aid from the Section unless other income supplied the need. Possibly Mrs. Connolly was by this time well enough to work, possibly checks began to come from the brother or the government—we are not told, the record ending abruptly without explanation, as did so many in those hurried war days. (Cross-section record. Not known to any social agency.)

Mrs. Ingram, with two small children, lived in three rooms described as "bright, clean and comfortably furnished," in a "well kept apartment house" though they rented for $9.00. Her husband, a sergeant, had made allotment and applied for an allowance two months before she was referred to Home Service, but she received no check from the War Risk Bureau until five months later, during which period two checks for $50 each, received from her husband through the Quartermaster's Department, seem to have constituted all her income apart from Red Cross aid. Fortunately this was prompt and seems to have been adequate. Rent was paid, a much-needed baby carriage was purchased, a budget planned, and a list of debts made out. The sums given were not the same as the one originally named nor were they given with the regularity usually characteristic of an allowance, but they are repeatedly referred to in the record as allowance payments and seem to have been essentially of this character. They were definitely understood to be a loan, and the record ends (as such records should, but, alas, do not invariably!) by the receipt of a large check ($480) which Mrs. Ingram brought to the office asking to have it cashed and the $106.50 owed to the Section deducted. (Cross-section record. Not known to any social agency.)

Another wife, with a small baby and a little girl of ten, who rented four of her eight well-furnished rooms, receiving approximately enough to meet her rent of $45, has already been mentioned. (See pages 52 and 188.) She was given a regular allowance, beginning in July, 1918, of $11.25 a week, which was continued until she began to receive her allotment and allowance checks in the following December. Again, when Mrs. Niles insisted that she could not manage on these, a smaller sum of $2.50 was given weekly beginning in January, 1919, for a period of several months. In May the dietitian was consulted (the government checks having ceased to come due to a mistaken report of the man's discharge) and a tentative budget of $8.50 was planned, subject to correction after account slips had been kept for a time. This was continued up to July, until after the husband had come home and gone to work. It is interesting to note that here the dietitian arrived at a lower estimate of weekly needs than had the visitor in her earlier calculations, though possibly some small addition to income explains the reduction. (Cross-section record. Known only to a diet kitchen.)

The examples which have been given sufficiently indicate the good and evil in the earlier administration of continued relief. Some allowances were carefully planned after full discussion of household problems with the mother, and probably represent conclusions not very different from those a trained dietitian would have arrived at. Others seem to have been more or less arbitrarily determined, and it is difficult to see how they could have met the needs of the family to which they were given.

There were also a number of after-care cases in which more or less disabled discharged soldiers were helped through a difficult period. The stories of several of these men have already been told under other heads. We may say of the cases of this class that, owing to their coming to attention at a late period of Home Service activity, when supervisors and visitors were less overburdened and had been educated in budget-making and dietetic standards, and owing perhaps also in part to the special appeal made by the disabled soldier, they were very liberally helped. This is equally true of the cross-section and of the selected cases that have come to our attention; nor does there seem to be any marked difference in the treatment given such of them as had their allowances determined solely by the workers in the various divisions and such as were made the subjects of budget study by the dietitian.

The Canadian and British allowances, on the other hand, were nearly all given before the dietitian joined the staff of the Section. Among the eight cross-section cases which received allowances, all but one originated in 1918, and of the two selected Canadian cases in which allowances were given one came to Home Service in 1918, one in 1917. All ten families received flat allowances of $10, $15, or $20 for periods varying from two or three months to a year—sometimes until the receipt of pay and separation allowance, sometimes until the return of the man. As a rough tentative standard in determining the size of an allowance given pending the receipt of a government separation allowance, the amount the wife or mother would have had a right to if her husband or son had been in the United States service was used, subject to modification to fit the special facts of the case. The investigation which preceded the granting of an allowance was usually somewhat less extensive than those made in allowance cases in other divisions; sometimes there was none at all. This difference is in part explicable by the fact that the status of the recipient was in all cases established through British or Canadian official sources. Then, too, these women were often comparatively newcomers in New York and far from kith and kin. The preference of the Patriotic Fund, which reimbursed the Red Cross, for regular monthly payments of fixed amounts naturally had a great influence in determining these allowances. The insistence of wives upon help which had been promised their husbands or themselves by the recruiting officers or representatives of the Fund was also a factor in some cases.

Families which have been made the subjects of budget study by the dietitian of the Section now demand our attention. In contrast to the cases previously discussed, which represent almost every possible method of approach and degree of liberality or its lack, the treatment of these is standardized, and we found the deviations from the standard few and slight. Therefore a comparatively small number of examples will represent the much larger number of such cases. It should be kept in mind that these comparatively few cases are actually typical of Home Service treatment during 1919 and later, when conditions of work, including proportion of visitors to cases, had been improved until they approached those in the better type of permanent family agency and when the pooling of ideas by the supervisors, taken with the labors of the dietitian, had brought about an approach to uniformity throughout the Section lacking in the first hurried years.

In most families whose men were absent in service the carefully planned budget was subject to constant readjustment; for not only did illness, loss of work, new positions at higher salaries, and other incidents common to families under peace-time conditions frequently upset calculations, but government checks were likely to arrive late or fail to arrive at all for an indefinite number of months. Especially in the very poor family consisting of a mother and small children where the allotment and allowance was the sole income, the irregularly arriving checks had to be largely paid out to meet accumulated debts or to buy clothing and other long-neglected necessities. In many cases, both of this and other types, there is hence little connection between the budget card of a certain date, with its indicated deficit in income, and the amounts actually given during the months that follow.

Thus Mrs. Torquato and her family of three small children were found in December, 1918 (on the assumption that $12.11 weekly was available from her allotment and allowance), to need $2.52 a week. Milk was ordered to supply the deficiency; but during the succeeding months many allowance payments in cash had to be made to take the place of delayed checks. It was also found necessary to supply much clothing and another bed with bedding, for the budget allowance provides only for repairs and other current needs in clothing, assuming a normal stock to start with; and where long poverty has led to the depletion of wardrobes, careful individual study of needs must be made and special grants arranged to cover them. (Cross-section record. Known to a family society and another agency.)

A very different type of family was that of Mrs. O'Toole: two sons were absent, one in service and one in prison, and a third, twenty-four years old, was at home alone with the mother. In May, 1919, when the budget study was made, he was earning $10 and Mrs. O'Toole was supposed to be receiving the equivalent of $5.77 weekly in allotment checks; the total of calculated expenses coming to $18.40, there was a deficit of $2.63. It was decided to give $4.00 weekly to cover certain medicine the mother needed, and this was done for two weeks, after which $2.00 was given for two more. A much larger allowance had been paid during the preceding six weeks before the son found work. (Cross-section record. Known to a family society.)

Two families of a better-to-do class may be mentioned.

Mrs. Ives had two sons in service but had received nothing in the way of allotment and allowance payments in so many months that in February, 1919, when her budget was made, these were not counted as part of the prospective income, which was composed of the earnings of three children at home. The deficit shown was $7.05; but as one of the children was then recovering from an appendicitis operation and could not work, his full wages of $15 were supplied until he was again earning. Much help had been given before this time, and the grand total of $240 loaned was later returned by Mrs. Ives. (Selected record. Not known to any social agency.)

Mrs. Underhill, a charming and cultivated woman, was an actress with a reputation for absolute honesty and fair dealing. She was in bad health and unable to work, and so was wholly dependent upon her $30 allotment and allowance check when she was referred to Home Service. Budget study revealed a deficit of $12 a week, the dietitian recommending a "building-up diet." The exact amount indicated was supplied for many weeks and help was continued down through the time of Mr. Underhill's return until he had found, after one or two abortive attempts, a permanent job. Though everything possible had been done to keep this couple from feeling overburdened by the debt they were contracting, they took the greatest pride, as soon as they were able, in repaying as much of the total sum expended as they were given to understand had been a loan; not by any means all that was so recorded on the cash-card—that would have been to overburden too heavily a family of small means already handicapped by the wife's ill health. (Selected record. Not known to any social agency.)

The somewhat exceptional case of a soldier in the army who was living at home, and that of a representative discharged man, follow.

The story of Sergeant Ritchie and his three children—two his own, one adopted—has been partly told on page 115. He came to the Section's attention in May, 1919, when he was stationed in the city where he had taken an apartment and was trying to manage his household single-handed. In the following month a budget was made which showed that his pay, amounting to $10.38 weekly, was $6.43 short of the sum he needed properly to care for his small family and keep up his payments on a Liberty Bond. Accordingly an allowance of $6.50

was at once started. He had been feeding the children on $1.00 a day and had said when the budget idea was suggested that if this meant that the Red Cross would lend or give him money he would rather get along as he was. However his scruples were evidently overcome and the allowance—accompanied by visits from one of the dietitians who helped prepare meals and look out for the children—continued until he was transferred to duty elsewhere and placed his children in an institution. He has since repaid his debt in full. (Cross-section record. Not known to any social agency.)

Young Godonov, as related elsewhere (see page 161), was suffering from deafness and without any income whatever when Home Service took up his case. The dietitian's budget shows a needed expenditure of $24.06, but as Mrs. Godonov met with an accident just at this time and was taken to the hospital for a stay of several months, he never received the full amount. Weekly loans of $10 to $12 were given regularly for two months until his compensation check arrived, when he repaid in full. This reduction seems a greater one than was to be expected, but we note that the dietitian was consulted at one point and approved the giving of $10 only. (Selected record. Not known to any social agency.)

Few as are the examples given, they are so thoroughly representative that to give more would be a waste of space. There are a few instances of allowances where considerably less than the indicated deficit was given in weekly cash payments, while special grants to cover clothing and other needs were made. In a few instances, also, we noted that the clothing item was dropped, once on the theory that at a recent more prosperous period there had been an opportunity for the family to stock up in clothes; this was clearly the result of a misunderstanding of the significance of this item which, as already stated, was intended to cover current expenses of renewal and repair only. With few exceptions, however, the standards set were lived up to.

One other after-care case may be mentioned to show the extreme of liberality to which Home Service occasionally has gone in dealing with exceptionally high-standard families. Louis Tannenbaum, with a wife and two small children, had been a salesman earning $200 to $250 a month, but now, on account of pain from an injured foot, was able to work only part time. He and his wife had reached the point of pawning things before they were referred to Home Service. She knew nothing of cooking or of food values and was utterly unable to economize, so that at first, the expected compensation (equal to $31.93 weekly) not having yet come, and the budget showing a needed expenditure of $35.25, practically this full amount was supplied. After a few weeks, however, the tactful labors of the visiting dietitian had produced such results that the man himself requested the reduction of the weekly allowance to $25. (Selected record. Not known to any social agency.)

The Question of Loans vs. Grants

A number of the citations under the general problem of relief have mentioned the return of loans. Some of the supervisors of the Section declare themselves strongly in favor of loans; others are just as strongly opposed, preferring to give outright if at all. These latter are those who feel most strongly the demoralizing effects of relief giving in any form, though in the latter years of Home Service some of the most liberally aided families were under their care; they are very deeply impressed with the instances of evasion and neglect to repay which have come to their attention, whereas the believers in loans joyously cite instances of conspicuous honesty and scrupulousness. A certain unconscious temperamental bias seems to enter into the point of view of each group.

The writer herself, from the standpoint of the judicially minded outsider, finds considerable ground both for the optimistic attitude of the one and the pessimistic attitude of the other party. A goodly number of instances can be cited—some have been cited—in which both large and small loans were returned quite spontaneously. These, however, we are bound to admit, are largely among the selected cases, and there has been a very large number of unreturned loans. While some of these reflect painfully upon the faultiness of human kind, many failures to repay were inevitable in view of the extraordinary rise in prices, the insufficiency of allotments and allowances to meet the needs of a large proportion of families, and the many personal misfortunes which have necessitated unforeseen expenditures. Recognizing this, visitors and supervisors, during the closing period, formally released many clients from the obligations assumed, while the debts of others were tacitly recognized as uncollectable.

However, all the supervisors would, we believe, agree that many so-called loans should have been grants. Desire to make things easy for clients who shrank from accepting relief, or the wish to compel clients of an opposite type to assume obligations which it was felt they ought to carry, led many, especially among the more inexperienced visitors, to use the term "loan" when there was very little reason to suppose that the recipients would ever be in a position to repay. Often, on the other hand, clients seem not to have understood that it was a loan they were receiving, so lightly was the point glided over by the visitor. One instance of especially mistaken policy may be cited for the light it casts on tendencies that have been obscurely at work in less extreme form.

This is a case in which the policy of lending money instead of giving it as a grant seems to have been an error. Young Mrs. Isaacs, referred to the Section a few days after her husband entered the service, was expecting a baby in three months and was living with her mother, father, and brother. Two relatives and two previous addresses were visited, but the situation of the family seems never to have been really studied. For example, the wife's statement in the first interview that her brother was an errand boy, contributing from $12 to $14 to the family, was accepted without further inquiry, and it was not until several months later that it was learned that he was a cutter, and had been out of work fourteen weeks; and not until even later did it appear that the father worked irregularly with a push cart, earning, his daughter said, often not so much as $3.00 a week. Not until the case had been under care over a year was the fact brought out that the wife had to help her parents.

These general points, with the defects in diagnosis involved, we mention chiefly as background for another point regarding the relief policy. After Mrs. Isaacs had received a number of small grants, sparsely distributed over a considerable period, she stated that "she had borrowed from everybody and did not know where to turn to now unless the Red Cross would help her. . . . Visitor asked whether she would accept money as a loan, but she said she feared to take it this way as she already owed so much that she could not repay it all." In spite of this very frank statement, the irregular allowance given after this time was largely treated as a loan, the cash card showing a total of $65 loaned between the date of the conversation quoted above and the date of our reading of the record. Gradually the pretense of a possible future repayment seems to have been assumed by Mrs. Isaacs. In June, 1919, she begged for the continuance of the allowance (though she was now receiving her allotment and allowance) "at least until her husband returns. . . . She could not think of paying anything back to the Home Service as yet." After her husband's return in July she asks again that it be continued, still talking of returning the loans made at some later date.

We may be wrong, but we felt strongly, in reading this record, that Mrs. Isaacs' spirit of independence and honesty had been undermined as it would not have been if her first frank statement had been frankly met and the money she needed (whatever full study might have revealed it to be) given her in the form of grants. (Cross-section record. Not known to any social agency.)

CHAPTER X

CONCLUDING STATEMENT

In the preliminary statement to Part II of this study the writer promised that no general summing up of the good and evil in the methods pursued by Home Service visitors in the cases to be cited would be attempted, but that the reader would be left free to judge, after reviewing each chapter, how adequate or inadequate had been the efforts of the Section to meet the needs of those who came to it in their difficulties. This promise has been kept, nor is it our intention to break it at this late day.

The reader may, however, be reminded of one feature of the task undertaken: that even more significant than the huge number of cases dealt with and the inadequacy of organization and staff, was the unexpectedness of the burden.

It is true that from the time of our entrance into the war Americans were forewarned that an army of several million men was to be raised by draft. But from an early date, also, we were led to expect that extraordinary measures would be taken by the federal government to meet the needs of the families of these men. The amount of the allowance that was to supplement the soldier's allotment from his pay was to be determined by the size and composition of his family, and it was hoped would prove large enough to insure independence to most families possessed of normal resourcefulness where illness or other special difficulties did not complicate the situation.[1] Wherever such special difficulties should arise Home Service expected to step into the breach; but it could hardly have anticipated, under the circumstances, how wide that breach was to be. The two principal unforeseen factors which entered in were the breakdown in the administration of the War Risk Insurance Act and the rise in the cost of living.

Upon the second of these factors there is no need to enlarge

[1] See footnote, page 87.

here: everyone knows what has happened to the purchasing power of the dollar during the last few years and can appreciate the significance of the change to the mother endeavoring in 1918 and 1919 to maintain her children in health upon an allowance which would have been barely sufficient in 1917. What, then, must it have meant to the wives and mothers of soldiers when even that minimum income was interrupted for three, six, nine months or a year, and what must it have meant for the Section when, with its lack of preparation to care for them, thousands of families whose incomes were thus reduced or entirely cut off by a failure in the government allowance came pouring into its doors!

To what extent is the work of any social agency to be judged by the best and most successful examples of that work which it can show? To what extent by its average, or by examples of its worst work? These are questions which will be differently answered according to temperamental bias, or bias of another kind; for not infrequently in our experience there is a tendency to apply the first standard suggested to one's own society, the second to other agencies.

In Part II of this study the aim has been to give the data by which Home Service case work may be judged, whichever standard the reader may choose to apply. To the writer what seems most typical of Home Service is the work which exhibits the qualities dwelt upon in the chapter on Characteristics in Part I; namely, flexibility in treatment, consideration for the point of view of the client, cordial co-operation with other agencies, emphasis on maintenance of normal standards, and a genuine democratic relation between visitor and visited. To every reader, however, the opportunity is offered to decide for himself how far the qualities enumerated are characteristic. This study represents, above all else, an experiment in frankness; and the fact that Home Service workers were anxious to have it made and were ready to welcome the publication of as much of the whole truth regarding the successes and failures of the Section as one impartial critic could see and express seems good evidence that no mistake was made in judging its best work to be its most truly typical work.

INDEX

INDEX TO FICTITIOUS NAMES OF FAMILIES MENTIONED IN THIS STUDY[1]

(Numbers refer to pages)

[1] Many other case records are cited without use of names, but the indexing of these is unimportant from the standpoint of cross-referencing.

www.ingramcontent.com/pod-product-compliance
Lightning Source LLC
LaVergne TN
LVHW050526100826
845148LV00002B/451